Struggling with Substance Use

Struggling with Substance Use

Supporting Students' Social Emotional Learning

Deborah Lynch

ROWMAN & LITTLEFIELD
Lanham • Boulder • New York • London

Published by Rowman & Littlefield
An imprint of The Rowman & Littlefield Publishing Group, Inc.
4501 Forbes Boulevard, Suite 200, Lanham, Maryland 20706
www.rowman.com

86-90 Paul Street, London EC2A 4NE, United Kingdom

British Library Cataloguing in Publication Information Available

Library of Congress Cataloging-in-Publication Data

Names: Lynch, Deborah (Teacher), author.
Title: Struggling with substance use : supporting students' social emotional learning / Deborah Lynch.
Description: Lanham : Rowman & Littlefield, [2023] | Summary: "Struggling with Substance Use presents evidence on the magnitude of the problem of student substance abuse and provides education professionals with information on the causes as well as the risk and protective factors that must be understood to address the issue"—Provided by publisher.
Identifiers: LCCN 2022032527 (print) | LCCN 2022032528 (ebook) | ISBN 9781475866094 (cloth) | ISBN 9781475866100 (paperback) | ISBN 9781475866117 (epub)
Subjects: LCSH: Youth—Substance use. | Teenagers—Substance use. | Substance abuse.
Classification: LCC HV4999.Y68 L965 2023 (print) | LCC HV4999.Y68 (ebook) | DDC 362.290835—dc23/eng/20220909
LC record available at https://lccn.loc.gov/2022032527
LC ebook record available at https://lccn.loc.gov/2022032528

Contents

Preface

I am a mother and a teacher. I taught high school when my own kids were high school students, so I know it's an exciting and challenging age. I loved it: the energy, the silliness, the curiosity, and, often, the kindness. I taught in a high-poverty high school and so the students had lots of struggles as well: family issues, poverty, neighborhood violence. And, of course, a lot of that came into the school as well: gangs, drugs, disinterest in academics, and trauma.

I often compared my students with my children. We lived in a safe area. I monitored their grades and made sure they did their homework. I kept tabs on their friends and their whereabouts—or at least I thought I did. They had the material things they needed, and they had love and support from our nuclear family and their extended family. None of this insulated my family from substance use, abuse, and addiction.

I was peripherally aware of student drug activity in my school. I heard of this student or that who got caught with marijuana and was turned over to the police. At the time I didn't realize I was watching the school-to-prison pipeline in action.

It was more insidious in my home. I didn't see it coming and was at a total loss as to what to do about it when reality hit—and hit hard. I wasn't the only one who didn't understand it, didn't see it coming, and didn't have the knowledge or the resources to fight it. None of my son's teachers ever seemed to notice either.

None of them ever called me or reached out with their concerns about my son's behavior in school or his increasing lack of interest in anything academic. But, as a teacher, neither did I. How many of my own students were ill-served by my lack of knowledge and understanding of the signs and symptoms of—and the reasons for—substance use and abuse?

As a parent, I was at a complete loss. I was totally unprepared for the changes I saw in my son. And I was terrified—more terrified than I had ever been in my life. I was living in a constant state of terror. The thought of losing my child to substance use was too much to bear. I thought love was enough, but it wasn't. We needed help, support, and an understanding of substance use. I finally saw the signs that something was very wrong and got him treatment.

After treatment, one of his teachers—and only one—spoke so positively about him at parent–teacher conferences. It was his culinary arts teacher, Judy Brower, who raved about what a great kid he was and how well he did in her class. He did so well that she arranged for him to have an independent study the following year, his senior year, as her assistant. I really believe that helped keep him in school until graduation, and then on to college.

He was able to graduate with a degree in hospitality management and even went on for another year of education after that. The substance use continued throughout college and young adulthood, however, becoming more and more problematic. After a couple of tries to quit by himself, he sought help at age twenty-six and committed himself to the very hard work of achieving sobriety. He is now going on five years of recovery. And, of course, I am so proud of him.

And that extra year of schooling I mentioned? He attended culinary school to become a chef. Today he is an executive chef, thanks, in large part, to the connection, support, and encouragement he had with his high school culinary arts teacher. Thank you, Mrs. Brower.

So, this book is for staff in a school setting who, like me, had no idea about the extent and impact of student substance use. For it is here, and it continues to destroy lives—and take lives. And it devastates every single person who loves every single child who loses their way and gets so involved with drugs or alcohol that there is no turning back.

As educators, we are often the first responders in this epidemic. It is my hope that with greater knowledge and understanding of student substance use, and an enhanced understanding and compassion for why students turn to substances in the first place, we can better support children who are struggling.

Doing so will greatly enhance their chances of a happy and fulfilling life. And isn't why we are in schools in the first place?

I recently completed a thirty-year full-time teaching career and am now an adjunct professor and a substance use counselor. I am also part of a professional advocacy group that offers conferences and workshops on student substance use and what can be done about it. Most educator-participants continue to report little or no preparation or training on this issue, and the vast majority report few resources being devoted to prevention or intervention in their schools.

It is my hope that sharing this vitally important information, as well as my experience getting here, will enable you to be better prepared to address this issue than I was. And I hope that, with greater understanding and insight, you will appreciate just how important you are to these students—and their families—and that you know just how much of a difference you can, and do, make in their lives.

Deborah Lynch
January 2022

Introduction

Struggling with Substance Use: Supporting Students' Social Emotional Learning begins with a presentation of the extent of the problem of adolescent substance use. Chapter 1 presents findings from various governmental agencies responsible for studying this issue, from the CDC (Center for Disease Control) to NIDA (National Institute on Drug Abuse) to SAMSHA (Substance Abuse and Mental Health Services Administration).

Their studies' findings paint a compelling picture of the evolving and varied use of substances by adolescents over the decades and illustrate a continuing, if ever changing, challenge for professionals and families alike. And while trends are ever changing, so is the terminology. For example, it is now accepted that alcohol is, indeed, a drug; so in many instances, data is combined for both alcohol and other drugs.

Experts have moved away from the term *abuse* toward terminology from the most widely accepted source of mental illness definitions, the DSM V (*Diagnostic and Statistical Manual*, 5th edition) developed by the American Psychiatric Association (2013). Previously there was a distinction between substance use and dependence, but the 2013 DSM V shifted and now considers these as part of one continuum, categorized as mild, moderate, or severe.

This volume, therefore, refers to *adolescent substance use*, not *abuse*, and to *substance use disorder* as well as the term *addiction*, in lieu of abuse and dependence. It includes alcohol, nicotine, and marijuana (the primary substances of adolescent use), as well as other drugs when referring to substance use. And while the focus is on adolescents, it also addresses use prior to adolescence—use that educators in elementary and middle schools can attest does happen.

After presenting the extent of the problem, the focus turns to some of the many issues that underlie substance use, issues relating to adolescent substance use that are of significant concern to an adolescent's social-emotional development and also to a successfully functioning classroom and school. These other issues, or co-occurring disorders (disorders that co-exist with a substance use disorder), include ADHD, Conduct Disorders, Anxiety, Depression, and the experience of childhood trauma.

Each of these chapters (chapters 2–5) examines the issue itself, its association with the initiation and use of substances, elaboration of risk factors, then protective factors, and, finally, an example of a promising program targeting the co-occurring disorder under discussion.

Chapters 6–9 cover the factors that go beyond the individual to the adolescent's larger environment, with a chapter on the impact of (and on) family, peers, the school environment, and the larger community in relation to adolescent substance use.

These chapters also follow the pattern of an introduction of the topic and its relationship to adolescent substance use, an extensive discussion of the risk factors involved in such use, the protective factors specific to the chapter's focus, and an example of a promising program designed to address the specific factor.

The ten promising programs (as well as additional resources identified in the appendix) all serve to provide examples, or exemplars of ways other educators, schools, and communities have successfully addressed the topic in question. They are meant to inspire those who want to take action by providing a road map of possibilities. They are meant to provide an understanding that quality, evidence-based programs already exist and there is no need to reinvent wheels.

The final chapter, chapter 10, presents a synthesis of the protective factors that have been discussed in relation to the specific topics of the previous chapters. While there are some protective factors unique to some of the issues covered, there are many that are common to all of them.

This synthesis of protective factors provides an overview, and can be a starting point, for those wishing to take a critical look at the protective factors currently in place—what is—and then identifying what could be. And while there are programs and practices that will require more resources and personnel, there are many ways protective factors can be identified, incorporated, and enhanced in existing systems and structures.

Recognizing that there is a problem, perhaps a problem no one wants to look at, takes courage. It takes knowledge and understanding and passion to do something to address the problem. Because this problem is so much more than numbers and percentages of students at various grade levels. It is real children and real family members who are in pain—so much pain.

For too many of these children and their families, school is their *only* connection to help. And if caring and committed education professionals cannot provide that help, who will?

Chapter 1

Understanding Adolescent Substance Use

ADOLESCENT SUBSTANCE USE: PREVALENCE

Overall Adolescent Substance Use Prevalence

Student substance use involves the use of addictive substances, most commonly alcohol, marijuana, and nicotine. While these are the most frequently used substances by students, student substance use has changed over time, in some positive ways nationally, due to policy changes implemented by national, state, and local agencies.

According to the Monitoring the Future (MTF) Survey (2019) of the National Institute on Drug Abuse, cigarette smoking in grades eight, ten, and twelve was close to the lowest levels since this survey began in 1975 (see Figure 1.1). Thirty-day prevalence of cigarette use which was at its peak in the mid-1990s has fallen by 84 percent according to the survey, which says that current prevalence for half-pack-a-day smoking was 0.3 percent for eighth graders, 0.7 percent for tenth graders, and 1.5 percent for twelfth graders.

The MTF attributed this decline in cigarette smoking to the adverse publicity the tobacco industry has experienced, a reduction in cigarette advertising and youth anti-smoking campaigns. This success is very encouraging and something we can look to as advocates explore ways to address, prevent, and reduce adolescent substance use and its dangerous and life-threatening consequences.

2019 Monitoring the Future Survey
Key Findings: Percent Reporting Use of Selected Substances

	8th Grade	10th Grade	12th Grade		8th Grade	10th Grade	12th Grade
Vaping, Any				**Tobacco w/Hookah**			
Past Year	20.1	35.7	40.6	Past Year			5.6
Past Month	12.2	25.0	30.9	Past Month	1.3	2.4	4.0
Vaping, Nicotine				**Flavored Little Cigars**			
Past Year	16.5	30.7	35.3	Past Month	2.2	3.7	7.7
Past Month	9.6	19.9	25.5	**Narcotics Other than Heroin**			
Vaping, Marijuana				Past Year			2.7
Past Year	7.0	19.4	20.8	Past Month			1.0
Past Month	3.9	12.6	14.0	**Marijuana**			
Vaping, Just Flavoring				Past Year	11.8	28.8	35.7
Past Year	14.7	20.8	20.3	Past Month	6.6	18.4	22.3
Past Month	7.7	10.5	10.7	Daily	1.3	4.8	6.4
Cigarettes				**Alcohol**			
Past Month	2.3	3.4	5.7	Past Month	7.9	18.4	29.3
Daily	0.8	1.3	2.4	Daily	0.2	0.6	1.7
½ Pack +/Day	0.2	0.5	0.9	Binge	3.8	8.5	14.4

Change from 2018 to 2019

☐ Significant Increase   ☐ Significant Decrease

Figure 1.1   Monitoring the Future 2019: Percent Reporting Use of Selected Substances.
Source: National Institute on Drug Abuse; National Institutes of Health; U.S. Department of Health and Human Services. (December 2019). https://nida.nih.gov/sites/default/files/drugfacts-mtf.pdf

This positive news is offset, say MTF authors, by significant increases in vaping, which involves using a device that heats nicotine, marijuana, or flavoring creating an inhalable aerosol. The MTF survey found substantial increases, including what the authors describe as some of the largest absolute increases MTF has ever tracked for any substance.

Nicotine vaping prevalence rates, for example, were 11 percent for eighth graders, 25 percent for tenth graders, and 30 percent for twelfth graders. Marijuana prevalence was: 4.4 percent, 12.4 percent, and 13.1 percent for those grades, respectively. A concern here is that adolescents don't see much harm in vaping, rating its risk very low. As is now known, nicotine is highly addictive. It has negative effects, too, including behavior and mood changes, lung injury, increased heart rates, to name a few.

Annual prevalence for use of marijuana in 2019, per MTF, was 11 percent, 28 percent, and 36 percent for grades eight, nine, and twelve, respectively. Daily use rates are 1 percent, 3 percent, and 6 percent. Annual prevalence rates for illicit drugs other than marijuana held steady at 9 percent, which saw a decline since 2001 when it was 16 percent.

Alcohol is the most frequently used drug by adolescents. The MTF states that by the end of high school, about 60 percent of students have consumed alcohol (and 24 percent by the end of eighth grade). There have been some gradual declines in thirty-day prevalence since the peak use of the mid-1990s, though the decline has halted in the two lower grades.

This is a real concern due to the negative effects of alcohol use on adolescents, including lowered inhibition, impaired judgment, alcohol poisoning, with prolonged and heavy use leading to severe health consequences and addiction.

The full effects of the COVID-19 pandemic are still relatively unknown. A study funded by NIDA, which covered the first six months of the pandemic, found that substance use by adolescents aged ten and fourteen was stable during the first six months of the pandemic. According to the study, adolescents who experienced pandemic-related severe stress, depression, or anxiety, or whose families experienced material hardship during the pandemic, or whose parents uses substances themselves, were most likely to use them too.

The 2021 MTF study reported the percentage of adolescents reporting substance use as having decreased significantly during 2021. According to Dr. Nora Volkow, NIDA's Director, this is an unexpected potential consequence of the pandemic.

> The 2021 survey reported significant decreases in use across many substances, including those most commonly used in adolescence – alcohol, marijuana, and vaped nicotine. The 2021 decrease in vaping for both marijuana and tobacco follows sharp increases in use between 2017 and 2019, which then leveled off in 2020. This year, the study surveyed students on their mental health during the COVID-19 pandemic. The study found that students across all age-groups reported moderate increases in feelings of boredom, anxiety, depression, loneliness, worry, difficulty sleeping, and other negative mental health indicators since the beginning of the pandemic. (NIDA, 2021, p.1)

Volkow said that it will be crucial to identify the pivotal elements of this past year that contributed to decreased drug use—whether related to drug availability, family involvement, differences in peer pressure, or other factors—and harness them to inform future prevention efforts.

Another concern is the use of more than one substance by adolescents. A study by Feinstein et al. (2012) found that by grade twelve, 82.3 percent of students reported ever having used an addictive substance. Two-thirds were identified as using more than one substance. They found that one in eight high school students, or 11.9 percent, suffers from an addictive disorder. That is, in a high school of, say, 2,000 students, would amount to 240 kids walking the halls with a serious problem. This doesn't count those who are just using/misusing substances.

In a more recent study, Johnson et al. (2017) found that almost half of twelfth graders (46 percent) and 9 percent of eighth graders reported having been drunk at least once in their life. Six percent of twelfth graders are daily marijuana smokers and 11 percent are current cigarette smokers. By age twenty-one, about 55 percent of American young people report marijuana use at least once, and twenty-two percent report being current marijuana smokers (Chen et al., 2016).

The U.S. Substance Abuse and Mental Health Services Administration (SAMSHA) describes the use of substances and substance use disorders (SUDs) as chronic health problems and estimates the annual economic cost is in the billions. SAMSHA notes that in 2017 more than 140 million people aged twelve and older, about 52 percent of this population, reported using alcohol in the past month and almost half reported binge drinking. And, about 14.5 million meet the diagnostic criteria for alcohol use disorder (AUD). And 48.7 million in this age group use cigarettes (Center for Behavioral Health Statistics and Quality, 2018).

Regarding illicit substances, SAMSHA reports that in 2017, more than thirty million people aged twelve and older used illicit substances in the last month (85 percent used marijuana, 10 percent used an opioid). Further, SAMSHA estimates that almost half of the estimated 18.7 million individuals who met the criteria for a substance use disorder also experienced a mental health illness such as depression or anxiety.

The death rates are staggering annually, with more than 480,000 deaths due to cigarette smoking, 89,000 attributable to alcohol-related causes, and (in 2017), 63,000 due to drug overdose. During 2020, the first year of the COVID-19 pandemic, those overdose deaths increased by an astounding 30 percent in this country.

These numbers reflect our lack of previous knowledge about prevention and lack of prioritizing substance use prevention and intervention. There is new data and evidence of effective approaches, like the anti-smoking campaigns of the recent past. What is needed now is the prioritizing of these effective approaches to minimize harm in future generations. For the harm begins starts in early adolescence, as over 96 percent of adults with a substance issue disorder began using substances on adolescence, when their brains are most vulnerable (Nash et al., 2015).

Substance Use Prevalence in Various Racial/Ethnic Groups

According to the MTF report (2020), prevalence rates vary by racial and ethnic groups. This report notes that, generally, White adolescents use more alcohol and tobaccos than do Hispanic adolescents, and that African American adolescents appear to use the least. The MTF report says that differences in marijuana use among racial/ethnic groups have essentially disappeared, with all three groups using marijuana at about the same levels.

Mason et al. (2017) describe the impact of discrimination on minority groups, stating that it is a common stressor and may increase vulnerability to risk behaviors such as early initiation of substance use, and substance use problems. Their work found a link between racial and socioeconomic discrimination and risk behavior in African American youth, which, they say, may be used as a coping mechanism.

The MTF study has also found that younger Hispanic adolescents may be somewhat more vulnerable to engaging in substance use, with Hispanic eighth graders reporting higher lifetime prevalence of substance use than White students (e.g., 27.4 percent for alcohol, compared to 23.2 percent, and African American students, 20.1 percent). They also reported higher last thirty-day prevalence of alcohol, cigarettes, and marijuana.

Figure 1.2 presents the overall prevalence and rate of alcohol use by race, as alcohol is one of the most used substances for ages twelve and older. It indicates that the highest use is among Native Hawaiians and the lowest is among Asians.

Research confirms that Black and Brown adolescents also face more severe consequences for their use that White adolescents, given the structural racism that has yet to be eliminated from our criminal justice system. Many minority group members also live in poverty and experience economic discrimination as well further compounding adolescent stress and tendency to use substances to escape the stressors (Mason, 2017). The impact of poverty and its

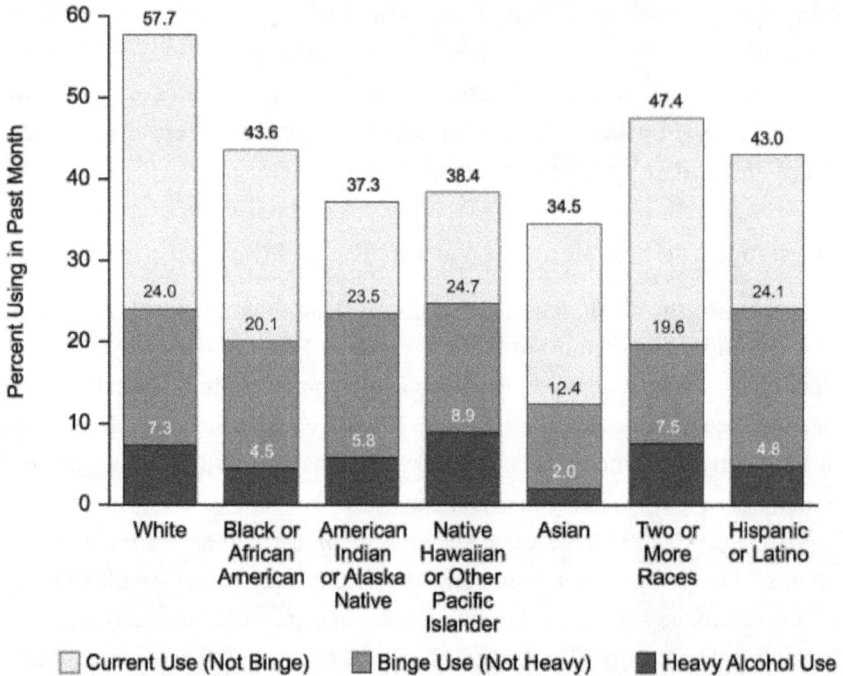

Figure 1.2   **Current, Binge, and Heavy Alcohol Use among Persons Aged Twelve or Older, by Race/Ethnicity: 2013.** www.samhsa.gov/data/sites/default/files/NSDUHresult sPDFWHTML2013/Web/NSDUHresults2013.htm

associated factors (e.g., neighborhood dysregulation, crime, violence) will be addressed further in chapter 9.

These numbers presented in this section reflect a very significant problem among middle and high schoolers. Even many educators are surprised to learn just how significant it is and how early many students begin using substances. This is particularly problematic due to the vulnerability of the adolescent brain and the long-term impact of early use.

THE ADOLESCENT BRAIN AND EARLY SUBSTANCE USE

The adolescent brain is known to be more vulnerable to the effects of sub-stances than the adult brain. The research on early substance use, and the impact of such use on the adolescent brain, is extremely troubling. Early use is dangerous and predictive of greater problems in young adulthood. Studies have confirmed that early adolescent substance use dramatically increases the risk of lifelong substance use disorder.

Alcohol, for example, is the most frequently misused drug by students. The National Institute of Alcohol Abuse and Alcoholism (NIAAA) notes that about 40 percent of teens who start drinking by age thirteen develop alcohol addiction, but only 10 percent of those who begin after the age of seventeen will be diagnosed with an AUD. Feinstein et al. (2012) found that nine out of ten people who meet the clinical criteria for SUDs began using substances before they were eighteen. They also found that individuals who began using substances before the age of fifteen were 6.5 times as likely to develop an SUD as those who delay use until age twenty-one or older.

The SAMSHA chart (figure 1.3) indicates rates of use of illicit drugs (including marijuana) by age over the past month.

Jordan and Anderson (2017) also confirm that risk taking and subsequent drug experimentation during adolescence increase the likelihood of developing a lifelong addiction. Their review of research found that, as individuals

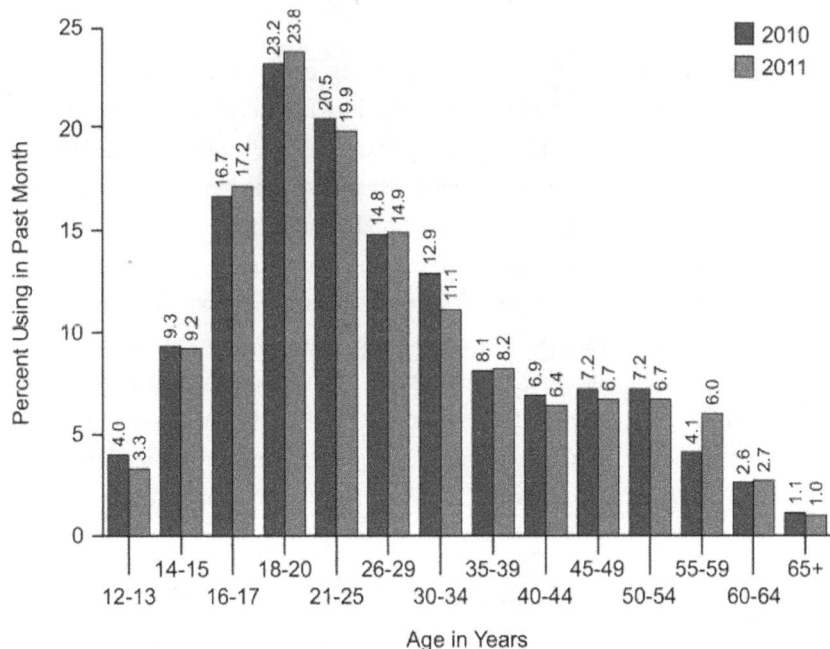

Figure 1.3   Past Month Illicit Drug Use among Persons Aged Twelve or Older, by Age: 2010 and 2011. www.samhsa.gov/data/sites/default/files/NSDUHresults2010/NSDUHresults2010.htm#fig2-4

continue to mature between thirteen and twenty-one years, the likelihood of lifetime substance abuse and dependence drops 4–5 percent for each year that initiation of substance use is delayed further suggesting early drug use conveys the greatest risk.

Researchers now know a lot more about the adolescent brain, and the fact that the brain doesn't fully mature until around the age of twenty-five. Winters and Arria (2012) refer to the front of our brains, the pre-frontal cortex, as the center of logical reasoning and impulse regulation. They say that, during adolescence, the regions further back including the limbic system (which controls emotions) mature earlier than the pre-frontal cortex.

Therefore, they say, the risk-taking, efforts at independence, lack of impulse control, the high emotions, the peer pressure, and the desire for instant gratification characteristic of adolescence can also contribute to a teen's risk for substance use and, potentially, a substance use disorder. Winters and Arria agree that adolescence as a developmental period is associated with the highest risk for developing a substance use disorder, and, that early age of onset, rather than duration of use, is a stronger predictor of the rapid progression of SUDs.

Winters and Arria also reference a growing body of research suggesting that learning may be adversely affected by drug use during adolescence, particularly if it is frequent and heavy. They also evidence indicating that adolescents who had treatment for a substance use disorder had poorer performance on verbal and non-verbal memory compared to controls.

The vulnerability of the adolescent brain, in combination with the invulnerable developmental stage of the adolescent, makes this a potentially dangerous combination. Starting substance use prevention very early is vital, with some advocates encouraging some form of prevention messaging continuously from pre-K to twelfth grade. There are critically important emotional regulation and coping skills that can be taught to even very young children, which can serve them in adolescence when the stakes are even higher.

RISK FACTORS FOR SUBSTANCE USE

What are some of the reasons students use substances? Most designations of risk factors break them down into five categories: individual, peers, family, school, and community.

Individual Factors

In addition to age at first use, other individual risk factors include temperament (e.g., early behavioral problems, impulsivity, and rebelliousness); mental health disorders (e.g., depression, ADHD); genetic predisposition; and/or early childhood trauma.

Temperament

Childhood temperament, characterized by behavioral disinhibition (a lack of control over one's behavior) and impulsivity, has been identified as a possible correlation to later onset of a substance use disorder. Such behavioral disinhibition, emotional dysregulation, and negative emotionality are described by Hussong et al. (2011) as characteristics leading to increased risk for internalizing symptoms that increase the risk of substance use. In the classroom, this can look like temper tantrums, inconsolable crying, or an inability to self-soothe.

According to Scheier (2010), there are unique aspects of temperament that can predict later substance use. These include activity level, emotionality, attention, rigidity, and sociability. They begin early in life, from ages two to four and then become impacted in life by environmental and familial contexts. Scheier cites research which shows that "future drug users were characterized as high on activity and restlessness, negativism and hostility, reactivity to frustration, independence, self-indulgence and rebelliousness... measures obtained at ages 3–5 predict substance use and even disorder in late adolescence and young adulthood" (p. 130).

These findings provide support for early identification and intervention for children continually exhibiting these behaviors to reduce later negative consequences. Increasing screening for these indicators in early childhood and providing intensive, evidence-based supports can reduce later problems.

Mental Health Disorders

Hussong et al. (2013) also found depressive symptoms as consistent predictors of adolescent substance use, along the lines of the self-medication theory. This theory suggests that individuals use substances to self-medicate negative experiences and emotions. They note that adolescent depression, more than anxiety, increases the odds of substance use onset.

ADHD has also been identified as a risk for substance use disorder and nicotine dependence in adolescence. A meta-analysis (i.e., a statistical comparison of studies) of multiple studies on the role of ADHD and substance use found that adolescents with ADHD are at 1.35 times increased risk of developing an AUD, at 2.36 times increased risk for developing nicotine use disorder, and at 3.48 times increased risk for non-alcohol drug use disorder (Groenman et al., 2013).

Finally, Molina and Pelham (2003) found that ADHD was of particular concern because children with ADHD often use substances at a younger age and experience more substance-related problems than their peers. Other disorders associated with substance use include conduct disorders, such as oppositional defiance disorder.

In a school setting, students with anxiety and depression zone out, opt out, and shut down. They are there but they are not there. Those with ADHD or conduct disorders, on the other hand, act up, disrupt, and often push away those who try to help them. Adding substance use into the mix makes these very challenging behaviors even more difficult to manage. And, of course, they interfere with the child's social and emotional development in terms of strained peer and adult relationships and disrupted learning environment.

Genetic Predisposition

Genes play a role in development of a substance use disorder. Initiation and early patterns of drug use are strongly influenced by family and social factors, whereas progression to heavy and compulsive use is strongly influenced by genetics (Hammond et al., 2014). Hammond et al. also note that genetic contributions to addictive disorders are significant, although few studies in adolescents are available.

Twin studies, studies of identical twins being raised in different environments and still experiencing addiction, suggest that genetic factors account for 30 percent to 70 percent of the variance in addiction, according to the National Institute on Drug Abuse (NIDA). According to NIDA, exposure to chronic environmental stress can actually alter gene function, while genes can also play a part in how someone responds to their environment. A genetic predisposition combined with an environment of trauma or chronic stress can increase the probability of developing a substance use disorder.

Childhood Trauma

Important work on adverse childhood experiences (ACEs) has informed ongoing research related to adolescent substance use. The seminal CDC-Kaiser ACE Study (Felitti et al., 1998) identified ten ACEs belonging to three broad categories: abuse (physical, emotional, sexual), neglect (physical, emotional), and household dysfunction (caregiver substance abuse, caregiver mental illness, caregiver divorce or separation, caregiver incarceration, domestic violence).

Of the thousands of adults surveyed regarding experiences with abuse and household dysfunction, over half reported experience with at least one ACE, and one-quarter reported experiencing two or more ACEs. Felitti et al. found that individuals who experienced four or more ACEs before age eighteen were at high risk for adverse physical and behavioral health outcomes, including heart disease, alcoholism, drug use, depression, sexually transmitted diseases, and premature death.

In addition, Chatterjee et al. (2018) found exposure to any abuse or household dysfunction predicted early initiation of alcohol and marijuana use, and exposure to any type of abuse or neglect and specific types of household dysfunction (i.e., parental incarceration and binge drinking, exposure to violence) was associated with adolescent marijuana and cocaine use. They also said that dose response relationships were observed, supporting the assertion that exposure to more types of ACEs was associated with drug use.

Then there is the additive effect to consider. In their review of studies on ACEs and substance use, Folk et al. (2020) found a strong positive relationship between ACEs and psychiatric symptoms or mental health problems. They identified evidence of an increased risk of psychiatric symptoms for adolescents who experienced four or more ACEs.

These additive effects of ACE show up in many ways in the classroom. Students either tune out and shut down or act up and strike out. They can be hyper-vigilant and explosive. They behave this way because they do not have the skills to self-soothe. They are in survival mode. A deeper understanding of the underlying causes of their behavior can result in solutions and strategies that will help them. These will be explored in later chapters.

The Influence of Peers

Parents and educators know peers and their influence are especially important in middle and high school. Peers often begin to have more influence over student behavior than their own family members. Friendships are vitally important for social-emotional development and helping students begin the process of greater and greater independence.

Peers may also influence student behavior in both negative and positive ways. Burrow-Sanchez and Hawken (2007) identify the risks peers can pose when it comes to substance use as including the following: peers who use or abuse drugs themselves, peers with favorable attitudes toward drugs, peers who engage in delinquent behaviors, peer rejection, and peers with deficits in social skills and problem solving.

Deutch et al. (2015) looked at the concept of closeness of friends and substance use and concluded that closeness significantly moderated the influence of problematic behaviors for tobacco and marijuana use. Mason et al. (2017) found that having friends who offer substances significantly increases the risk of use, so much so that being offered substances at age thirteen had a lasting effect on cigarette and marijuana use at age fifteen. They say that "it is reasonable to assume that a direct invitation to use substances carries influence, particularly if an adolescent is seeking to become established or fit in with an aspiring peer group" (p. 8).

Peer influence can affect substance use in a different way. There is something known as the "false consensus effect" when adolescents believe that one's peers are engaging in behaviors and at the same levels as oneself. This, says Mason et al., results in an adolescent's perceptions of friends' use that may greatly affect his or her own, even if those friends do not use or use infrequently.

Then there is the issue of unstructured time peers spend together. Mason et al. reference research that shows that involvement in unstructured socializing is associated with increased risks for delinquency and substance use. They claim that, of these three elements of unstructured time, (the absence of authority figures, the lack of structured activity, and the presence of peers), it is the effect of the peers that explains variation in substance use, as peers can instigate, reinforce, or provoke deviant behavior.

Hoeben et al. (2021) cite Warr's three motives to consider when adolescents are instigated or provoked to engage in these behaviors by their peers:

1) fear of ridicule; 2) status competition; and 3) desire to remain loyal to their friends. Examining these motives may help education professionals identify ways to counter these pressures on kids.

The Family

Addiction has been called a family disease and many of today's students are living in families with a parent or caregiver who is struggling with a substance use disorder themselves. Lipari and Van Horn (2017) report that about one in eight children seventeen or younger live with at least one parent who had a past year substance use disorder.

Whether it is the parent or the student, or both, the disorder affects every single person in the family constellation. The factors go back to in utero, and even back to generations, when genetic predisposition is involved. There are many factors to consider when it comes to the role of the family in adolescent substance use.

Bozzini et al. (2021) did a systematic study of risk factors associated with risk behaviors in adolescence, including substance use, and identified proximal (near) and distal (far) factors for various risk behaviors. They describe three basic ways in which lifelong effects of distal, or far, factors impact a child's future health and behavior:

1. prenatal factors such as maternal depression, tobacco, alcohol, caffeine, and other substance use during pregnancy;
2. birth conditions such as prematurity and low birth weight; and
3. experiences during early life such as adverse experiences (abuse, neglect, family violence, adoption), low family income and maternal or caregiver emotional problems (p. 216).

The distal family-related risk factors for adolescent alcohol use, for example, were:

- intrauterine alcohol exposure maternal depression in early childhood,
- low maternal age at birth, cumulative adverse experiences in early childhood,
- externalizing symptoms, and low family income at birth.

Proximal (or near) family-related risk factors for adolescent alcohol use included:

- sibling and peer alcohol use
- parental alcohol use or abuse, parental separation
- a single mother family
- parental style (overprotection) was associated with regular alcohol use in adolescence
- poor parental attachment (pp. 213–214).

Proximal family-related risk factors such as maternal smoking, friends who smoke tobacco, low parental monitoring, and having smoked tobacco by age eleven contributed to marijuana use by age seventeen to eighteen.

The distal risk factors for cigarette smoking in adolescence were behavioral and emotional problems during infancy, maternal smoking during pregnancy, boys born to single mothers, girls with high stress at age three, and exposure to maternal depression at four to five years old. The proximal risk factors for smoking in adolescence were child depression, maternal depression, current maternal smoking, peer drug use, parental separation, thrill-seeking behavior, stress, other risk behaviors, and the father's use of snuff.

As we can see, so many of these factors occur way before the child even thinks about taking that first sip or puff. Embedded in these lists are the factors that can be addressed in the present: parenting style, parental intimacy, parental knowledge, parental use, and parental attitudes toward substance use—elements that can be incorporated into school parent education programs.

Studies of traditional parenting styles, for example, have explored the correlations between authoritative, authoritarian, permissive, and neglectful parenting approaches. And have found that inconsistent parenting and hard parenting were risk factors for substance use, as were low parental knowledge, or monitoring of the child's behavior, whereabouts, and friends (Burrow-Sanchez and Hawkins, 2007).

A lack of parent–child bonding and intimacy is also associated with substance use. Studies also show that substance use and parents' neglect are greater in middle adolescence than in early adolescence. Support and family communication and perceived academic self-efficacy are lower. Substance use is positively related to parents' neglect, psychological control, and rejection. Also, a lack of rules with respect to substance use and permissiveness toward substance use in indulgent parenting increase the risk of substance use (Turpokar et al., 2019).

In subsequent chapters we will explore the vitally important role of the school as one of the few societal institutions with ability to reach parents and families on these issues.

The School

Burrow-Sanchez and Hawken (2007) highlight the school-related risk factors related to student substance use:

- academic failure
- low commitment or bonding to the school
- inappropriate classroom behavior (i.e., withdrawn, overly aggressive)
- low teacher expectations
- school disorganization
- unsafe school climate
- unclear school policies on substance use. (p. 34)

As seen by this list, schools represent a key context that influences adolescent substance use. Several studies have found that feeling connected with school (resulting from supportive relationships with peers and teachers) is associated with lower substance use.

It is also important to remember that the numbers presented in the various studies such as the MTF report only include students who are currently in school. They do not include the significant number of students who have dropped out (or who have been pushed out). Past studies of school dropouts noted that they were at even greater risk for substance use than students who remained in school.

The presence of substances in school is another risk factor. One survey of adolescents' perspectives on substance use (Debnam et al., 2018) found that many students identify substance use as a significant problem in their schools. They also reported finding substances easily accessible. They found that students also underestimate their associated harms. The risks appear, the survey authors note, to be greatest for males and as youth advance in grade level.

When it comes to student achievement, there is very strong evidence of an association between substance use, perceived self-efficacy in terms of academic performance, and resulting academic problems, with low perceived academic performance increasing negative emotions in substance users (Bozzini et al., 2021). And then many students come to school with multiple issues. Students who exhibit behavior problems, low internal control, depressive symptoms, poor parental attachment, *and* low school connectedness are significantly associated with alcohol use, they say.

Another issue is the preparedness of school staff to deal with adolescent substance use. Given the prevalence of student substance issues and the myriad of risk factors predisposing children to substance abuse, it is a concern that schools and professional preparation programs do not prepare educators on this issue. Professionals in a school building who might have the necessary expertise to address these issues with students (e.g., school psychologists, counselors, and social workers) report little or no preparation in this area.

For example, Burrow-Sanchez (2007) surveyed a group of school psychologists who reported that their lowest perceived competencies were in the provision of direct intervention services for SUDs (e.g., individual, group, and teaching curriculum). Most survey participants (76.3 percent) had not received such a course as part of their graduate training, nor had most (53 percent) received any training from their school or district on it in the prior three years, even though they were working with students who experienced substance use concerns.

The Community

Burrow-Sanchez and Hawken also identified community-level risk factors for student substance use. These include norms favoring substance use, disorganized and unsafe neighborhoods with high rates of crime, poverty and lack of resources, high levels of family transition and mobility, and disenfranchised cultural groups.

Findings on these community factors show that families and communities have more influence on substance use among children and young adolescents, whereas peer and school factors seem to have more influence for older adolescents. As children spend more time outside of the home, community and peer influences become more significant (Abadi et al., 2011). Abadi et al. also found that perceived availability of substances, positive community norms, and the risk of getting caught were significant predictors of several substance use outcomes.

There are many community risk factors that align with adverse childhood experiences: exposure to crime, a lack of feeling safe, disorganization and instability in family and neighborhood, and societal neglect when it comes to resources and supports for physical and emotional health. One in five children still lives in poverty in this country, and, as the pandemic made it undeniably obvious, there are a myriad of societal structures and supports that must be radically overhauled due to the disparate and negative impact they currently have on underserved communities.

Other community and societal structures such as policies and practices need to be reexamined. Laws governing age of purchase of legal substances, taxation of these substances, and enforcement of community standards can make a difference. Communities need to address crime and neighborhood safety, lack of resources, and availability of enriching activities for young people to engage in as some of the strategies that will help reduce adolescent substance use.

These are just a few examples of how community members can begin to recognize that the lack of these protections contributes to student substance use. Understanding the magnitude of the problem, for current and future generations, can increase commitment to making communities safer and more welcoming places for children and families.

PROTECTIVE FACTORS AND PROMISING PROGRAMS

Now that the dimensions of the challenge of student substance use have been identified and quantified, what should be done about it? The list of risk factors provides clues for us to explore how our schools and communities are structured to either increase or decrease exposure to the risk factors. With increased knowledge and understanding of the many dimensions of student substance use, these can be modified accordingly. Equally important are the protective factors, which the rest of this handbook will identify and develop, with implications for the classroom, the school, and the community.

The next several chapters will first look deeper at the individual factors in substance use and the many co-occurring conditions that accompany it (e.g., trauma, ADHD, conduct disorders, depression, and anxiety). Next, the recent research on the other factors (i.e., family, peers, school, and community) will be covered. These will be contrasted with the protective factors as a way to develop solutions to address them. Each chapter will include a profile of a promising, evidence-based program that educators might consider for addressing an identified need.

Addressing student substance use is not one of most educators' goals going into the profession. As illustrated here, it is one of the realities needing to be addressed if education professionals hope to reach and teach our students successfully. But educators don't have to do this work alone. There are resources, both within and outside of the school building. This volume will identify many of them.

What is needed is an understanding of what's going on with these children, a recognition of the signs and symptoms that they are in trouble, and knowledge of who and where to go for help and backup. The students before us in our classrooms are counting on us to see them, to understand them, and to help them when they cannot help themselves.

REFERENCES

Abadi, M. H., Shamblen, S. R., Thompson, K., Collins, D. A., & Johnson, K. (2011). Influence of Risk and Protective Factors on Substance Use Outcomes across Developmental Periods: A Comparison of Youth and Young Adults. *Substance Use & Misuse*, 46(13), 1604–1612. https://doi.org/10.3109/10826084.2011.598598. Epub 2011 Sep 7. PMID: 21899434.

Boman, IV J. H., Stogner, J., & Lee Miller, B. (2013). Binge Drinking, Marijuana Use, and Friendships: The Relationship between Similar and Dissimilar Usage and Friendship Quality. *Journal of Psychoactive Drugs*, 45(3), 218–226. [PubMed] [Google Scholar]

Bozzini, A. B., Bauer, A., Maruyama, J., Simões, R., & Matijasevich, A. (2021). Factors Associated with Risk Behaviors in Adolescence: A Systematic Review. *Revista brasileira de psiquiatria (Sao Paulo, Brazil: 1999)*, 43(2), 210–221. https://doi.org/10.1590/1516-4446-2019-0835

Burrow-Sanchez, J. J., & Hawken, L. S. (2007). *Helping Students Overcome Substance Abuse: Effective Practices for Prevention and Intervention (May 9, 2007)*. New York, NY: The Guilford Press.

Center for Behavioral Health Statistics and Quality. (2018). *2017 National Survey on Drug Use and Health: Detailed Tables*. Rockville, MD: Substance Abuse and Mental Health Services Administration.

Chatterjee, D., McMorris, B., Gower, A. L., Forster, M., Borowsky, I. W., & Eisenberg M. E. (2018). Adverse Childhood Experiences and Early Initiation of Marijuana and Alcohol Use: The Potential Moderating Effects of Internal Assets. *Substance Use & Misuse*, 53(10), 1624–1632. https://doi.org/10.1080/10826084 .2017.1421224. Epub 2018 Jan 24. PMID: 29364764.

Chen, X. (2016). Information Diffusion in the Evaluation of Medical Marijuana Laws' Impact on Risk Perception and Use. *American Journal of Public Health*, 106(12), e8.

Debnam, K. J., Saha, S., & Bradshaw, C. P. (2018). Synthetic and Other Drug Use among High School Students: The Role of Perceived Prevalence, Access, and Harms. *Substance Use & Misuse*, 53(12), 2069–2076. https://doi.org/10 .1080/10826084.2018.1455699. Epub 2018 Apr 6. PMID: 29624111; PMCID: PMC6136142.

Deutsch, A. R., Chernyavskiy, P., Steinley, D., & Slutske, W. S. (2015). Measuring Peer Socialization for Adolescent Substance Use: A Comparison of Perceived and Actual Friends' Substance Use Effects. *Journal of Studies on Alcohol and Drugs*, 76(2), 267–277. [PMC free article] [PubMed] [Google Scholar]

Feinstein, E. C., Richter, L., & Foster, S. E. (2012). Addressing the Critical Health Problem of Adolescent Substance Use through Health Care, Research, and Public Policy. *Journal of Adolescent Health*, 50(5), 431–436. https://doi.org/10.1016/j .jadohealth.2011.12.033. PMID: 22525104.

Felitti, V. J., Anda, R. F., Nordenberg, D., Williamson, D. F., Spitz, A. M., Edwards, V., Koss, M. P., & Marks, J. S. (1998). Relationship of Childhood Abuse and Household Dysfunction to Many of the Leading Causes of Death in Adults. The Adverse Childhood Experiences (ACE) Study. *American Journal of Preventive Medicine*, 14(4), 245–258. https://doi.org/10.1016/s0749-3797(98)00017-8. PMID: 9635069.

Folk, J. B., Ramos, L. M. C., Bath, E. P., Rosen, B., Marshall, B. D. L., Kemp, K., Brown, L., Conrad, S., & Tolou-Shams, M. (2021). The Prospective Impact of Adverse Childhood Experiences on Justice-involved Youth's Psychiatric Symptoms and Substance Use. *Journal of Consulting and Clinical Psychology*, 89(6), 483–498. https://doi.org/10.1037/ccp0000655

Groenman, A. P., Oosterlaan, J., Rommelse, N., Franke, B., Roeyers, H., Oades, R. D., Sergeant, J. A., Buitelaar, J. K., & Faraone, S. V. (2013). Substance Use Disorders in Adolescents with Attention Deficit Hyperactivity Disorder: A 4-year Follow-up Study. *Addiction,* 108(8), 1503–1511. https://doi.org/10.1111/add .12188. Epub 2013 Apr 22. PMID: 23506232.

Hammond, C. J., Mayes, L. C., & Potenza, M. N. (2014). Neurobiology of Adolescent Substance Use and Addictive Behaviors: Treatment Implications. *Adolescent Medicine: State of the Art Reviews*, 25(1), 15–32.

Hoeben, E. M., Osgood, D. W., Siennick, S. E., & Weerman, F. M. (2021). Hanging Out with the Wrong Crowd? The Role of Unstructured Socializing in Adolescents' Specialization in Delinquency and Substance Use. *Journal of Quantitative Criminology*, 37(1), 141–177. https://doi.org/10.1007/s10940-019-09447-4

Hussong, A., Burns, A., Solis, J., & Rothenberg, W. (2013). Future Directions in the Developmental Science of Addictions. *Journal of Clinical Child and Adolescent Psychology: The Official Journal for the Society of Clinical Child and Adolescent Psychology, American Psychological Association*, Division 53, 42. https://doi.org/10.1080/15374416.2013.838772

Jordan, C. J., & Andersen, S. L. (2017). Sensitive Periods of Substance Abuse: Early Risk for the Transition to Dependence. *Developmental Cognitive Neuroscience*, 25, 29–44. https://doi.org/10.1016/j.dcn.2016.10.004

Lipari, R. N., & Van Horn, S. L. (2017, August 24). Children Living with Parents Who Have a Substance Use Disorder. In: *The CBHSQ Report*. Rockville, MD: Substance Abuse and Mental Health Services Administration (US); 2013–. PMID: 29144715.

Mason, M. J., Zaharakis, N. M., Rusby, J. C., Westling, E., Light, J. M., Mennis, J., & Flay, B. R. (2017). A Longitudinal Study Predicting Adolescent Tobacco, Alcohol, and Marijuana Use by Behavioral Characteristics of Close Friends. *Psychology of Addictive Behaviors*, 31(6), 712–720. https://doi.org/10.1037/adb0000299

Miech, R. A., Johnston, L. D., Bachman, J. G., O'Malley, P. M., & Schulenberg, J. E. (2017). *Monitoring the Future: A Continuing Study of American Youth, 2017*. Ann Arbor, MI: Inter-university Consortium for Political and Social Research [distributor], 2018-10-29. https://doi.org/10.3886/ICPSR37183.v1

Miech, R. A., Johnston, L. D., Bachman, J. G., O'Malley, P. M., Schulenberg, J. E., & Patrick, M. E. (2020). *Monitoring the Future: A Continuing Study of American Youth, 2020*. Inter-university Consortium for Political and Social Research [distributor], 2021-10-26. https://doi.org/10.3886/ICPSR38156.v1

Molina, B. S., & Pelham, W. E. Jr. (2003). Childhood Predictors of Adolescent Substance Use in a Longitudinal Study of Children with ADHD. *Journal of Abnormal Psychology*, 112(3), 497–507. https://doi.org/10.1037/0021-843x.112.3.497. PMID: 12943028.

Nash, A., Marcus, M., Engebretson, J., & Bukstein, O. (2015). Recovery From Adolescent Substance Use Disorder: Young People in Recovery Describe the Process and Keys to Success in an Alternative Peer Group. *Journal of Groups in Addiction & Recovery*, 10(4), 290–312. https://doi.org/10.1080/1556035X.2015.1089805

NIDA Percentage of Adolescents Reporting Drug Use Decreased Significantly in 2021 as the COVID-19 Pandemic Endured, December 2021. Retrieved from:

Percentage of adolescents reporting drug use decreased significantly in 2021 as the COVID-19 pandemic endured | National Institute on Drug Abuse (NIDA).

SAMSHA Results from the 2011 National Survey on Drug Use and Health: Summary of National Findings. Retrieved from: Results from the 2011 NSDUH: Summary of National Findings, SAMHSA, CBHSQ.

SAMSHA Results from the 2013 National Survey on Drug Use and Health: Summary of National Findings. Retrieved from: Results from the 2013 NSDUH: Summary of National Findings, SAMHSA, CBHSQ.

SAMHSA, 2015. Behavioral Health Trends in the United States: Results from the 2014 National Survey on Drug Use and Health (HHS Publication No. SMA 15–4927, NSDUH Series H-50).

Scheier, L., ed. (2010). *Handbook of Drug Use Etiology*. Washington, DC: APA.

Tur-Porcar, A. M., Jiménez-Martínez, J., & Mestre-Escrivá, V. (2019). Substance Use in Early and Middle Adolescence. The Role of Academic Efficacy and Parenting. *Psychosocial Intervention*, 28, 139–145. https://doi.org/10.5093/pi2019a11

Winters, K. C., & Arria, A. (2011). Adolescent Brain Development and Drugs. *The Prevention Researcher*, 18(2), 21–24.

Wu, L., Woody, G. E., Yang, C., Pan, J., & Blazer, D. G. (2011). Racial/Ethnic Variations in Substance-Related Disorders Among Adolescents in the United States. *Archives of General Psychiatry*, 68(11), 1176–1185. https://doi.org/10.1001/archgenpsychiatry.2011.120

Chapter 2

Understanding Co-occuring Disorders

Trauma and Adolescent Substance Use

TRAUMA: DEFINITION AND PREVALENCE

In addition to little professional training on substance use prevention or addiction, today's teachers and school staff get little or no training on understanding and addressing childhood trauma. The concern related to the use of trauma-informed teaching and learning is a relatively new and important concept which has not yet been introduced in all school settings.

The CDC-Kaiser Permanente study on adverse childhood experiences (ACEs) was conducted in 1998, and is now replicated many times across different environments. Its groundbreaking finding is that the greater the number of bad things that happen to a child, the greater and greater problems the child experiences into adulthood.

The ACE study has had a great impact on the psychological community, and it is often discussed when referring to child development. It should be taught to anyone working with children. There are so many implications for educators and schools. For example, if four of the ten identified adverse experiences happen in a child's life, that child is thirty-two times more likely to have behavior problems in school (Burke et al., 2011).

The ACE study identified different experiences individuals could experience as children (e.g., abuse, neglect, and household challenges, such as domestic violence and parental divorce). The original study was conducted on middle-class, working adults who had health insurance. The number of negative experiences was found to be significantly and positively associated with adverse outcomes in adulthood, including chronic disease, mental illness, violence, health risk behaviors, and chronic health conditions such as heart disease (Dube et al., 2003). See Figure 2.1 for a visual look at the ACE pyramid of impact on health throughout the lifespan.

Adverse and traumatic experiences turn out to be very common: two-thirds of children have experienced at least one adverse event, and approximately and 13 percent of children have been exposed to multiple traumas (Burke et al., 2011). Emotional abuse (i.e., psychological abuse such as scaring, shaming, ignoring) was the most frequently reported trauma, observed among one in six.

Other traumas such as physical abuse and neglect, parental binge drinking or incarceration, being threatened with knife or at gunpoint, and witnessing a shooting or stabbing were each reported by 10 percent (Scheidell et al., 2018). They say that the ACE study, the first to evaluate a diverse range of childhood traumatic events as correlates of numerous health outcomes including

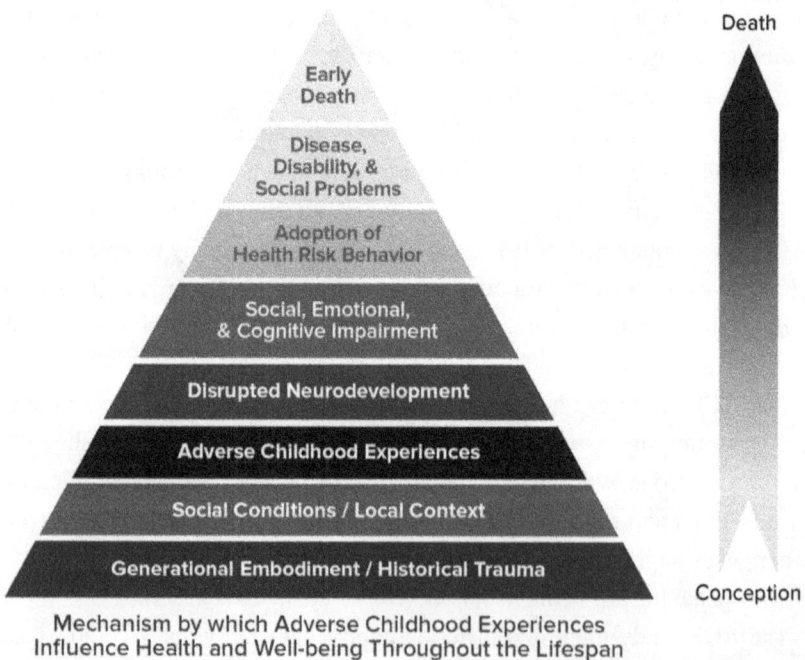

Mechanism by which Adverse Childhood Experiences
Influence Health and Well-being Throughout the Lifespan

Figure 2.1 The ACE Pyramid: Mechanism by which Adverse Childhood Experiences Influence Health and Well-being Throughout the Lifespan. The CDC-Kaiser Permanente adverse childhood experiences (ACE) study. *Content source: National Center for Injury Prevention and Control, Division of Violence Prevention.* https://www.cdc.gov/violenceprevention/aces/about.html

substance use, found that *each* of ten childhood traumas increased substantially the likelihood of adolescent and adulthood use of substances.

Shin et al. (2010) quantify the extent of child maltreatment. They note that in 2008 alone there were nearly six million referrals made to local child protective services for investigation. Over 888,000 children were known childhood maltreatment victims that year.

Beal et al. (2019) say that it is important to distinguish among risks related to unexpected trauma or tragedy (e.g., natural disaster, parental divorce), family instability (e.g., parental substance abuse or mental health concerns), and family violence (e.g., physical, or sexual abuse). They found that family violence was associated with poorer psychological well-being and quality of life, while family instability was associated with cigarette and marijuana use.

The ACE study has been replicated in a variety of diverse settings, including with low-income populations. Beal et al. found that vulnerability to adverse experiences is higher when children are exposed to poverty, family psychopathology, or other family relationship problems. They conclude that adverse or traumatic experiences occur frequently in childhood, are measurable, and are not randomly dispersed. Instead, some children are more vulnerable to exposure to traumatic events and environments than others.

This has tremendous implications for teachers and school staff, especially those in high-poverty urban areas. In Chicago, for example, one in every three children lives below the poverty level. That concentration of poverty and trauma, as measured by ACEs, calls for so much more than academics, the only thing most schools are set up for, even in more advantaged areas. The emotional effects seen in classrooms include *anxiety* and *depression* (called *internalizing behaviors*). Behavioral effects could be *hypervigilance, fighting,* and *acting out* (called *externalizing behaviors*).

These effects also affect their education progress. Traumatized and abused children are more likely to:

- Be in special education
- Have below grade level achievement
- Have poor work habits
- Are 2.5 times more likely to fail a grade
- Score lower on standardized tests

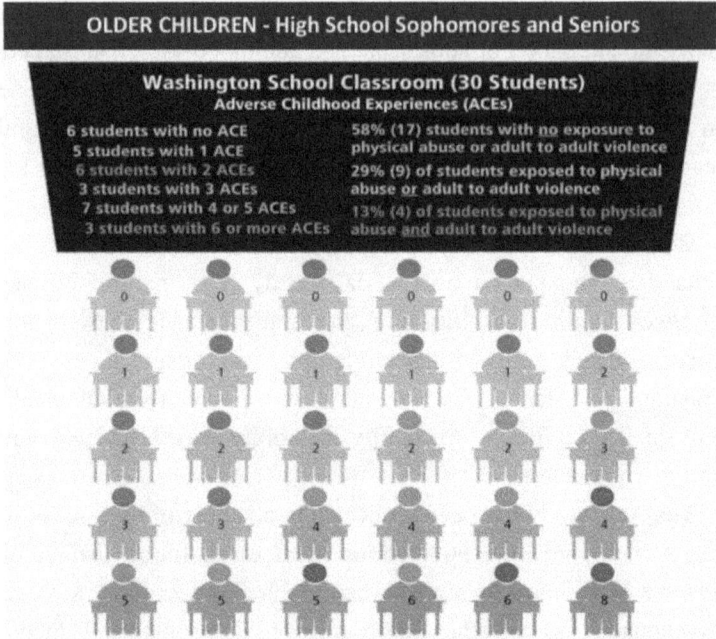

Figure 2.2   ACEs and High School Students. *Source: Washington State Family Policy Council* https://acestoohigh.com/2012/05/31/massachusetts-washington-state-lead-u-s -trauma-sensitive-school-movement/

- Have expressive or language difficulties (Massachusetts Advocates for Children, 2005)

Figure 2.2 illustrates what a typical high school would look like by the number of ACEs in a typical class of thirty students. Add in struggling with substance use, and this is a very serious problem that most educators are not prepared for. This indicates that an average of seven students out of a classroom of thirty students experience four or more ACEs, putting them at great risk for serious problems, including substance use.

TRAUMA AND SUBSTANCE USE

Correlation between Trauma and Substance Use

Internationally renowned physician Gabor Mate has treated and written extensively on *trauma* and *addiction*. He cites statistics which confirm that, for each adverse childhood experience, the risk for the early initiation of substance abuse increases between two- and fourfold. With five or more ACEs, there is a seven to ten times greater risk for substance abuse than those with none (Mate, 2012). He maintains that, rather than choice, chance, or genetic predetermination, it is childhood adversity that creates the susceptibility for addiction.

Why is this the case? Mate says that trauma in children, such as sexual, physical, or emotional abuse or abandonment, alters a child's physical stress mechanisms and, as a result, the child is more reactive to stress throughout his or her adult life. He finds that:

> "Studies of drug addicts repeatedly find extraordinarily high percentages of childhood trauma of various sorts, including physical, sexual and emotional abuse" and he says that one group of researchers was moved to remark that "our estimates . . . are of an order of magnitude rarely seen in epidemiology and public health" (p. 57.).

Another key factor, Mate notes, is the quality of the contact the parent provides, which in large part, is dependent on the parent's mood and stress level. Parental nurturing determines the levels of other key brain chemicals too. Even slight imbalances in these chemicals show up in aberrant behaviors such as fearfulness and hyperactivity and increase the individual's sensitivity to stressors for a lifetime. In turn, such acquired traits increase the risk of addiction.

Maternal deprivation and other types of adversity during infancy and childhood result in chronically high levels of the stress hormone cortisol, Mate says. Excess levels of stress hormone shrink important brain centers and impair structures important for memory and for the processing of emotions—and disturbs normal brain development. And these, of course, have lasting impacts on child well-being—and learning.

Villanueva et al. (2021) agree that the overall experience of suffering from adverse situations in childhood and adolescence is associated with a higher risk of substance abuse. As childhood adversity is strongly linked to social, emotional, and cognitive impairment, and to the adoption of health risk behaviors that promote these negative outcomes, these risky behaviors, such as the alcohol or drug abuse, become effective coping devices in the short term, due to their immediate benefits, to escape from the dramatic reality of negative experiences.

Shin et al. (2010) specify that childhood maltreatment not only influences the onset, but also shapes the longitudinal course of adolescent substance use. Their study found that adolescents with a history of childhood maltreatment were more likely to progress from less severe to more severe substance use than adolescents without such a maltreatment history. They also found

> that childhood maltreatment relates to the initial status of adolescent substance use . . . childhood maltreatment is related to deviations in several developmental processes related to optimal childhood development, which make maltreated children vulnerable to the initiation of substance use during adolescence.[[3], [46]] These deviations include increased expression of negative emotion,[[49]] poor emotion management skills,[51] behavioral dysregulation,[[52]] and internalizing symptoms like depression and anxiety.[54] Such compromised developmental competencies experienced by maltreated adolescents might also contribute to steeper increases in multiple-substance use and perpetuation of problematic patterns of multiple-substance use in adolescence. It is possible that the same developmental sequelae of childhood maltreatment that increase the likelihood of initiating substance use in adolescence might also harm individuals' resilience to recover and mature out of risky patterns of adolescent substance use (p. 460).

Such maltreatment has also been associated with acceleration of substance use and poly use (i.e., the use of multiple substances). Shin and colleagues found that adolescents who had been abused and/or neglected in childhood were more likely to transition into more severe substance use, and less likely to transition out of heavy polysubstance use than those without such a history.

Many researchers have found similar research confirmation of the link between trauma as evidenced in ACEs and substance use. For example, the Mills et al. (2013) research review confirms an association between child maltreatment and substance use disorders. Oshri et al. (2012) also identified multiple studies confirming that experiences of child maltreatment are associated with the development of less adaptive personality organizations, psychopathology, and alcohol and other drug use during adolescence and adulthood.

Yampolskaya et al. (2019) also advise of the need to look at both the severity and the chronicity of traumatic events in a child's life. They found that:

> The evidence for supporting adverse effects of maltreatment suggests differential effects of specific maltreatment types on substance use (Aarons et al., 2008; Cheng & Lo, 2010; Gabrielli et al., 2016). For example, Aarons et al. (2008)

found that three of the four types of maltreatment (physical, sexual abuse, and neglect) were related to significantly higher levels of substance use among youth ages 13-18 years. Emotional abuse was the only form of maltreatment that was not associated with substance use. Similarly, Casanueva, Stambaugh, Urato, Fraser, and Williams (2014) reported that physical abuse was related to both escalating marijuana use and any illicit substance during the follow-up period. Snyder and Smith (2015) have shown that youth who experienced physical abuse were at greater risk of abusing multiple drugs (p. 439).

Effect on Child and Adolescent Development

Mate (2012) says that many substance users self-medicate to soothe emotional pain and that their brain development is literally sabotaged by their traumatic experiences. The systems subverted by addiction—for example, the emotional brain, the stress apparatus, and the impulse control areas—are not able to develop normally under chronic stress. He notes that the brains of mistreated children have even been shown to be smaller than normal by 7 or 8 percent with below average volumes in multiple brain areas. This could show up in the classroom as impaired memory, learning disabilities, and/or a lack of control of emotions.

Scheidell et al. (2018) concur and describe a connection between the development and initiation (and continuation) of substance use and its effects on learning:

> Given that childhood is a highly formative development period, exposure to trauma and its co-occurring stress is associated with adverse effects on neurodevelopment and various neurological functions, including cognition, memory and affect regulation [25] [26] There is a complex hypothesized relationship between these functions and drug initiation and continued use. [27] (p. 44)

Even a relatively mild stress, claims Mate, can disturb a small child's physical stress mechanisms. Add neglect, abandonment, or abuse, and the child will be more reactive to stress throughout their life. He says that the stress-response mechanism is involved in addiction:

> Abandonment, neglect, or abuse (emotional, physical or sexual) can alter physical stress mechanisms and the child often becomes more reactive to stress throughout their life. Substance abuse or dependence is related to stress

response to self-soothe. Childhood emotional loss and trauma, then, provide both the experiential, psycho-emotional and physiological template for addiction. (p. 61)

Gender Considerations

Shin et al. (2010) conducted research on trauma, child sexual abuse, and substance use. They found that male adolescents were more likely to start from a multiple substance use type than were female adolescents. Their review of research shows that male adolescents had higher rates than females for current use of marijuana, cocaine, opioids, and hallucinogens. They also found that being male was associated with elevated probabilities to transition to more severe substance use.

Mallett (2015) explored the incarceration of seriously traumatized adolescents. These young people reported up to twice the incidence of mental health disorders, and up to sixty times the level of trauma. Mallett says that girls and boys share some risk factors for delinquency, but their exposure rates and levels differ. He found that significantly more incarcerated girls, for example, are victims of maltreatment (especially sexual abuse) compared with incarcerated boys.

Mate (2012) notes that rates of victimization among women substance abusers range from 50 percent to nearly 100 percent and found that those experiencing both physical and sexual abuse were at least twice as likely to be using drugs than those who experienced either abuse alone. Those who had suffered sexual abuse were three times more likely to begin drinking in adolescence than those who had not. For each emotionally traumatic childhood circumstance, Mate found, there is a two-to-threefold increase in the likelihood of early alcohol abuse.

Race and Culture Considerations

As mentioned, the ACE study has been replicated in many diverse settings with diverse populations, including minority and low-income communities. Villanueva et al. (2021) reviewed this research and found that:

Although some studies found that young people from racial/ethnic minorities were at a greater risk of experiencing higher levels of adversity [[10], [34]], other studies also highlighted subtle differences between these minority ethnic groups. For example, Native Americans reported the highest rates of total adversity, and Hispanics the lowest [[33]]. Moreover, Forster et al. [[29]] found that among Pacific/Asian emerging adults, increasing ACE enhanced vulnerability to different substance use behaviors and polysubstance use (p. 424).

Drake et al. (2009) found that Black children and youth (ages seven to eighteen) are disproportionately exposed to abuse, neglect, and other victimizations and that this disproportionate exposure places Black children and youth at elevated risk for negative health outcomes.

Hicks et al. (2021) also studied ACEs among minority youth. Using the U.S. Department of Health and Human Services data, they show that Black children and youth are the most vulnerable to victimization compared to other racial/ethnic groups: Black children and youth were victimized 82 percent more than their White counterparts and 74 percent greater than Hispanic children and youth. Mersky et al. (2013) found associations between ACEs and substance use among ethnically minority children, which included Black and Hispanic children.

In the Hicks et al. study, ACEs were found to be directly and positively associated with psychological distress that is, the more children experience ACEs, the rate of psychological distress reporting is higher. Then, psychological distress was directly and positively linked to substance use and delinquency. They confirmed a cumulative increase in risk for negative mental health, and internalizing and externalizing behaviors, with each additional ACE experienced. As Black children and youth experience more instances of ACEs, they reported higher levels of psychological distress, substance use, and delinquency.

Staff in high-poverty, minority elementary and high schools see the impact of stress and trauma on students every day, in a disproportionate number of dysfunctional homes, chronic exposure to community violence, and physical and sexual abuse. Many students act out, but there are just as many who shut down. For example, one high-poverty, urban high school analyzed the failure rates of its freshman students and found fully one-third of them were failing *more* than one class even though they had good attendance and did not exhibit behavior problems (Lynch, 2017). Teachers were stymied.

The students showed up every day and did nothing. Had they been screened for ACEs, it might have revealed many issues that the school staff might have been able to address, had they had a trauma-informed strategy.

That same year a survey was conducted of all 2,000 students. The staff was shocked to learn that about 40 percent of the students reported that they did not have an adult in the school they felt they could connect with. That school had some work to do.

Types of Trauma and Type of Drug Used

As previously noted, not all types of trauma, or ACEs, have the same effect. Some studies speak to general maltreatment, which others have been able to sift out which type of trauma has an association, or a correlation, to a certain of substance use.

Marijuana

Mills et al. (2014) identified a study of maltreated children and found they were more likely to use marijuana before the age of seventeen, use marijuana as an adult, use marijuana daily, and meet medical criteria for marijuana dependence. This study found that marijuana use in young adults is associated strongly with exposure to child abuse and neglect. There is a strong association between child maltreatment and early onset of marijuana use, independent of behavior problems and other adolescent substance use.

Marijuana and Cocaine

Scheidell et al. (2018) describe a study of court-documented cases of abuse and neglect before the age of twelve years, which demonstrated that trauma was associated with an approximately 50 percent increase in past-year marijuana in adulthood. They found that individual types of maltreatment, as well as the total number of ACEs experienced, were associated significantly with marijuana and cocaine use.

Cocaine

Scheidell et al. looked at the relationship between trauma and drug use, in particular cocaine. Each trauma was associated with elevated odds of early initiation (defined as fourteen years or younger) and lifetime use of street drugs. Each traumatic event was associated with an increase in the odds of adolescent and adult use of cocaine.

Alcohol

Villanueva et al. (2021) studied parental and sibling alcoholism and illegal drug use. They found that they increased the risk of both alcoholism and drug use. Emotional abuse and substance abuse in the household were significant predictors of alcohol consumption, and sexual abuse and emotional neglect were significant predictors of drug consumption. Shin et al. (2010) found physical abuse associated with alcohol. And Dube et al. (2003) also concluded that stress and trauma were associated with consumption of alcohol at an early age to self-regulate negative or painful emotions.

These findings really show that there are so many children struggling with trauma and, possibly, in danger of or struggling with substance use. And it is not only about the students with the externalizing (and aggravating and annoying) behaviors. The quiet ones, those staring off into space, in another world may be suffering and in danger of substance use too. How many more could be helped if more school staff know about and understand the associations between, ACEs, trauma, and substance use?

The next necessary step is to have a deep understanding of the risk factors. For if educators understand the risk factors, they may be able to identify ways to minimize, reduce, or eliminate their potentially deadly impact on children.

TRAUMA AND SUBSTANCE ABUSE: RISK FACTORS

Family Dysfunction and Discipline

Educators understand how vital families are to student success. They also see the terrible cost that family dysfunction has on so many students: students unable to handle their emotions, students lashing out at others, students so withdrawn that their teachers hardly know that they are there.

Exposure to family violence and inter-parental conflict may undermine the attachment security and lead to intensified anxiety, say Garland et al. (2013). Children growing up under these circumstances may engage in substance use behaviors as a means of coping with anxiety and anxiety-related symptoms, because they have not had an opportunity to handle them.

Shin et al. (2010) found that adolescents who had been abused and/ or neglected in childhood are more likely to transition into more severe substance use, and less likely to transition out of heavy use of multiple substances, than those without such a history. Neglect can also lead to substance-seeking behaviors, say Yampolskya et al. (2019) suggesting that due to neglect, a child might gravitate to other (possibly detrimental) figures and activities to get their attachment needs met.

Milburn et al. (2005) examined the influence of trauma and family factors (e.g., poor family functioning and family conflict) on mental health problems and externalizing behaviors (substance use, delinquent behaviors, and sexual risk) among 201 homeless adolescents, ages twelve to seventeen years. They found that trauma, poor family functioning, and family conflict significantly predicted greater mental health problems, delinquent behaviors, high-risk sexual behaviors, and substance use.

Parental Substance Use

Parental substance use has many repercussions on children. The parent's focus on the substance means less attention on or monitoring of the children, and less knowledge of what is going on with the child. Discipline becomes inconsistent and erratic. Parental substance use is often correlated with child abuse.

According to the Child Welfare League, approximately 25 percent of children live with a parent who uses alcohol or other drugs (Lam et al., 2004). Regardless of type of parental substance use, researchers conclude that children of a parent who abuses alcohol or illicit drugs are at increased risk for psychological and academic problems, and maladaptive behaviors, including substance use.

Francis (2011) also found that children of substance-abusing parents were at greatest risk for behavioral and physiological damage when exposed to substances in utero. Some of these issues, she warns, may last well beyond childhood. Educators often see students suffering with learning and behavior problems related to fetal alcohol syndrome, for example.

According to Johnson and Leff (1999), the single most potent risk factor for children is their parent's substance-abusing behavior. Biederman and colleagues (2000) found that adolescence is a critical developmental period for exposure to parental substance use. They say that independent of parental lifetime substance use history, exposure to parental substance use predicts substance use in children.

A review of the literature on parental substance use and its effects on children finds that children of substance-abusing parents have been found to be at higher risk for several negative outcomes, including:

- substance use
- delinquency
- negative health behaviors
- risky sexual activity and associated health problems
- school truancy
- academic problems
- psychological problems
- foster care placement
- homelessness

Merikangas and colleagues (1998) found that children of substance users had higher rates of conduct disorder, smoking, and drug use, and lower overall functioning than children of parents with no history of psychiatric disorders. Because of their substance use issues, parents are also at risk for having their children placed in the foster care system.

Related Problems: Foster Care and Homelessness

Many parents have lost custody of their children because of substance use. Estimates based on nationally representative samples indicate that up to 47 percent of child welfare-involved youth use alcohol and illicit drugs and that 19 percent have substance use disorders (Traube et al., 2012). Shin and colleagues also found that the speed of progression to problematic multiple substance use during adolescence may be much faster among high-risk populations, including adolescents involved in publicly funded service systems (i.e., foster care) than among the general population.

Older male adolescents (ages fifteen to eighteen) involved with foster care were at high risk for developing and maintaining multiple substance use. Shin et al. concluded that adolescents in foster care who have been exposed to childhood maltreatment are the most likely group to develop substance abuse and dependence in adulthood. Beal et al. (2019) also found that child maltreatment and entry into foster care were associated with increased acute and chronic health concerns as well as substance use.

Yampolskya et al. (2019) summarized studies that showed that child welfare-involved youth are among those who are at highest risk for substance use. Yampolskya et al. document other research confirming that between 50 and 80 percent of maltreated children involved in the child welfare system have emotional disorders, developmental delays, and other indications of behavioral problems. They say that the presence of behavioral and emotional problems, and externalizing problems such as fighting, may be a critical factor related to substance use.

Many families that struggle with parental substance abuse end up homeless, which adds another dimension of danger for their children. The National Alliance to End Homelessness says that adolescents comprise 22.1 percent of the homeless population in the United States, which translates to approximately 1.7 million young people being homeless on any given night (National Alliance to End Homelessness, 2014). Research has found that homeless adolescents report significantly high rates of mental health problems (approximately 19–53 percent), substance use, and trauma histories (Merscham, Van Leeuwen, & McGuire, 2009).

Milburn et al. found that homeless adolescents are more likely to report using substances, citing research which showed that, for example, 57 percent to 70 percent of samples of homeless adolescents report current alcohol use, 52 percent report consuming five or more alcoholic drinks a week, and 38 percent report having fifteen or more drinks per week. They also found data on high rates of marijuana use, injection drug use, polysubstance use, high-risk sexual behaviors and sexually transmitted diseases (STDs), and delinquency among homeless youth. They further warn that adolescents tend to engage in more than one risk-taking behavior at a time.

Risk-Taking, Delinquency, and Incarceration

Those who live or work with adolescents know that risk-taking and feeling invincible come with the territory. Francis (2011) says that adolescents engaging in risk behaviors such as substance use and risky sexual activity are at increased risk for contracting STDs, unplanned pregnancy, and other critical health problems. Francis describes studies of the relationship of adolescent substance use to sexual risk-taking behavior in late adolescence and young adulthood, which showed high correlations between them.

Conduct problems and delinquency have also been cited in the multiple risk factors experienced by traumatized youth and adolescents. Mallet (2015) studied incarcerated youth and, in addition to the disproportionate numbers of minorities in confinement, found that most incarcerated young offenders had impairing mental health problems, trauma histories, and educational deficits. Not only were these issues more prevalent (up to sixty times greater than the general adolescent population, according to one researcher), their disorders tended to be more severe as well.

Typically, says Mallet, a combination of risk factors, rather than any single experience, leads to delinquency and court involvement and, for some, incarceration. These risks include poverty, unstable and disorganized neighborhoods, violence, trauma history, mental health and substance abuse difficulties, school failure, learning problems (including learning disabilities), negative or delinquent peers, and dysfunctional families.

Mallet also notes an additional pathway from minor offending to the juvenile courts is the "school-to-prison pipeline," an outgrowth of the failed zero tolerance policies that grew out of the anti-crime 1990s. He says that "zero-tolerance policies prioritize disciplinary measures for disruptive behaviors in schools, including suspensions and expulsions, school-based arrests (mostly for misdemeanors), alternative special disciplinary schools and referrals to the juvenile courts—even though evidence increasingly indicates that these measures do not make schools safer or improve student behaviors" (p. 7).

School staff see multiple risk-taking behaviors playing out frequently in middle and high schools. Students using substances make many other, often dangerous, decisions: who to hang out with, whether to skip school today, whether to drive with someone under the influence, whether to pick up a weapon, or join a gang. Then, when caught with drugs or weapons, they get put into the school-to-prison pipeline as police are called, and their futures get dimmer and dimmer.

TRAUMA AND SUBSTANCE USE: PROTECTIVE FACTORS

Given the research on trauma and substance use, the following are research-based approaches and strategies that schools can begin to address, or better address, the twin issues of trauma and substance abuse. They are:

1. Screen for problems
2. Target at risk groups for support recognizing the quantity and quality of ACEs

3. Focus on the quality of attachment relationships
4. Provide staff training
5. Provide parent training
6. Adopt evidence-based interventions
7. Interrupt the school-to-prison pipeline
8. Promote trauma-informed teaching
9. Teach resiliency

Scheidell et al. (2018) emphasize that traumatic events during childhood have long-lasting detrimental effects. They remind us that while primary prevention of childhood trauma is the ultimate and ideal goal, interventions should address diverse types and the cumulative number of childhood traumas to reduce and prevent drug use.

To that end, Beal et al. (2019) recommend using existing measures of childhood adversity in a novel way to identify children at risk and deliver effective prevention services to the young people who are most likely to benefit. Strong bonds play a significant role in decreasing the likelihood that youths with engage in risky behaviors. School Staff can not only screen for students who need support, but work to ensure that staff-student connectedness is a priority across the board throughout every aspect of classroom and school culture.

Resiliency comes up repeatedly in the literature as a vital attribute that those struggling with trauma can learn to help them cope. *Resiliency*, the ability to bounce back from adversity, is a skill that can be taught, modeled, reinforced, and integrated through a child's school experience even without a substance use prevention curriculum.

Mallet (2015) calls for dismantling the school-to-prison pipeline. This, he says, requires reducing school (and juvenile justice) disciplinary actions and increasing preventative and non- exclusionary intervention strategies. Positive behavioral support, peer mediation, and conflict resolution programs, as well as other restorative justice models have shown to improve outcomes for adolescents with behavior problems.

A trauma-informed school starts with common training and a common understanding that, for so many children, school is their only hope to be heard and seen. Being connected with a caring adult at school when there isn't one at home can make all the difference for a child who is struggling. That connection builds trust, and that trust will enable that child to confide in that caring adult and, hopefully, get directed to the help and resources they need.

PROMISING PROGRAM: COGNITIVE-BEHAVIORAL INTERVENTION FOR TRAUMA IN SCHOOLS (CBITS)

The CBITS program is a school-based, group and individual intervention. As described on its website, it is designed to reduce symptoms of post-traumatic stress disorder (PTSD), depression, and behavioral problems, and to improve functioning, grades and attendance, peer, and parent support, and coping skills. This school-based program is designed to be delivered in school settings.

CBITS has been used with students from fifth grade through twelfth grade who have witnessed or experienced traumatic life events such as community and school violence, accidents and injuries, physical abuse and domestic violence, and natural and man-made disasters. CBITS uses cognitive-behavioral techniques (e.g., psychoeducation, relaxation, social problem solving, cognitive restructuring, and exposure).

CBITS is designed for delivery by mental health professionals in a school setting. The program consists of:

- 10 group sessions
- 1–3 individual sessions
- 2 parent psychoeducational sessions
- 1 teacher educational session

CBITS has been adapted for use with low-literacy groups, and children in foster care. It has been officially translated into Spanish and Arabic. CBITS has also been modified for delivery by non-clinicians and in a variety of settings (urban, rural, suburban, and tribal; see www.ssetprogram.org), and for younger elementary school students.

CBITS is described by the National Child Traumatic Stress Network as an ideal trauma intervention for underserved ethnic minority students who frequently do not receive services due to a whole host of barriers to traditional mental health services.

CBITS has also addressed the barrier of parent and family involvement that can be so common in many communities. They use a community-based participatory partnership model of including ethnic minority parents from the community being served along with community leaders, clinicians, and researchers to design the implementation plan so that the program is presented in a relevant and culturally congruent way.

Developers say that extensive research since 2000 has shown that students who participate in the program have significantly fewer symptoms of post-traumatic stress, depression, and psychosocial dysfunction.

TRAUMA AND SUBSTANCE USE: CONCLUDING THOUGHTS

Schools have a role in screening, prevention, and intervention so that our students don't end up in the juvenile justice system in the first place. Zero tolerance policies (except in the most extreme cases such as bringing a weapon to school) have failed the very children they were intended to help. The school-to-prison pipeline does not help students. It often warehouses and criminalizes them. The very students who need help the most are exiled to detention, suspension, and expulsion. Too often schools have pushed away the very children who, through their behavior, are crying out for help.

Thanks to the ACE study, so much more is known about childhood trauma and its impact of child development. The research described here details the pathway from trauma to risky behavior and substance use. Becoming more informed is a starting point. New information changes mindsets. This is essential to nurture the bonding and trust so that students can talk to concerned adults about what is going on with them, instead of answering a survey saying that they have not one adult in the school they can talk to.

That mindset shift is the question Jamie Meyer asks in her TED Talk. Instead of asking "What's the matter with you?!" when a student acts out, ask, "What happened to you?" That can make all the difference.

REFERENCES

Beal, S. J., Mara, C. A., Greiner, M. V., Wingrove, T., Lutz, N., & Noll, J. G. (2019). Childhood Adversity and Associated Psychosocial Function in Adolescents with Complex Trauma. *Child & Youth Care Forum*, 48(3), 305–322. https://doi.org/10.1007/s10566-018-9479-5

Biederman, J., Faraone, S. V., Monuteaux, M. C., & Feighner, J. A. (2000). Patterns of Alcohol and Drug Use in Adolescents can be Predicted by Parental Substance Use Disorders. *Pediatrics*, 106(4), 727–797.

Burke, N. J., Hellman, J. L., Scott, B. G., Weems, C. F., & Carrion, V. G. (2011). The Impact of Adverse Childhood Experiences on an Urban Pediatric Population. *Child Abuse & Neglect*, 35(6), 408–413.

CBITS (Cognitive Behavioral Intervention for Trauma in Schools). Center for Resiliency, Hope and Wellness in Schools. www.https://traumaawareschools.org

Dube, S. R., Felitti, V. J., Dong, M., Chapman, D. P., Giles, W. H., & Anda, R. F. (2003). Childhood Abuse, Neglect, and Household Dysfunction and the Risk of Illicit Drug Use: The Adverse Childhood Experiences Study. *Pediatrics*, 111, 564–572.

Francis, S. (2011). Using a Framework to Explore Associations Between Parental Substance Use and the Health Outcomes of their Adolescent Children. *Journal of Child & Adolescent Substance Abuse*, 20(1), 1–14. https://doi.org/10.1080/1067828X.2010.517736

Garland, E. L., Pettus-Davis, C., & Howard, M. O. (2013). Self-medication among Traumatized Youth: Structural Equation Modeling of Pathways between Trauma History, Substance Misuse, and Psychological Distress. *Journal of Behavioral Medicine*, 36(2), 175–185. https://doi.org/10.1007/s10865-012-9413-5

Hicks, M. R., Kernsmith, P., & Smith-Darden, J. (2021). The Effects of Adverse Childhood Experiences on Internalizing and Externalizing Behaviors among Black Children and Youth. *Journal of Child & Adolescent Trauma*, 14(1), 115–122. https://doi.org/10.1007/s40653-020-00316-y

Johnson, J. L., & Leff, M. (1999). Children of Substance Abusers: Overview of Research Findings. *Pediatrics*, 103(Suppl), 1085–1099.

Lam, W. K. K., Wechsberg, W., & Zule, W. (2004). African American Women Who Use Crack Cocaine: A Comparison of Mothers Who Live With and Have Been Separated from their Children. *Child Abuse and Neglect*, 28(11), 1229–1247.

Lansford, J. E., Dodge, K. A., Pettit, G. S., & Bates, J. E. (2010). Does Physical Abuse in Early Childhood Predict Substance Use in Adolescence and Early Adulthood? *Child Maltreatment*, 15(2), 190–194.

Lynch, D. (2017) Schooled in Fear: Lessons Learned About Keeping Students and Staff Safe. Rowman and Littlefield, Landham, MD.

Mallett, C. A. (2015). The Incarceration of Seriously Traumatized Adolescents in the USA: Limited Progress and Significant Harm. *Criminal Behavior & Mental Health*, 25(1), 1–9. https://doi.org/10.1002/cbm.1946

Massachusetts Advocates for Children. (2005). Helping Traumatized Children Learn 1&2: Supportive School Environments for Children Traumatized by Family Violence. Retrieved from http://traumasensitiveschools.org/tlpi-publications/download-a-free-copy-of-helping-traumatized-children-learn/

Merikangas, K. R., Dierker, L. C., & Szatmari, P. (1998). Children of Parents with Substance Abuse Disorders had Higher Rates of Conduct Disorder and Substance Use. *Journal of Child Psychology and Psychiatry*, 39, 711–720.

Merscham, C., Van Leeuwen, J. M., & McGuire, M. (2009). Mental Health, and Substance Abuse Indicators among Homeless Youth in Denver, Colorado. *Child Welfare*, 88(2), 93, 110.

Mersky, J. P., Topitzes, J., & Reynolds, A. J. (2013). Impacts of Adverse Childhood Experiences on Health, Mental Health, and Substance Use in Early Adulthood: A Cohort Study of an Urban, Minority Sample in the US. *Child Abuse & Neglect*, 37(11), 917–925.

Milburn, N. G., Rotheram-Borus, M. J., Batterham, P., Brumback, B., Rosenthal, D., & Mallett, S. (2005). Predictors of Close Family Relationships over One Year among Homeless Young People. *Journal of Adolescents*, 28, 263, 275.

Mills, R. J., Scott, J., Alati, R., O'Callaghan, M., Najman, J. M., & Strathearn, L. (2013). Child Maltreatment and Adolescent Mental Health Problems in a Large Birth Cohort. *Child Abuse & Neglect*, 37, 292–302. (National Alliance to End Homelessness, 2014).

National Alliance to End Homelessness. (2014). *An Emerging Framework for Ending Unaccompanied Youth Homelessness*. National Alliance to End Homelessness, Washington, DC.

Oshri, A., Tubman, J. G., & Brunette, M. (2012). Childhood Maltreatment Histories, Alcohol and Other Drug Use Symptoms, and Sexual Risk Behavior in a Treatment Sample of Adolescents. *American Journal of Public Health*, 102(Suppl. 2), S250–S257. https://doi.org/10.2105/AJPH.2011.300628

Scheidell, J. D., Quinn, K., McGorray, S. P., Frueh, B. C., Beharie, N. N., Cottler, L. B., & Khan, M. R. (2018). Childhood Traumatic Experiences and the Association with Marijuana and Cocaine Use in Adolescence through Adulthood. *Addiction*, 113(1), 44–56. https://doi.org/10.1111/add.13921

Sharp, S. F., Peck, B. M., & Hartsfield, J. (2012). Childhood Adversity and Substance Use of Women Prisoners: A General Strain Theory Approach. *Journal of Criminal Justice*, 40(3), 202–211.

Shin, S. H., Hong, H. G., & Hazen, A. L. (2010). Childhood Sexual Abuse and Adolescent Substance Use: A Latent Class Analysis. *Drug Alcohol Depend*, 109, 226–235.

Traube, D. E., James, S., Zhang, J., & Landsverk, J. (2012). A National Study of Risk and Protective Factors for Substance Use Among Youth in the Child Welfare System. *Addictive Behaviors*, 37(5), 641–650. https://doi.org/10.1016/j.addbeh.2012.01.015

Villanueva, L., & Gomis-Pomares, A. (2021). The Cumulative and Differential Relation of Adverse Childhood Experiences and Substance Use During Emerging Adulthood. *Child Psychiatry & Human Development*, 52(3), 420–429. https://doi.org/10.1007/s10578-020-01029-x

Washington State Family Council, The Washington State Family Policy Council Legacy, ACE Response. Retrieved from: Washington State Family Policy Council (aceresponse.org)

Yampolskaya, S., Chuang, E., & Walker, C. (2019). Trajectories of Substance Use among Child Welfare Involved Youth: Longitudinal Associations with Child Maltreatment History and Emotional/Behavior Problems. *Substance Use & Misuse*, 54(3), 437–448. https://doi.org/10.1080/10826084.2018.150407

Chapter 3

Understanding Co-occurring Disorders

ADHD and Adolescent Substance Use

ADHD: DEFINITION AND PREVALENCE

Margherio et al. (2014) describe ADHD as a highly chronic neurocognitive behavioral disorder. Varying estimates of the number of schoolchildren diagnosed with ADHD are between 5 and 10 percent. In a typical class of thirty, that would be at least two students, in addition to all the other children with behavioral difficulties and special needs. The symptoms and associated impairment often continue into adolescence and adulthood.

The symptoms of ADHD cause many challenges for students so diagnosed. Common symptoms include hyperactivity, of course, but also impulsivity, lack of self-control, impaired executive functioning, hyperarousal, low frustration tolerance, and unpredictable moods. Any one of those symptoms would be distressful. Several of them negatively impact social emotional development, as well as academic achievement. Figure 3.1 presents a list of other disorders also associated with ADHD.

According to Virtulano et al. (2014), students with ADHD are likely to experience poorer academic performance, which may be a function of associated neurocognitive deficits. In addition to increased conflict in school, students with ADHD symptoms demonstrate less academic engagement compared with their peers.

The challenges such students face include school failure and its associated disconnectedness, peer rejection, and anxiety and depression (Flory et al., 2003). Students who have behavioral problems in the classroom, such as

Percentage of children with ADHD and another disorder[1]

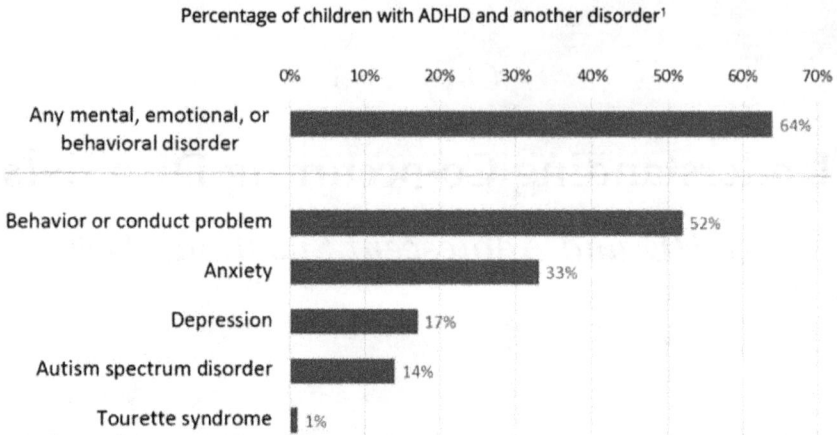

Figure 3.1   **Percentage of Children with ADHD and Another Disorder**. Content source: National Center on Birth Defects and Developmental Disabilities. https://www.cdc.gov/ncbddd/adhd/data.html

those with ADHD, often experience school adjustment problems and rejection by peers as a result. Children with ADHD are, in fact, rated lower on social preference, disliked by children of higher status, and over 50 percent are rejected by peers (Hoza et al., 2005).

The rejection often comes as a result of poor emotional regulation. ADHD is associated with emotional lability which includes symptoms such as irritability, hot temper, low frustration tolerance, and sudden unpredictable shifts toward negative emotions such as anger and sadness. The Virtulano et al. review found that a failure to bond with peers, teachers, and the academic system has been shown to influence social and emotional adjustment, including increased depression and other internalizing symptoms, symptoms, they say, are directly linked to substance use.

In fact, one of the most concerning issues associated with ADHD symptoms is the risk for early substance use (Molina & Pelham, 2003).

CO-OCCURRING DISORDER: ADHD AND SUD

These challenges of ADHD result in a great deal of stress on the individual student, the class, and the teacher. That stress for students with ADHD often leads to earlier substance use compared to their peers—and greater problems for them. Most educators report very little training or competence when it comes to dealing with children's mental health and compounded problems such as this.

Several research studies have found an association between ADHD and substance use—especially early use. Howard et al. (2014) conducted a meta-analysis and concluded that childhood ADHD predicted substance use and disorder. Groenman et al. (2013) also concluded that childhood ADHD is a risk factor for substance use disorder and nicotine dependence in adolescence. Their research review found that students with ADHD may initiate substance use at a younger age, report more frequent alcohol problems, have a more rapid escalation to a substance use disorder, and have a more difficult time quitting (with recovery rates twice as long as those who do not have ADHD).

Groenman et al. also demonstrated that adolescents with ADHD have greater vulnerability to smoking, alcohol, and illicit drug use. Adolescents with ADHD have a 1.35 greater chance of ending up with an alcohol use disorder, a 2.36 times greater chance of having a nicotine use disorder, and a 3.48 greater chance of another drug use disorder, they say. And many of these adolescents are poly substances users (i.e., they use more than one substance).

The progression seems to start in early childhood with associated ADHD symptoms, then behavior problems emerge, followed by early substance use and rapid escalation to abuse and dependence. Understanding what is going on with the child diagnosed with ADHD and what it is they are experiencing, as well as why they might turn to substance use, can increase our empathy for the distress. Such knowledge can also empower educators to find ways that such distress might be reduced and managed, reducing their own stress levels, benefiting the entire class.

TYPES OF SUBSTANCES USED BY STUDENTS WITH ADHD

Being an *early user* predicts faster increases in alcohol, marijuana, cigarettes, and other illicit drugs, and large differences in rates of use by age twenty-five for adolescents with and without childhood ADHD. Groenman et al. also found more early substance users in adolescence for ADHD (57.9 percent) than those with no ADHD (41.9 percent), including younger first use of alcohol, cigarettes, marijuana, and illicit drugs.

Cigarette smoking is the substance outcome most associated with childhood ADHD, say Howard et al. (2014). They note that cigarettes also mimic central nervous system stimulant properties of typical medication treatments for ADHD. The SAMSHA (2018) report concluded that marijuana, which has historically been illegal and less widely available but less so now with legalization in many states, currently ranks after alcohol as the second most used substance in adolescence. Illicit drug use—including prescription misuse—seems to be less common compared with other substances.

Cigarettes and Nicotine

Nicotine use can be a gateway to other drugs in students with or without ADHD. Groenman et al. cite several studies indicating that adolescents who smoke cigarettes have an increased risk for alcohol and drug use disorders. The high risk of smoking among ADHD youth suggests, they say, that this group is also at high risk for future alcohol and drug use disorders. Their own study of sixteen-year-olds showed a higher prevalence of both substance use disorder and nicotine dependence. The adolescents with ADHD were at higher risk of developing dependence on both substances than healthy controls.

Howard et al. (2014) say that by age twenty-five, twice as many young adults with childhood ADHD were daily smokers compared with their non-ADHD counterparts (38 percent vs. 19 percent, respectively). Another meta-analysis of longitudinal studies done by Lee et al. (2011) similarly showed that the odds of later developing nicotine dependence were actually three times as high in children with versus without ADHD.

Since nicotine is said to mimic central nervous system stimulant properties of typical medication treatments for ADHD, Howard et al., assert that individuals with ADHD may self-medicate with nicotine to manage their symptoms. They suggest that the adolescents' reactions to initial cigarette use may sensitize them more strongly to the effects of nicotine compared with non-ADHD peers, thereby increasing nicotine cravings.

Researchers have also found that students with a childhood diagnosis of ADHD and a conduct disorder (CD), a commonly co-occurring behavior disorder with ADHD, are at much higher risk of developing both a substance use disorder and nicotine dependence compared to ADHD subjects without a conduct disorder. This will be discussed more thoroughly in chapter 4.

Figure 3.2 depicts the extent of tobacco and nicotine use among high school students. Students with ADHD have higher than average use, as noted previously.

Alcohol

A particular concern among adolescents with ADHD is alcohol-related behaviors because these youth may initiate substance use at a younger age (Sibley et al., 2014) and endorse more frequent inebriation and alcohol-related problems than their same-aged peers. Some researchers have found alcohol use patterns to be particularly strong among older (e.g., fifteen to seventeen years) rather than younger adolescents with ADHD (Molina et al., 2007).

This pattern of risky alcohol use may continue to increase across the life span, suggest Howard et al. Their research review confirmed that childhood ADHD is predictive of the development of an alcohol use disorder in adulthood. Several theories of alcohol use point to the role of emotional difficulties in contributing to alcohol use, they say. This suggests that alcohol use may serve as a means of coping with or avoiding the experience of negative affect or as a means of amplifying pleasurable emotions.

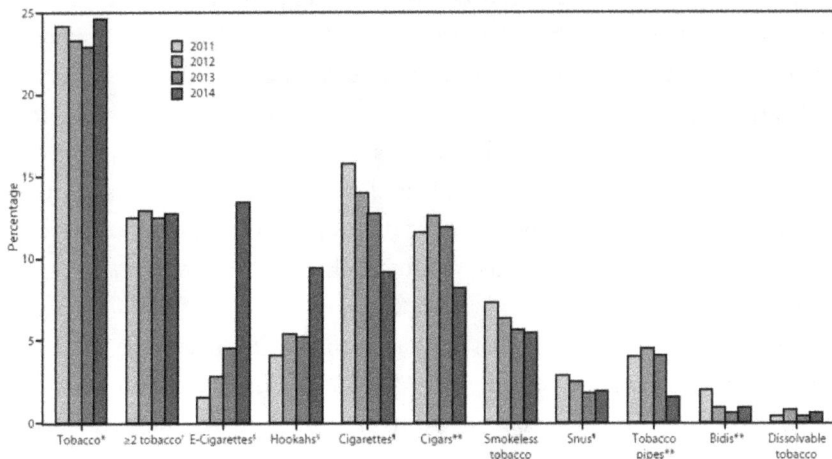

Figure 3.2 Estimated Percentage of High School Students Who Used Tobacco in the Preceding Thirty Days, by Tobacco Product (National Youth Tobacco Survey, United States, 2011–2014). *"Tobacco Use Among Middle and High School Students—United States, 2011–2014" in 'Morbidity and Mortality Weekly Report' (MMWR), April 17, 2015 / 64(14);381-385.* https://www.cdc.gov/mmwr/preview/mmwrhtml/mm6414a3.htm.

Sobanski et al. (2010) argue that the role of emotion regulation in alcohol use may be particularly pronounced among individuals with ADHD. Adults with ADHD are twice as likely as adults without ADHD to report using alcohol to enhance positive mood and reduce negative mood. Taken together, emotion regulation difficulties appear to play a role in alcohol use and the progression toward substance use disorders among individuals with ADHD (Margherio et al., 2014).

Marijuana

Groenman et al. (2014) maintain that an ADHD diagnosis confers risk for heavy substance use in adulthood and found the strongest evidence to be for marijuana and cigarette use. Vitulano et al. (2014) agree that ADHD symptoms also seem to be associated with the risk for early initiation of marijuana. Although not directly correlated with initiation of use at ninth grade, starting in the sixth grade, ADHD symptoms appear to increase the risk for marijuana use in each year except for the eighth grade.

Their findings suggest that ADHD is associated with an earlier onset of substance use disorder (most commonly marijuana as well as marijuana use and dependence symptoms). The ADHD risk for early marijuana use found in their study is particularly concerning, they note, as the recovery time in substance use treatment has been estimated to be more than twice as long in individuals with ADHD compared with those without ADHD.

If left untreated, Vitulano et al. warn, ADHD symptoms can spiral into this pathway toward early initiation of substances, particularly marijuana and tobacco use. They emphasize that when children with ADHD mature, they have a greater than 50 percent chance of developing a substance use disorder if left untreated. This is twice the risk of adults who received treatment for ADHD.

Molina et al. (2018) found that in adulthood, weekly marijuana use (32.8 percent ADHD vs. 21.3 percent non-ADHD) and daily cigarette smoking (35.9 percent vs. 17.5 percent, respectively) were more prevalent in the ADHD group than the non-ADHD group. They also found:

(a) more regular use of marijuana and cigarettes by adulthood in cases with childhood ADHD diagnosis; (b) no increased risk for use/misuse of other classes of substances including alcohol, cocaine, and prescription stimulants;

(c) more early substance use in adolescence for the ADHD group than local normative comparative groups; (d) slightly faster escalation of substance use in adolescence for the ADHD group; and (e) more adult substance use of all types (e.g., alcohol and marijuana) following early use regardless of childhood ADHD history. Frequent marijuana use and daily cigarette smoking stand out as key adult substance use outcomes associated with childhood ADHD. Use of any substances at especially early ages predicts these outcomes (p. 701).

RISK FACTORS FOR ADHD AND SUBSTANCE USE

In reviewing this research on the co-occurring disorders of ADHD and substance use, a variety of possible reasons emerge, and possible combinations of reasons, that students with ADHD are at greater risk for substance abuse than their peers. These include:

- Genetic predisposition
- Neurocognitive impairment
- Need to self-medicate
- Internalizing problems: depression, anxiety
- Externalizing problems: impulsivity and behavioral disinhibition
- Behavior disorder (CD or ODD)
- Early use
- Emotional dysregulation and few or no coping skills
- Poor social skills and peer rejection
- Poor or ineffective parenting
- Lack of school connectedness
- Poor academic achievement

Genetic Predisposition

Numerous studies indicate that ADHD symptoms are highly heritable and that most of the individual variation in ADHD assessments is attributable to genetic influences. Thapar and Stegiacouli (2008) say that non-inherited influences must however contribute, as well, because genetic factors do not account for 100 percent of the variation in ADHD. They maintain that, while there is consistent evidence of a strong genetic contribution to ADHD from family, twin, and adoption studies, ADHD is also influenced by non-inherited factors.

Family studies are also used to look at both co-occurring disorders. The previously mentioned Groenman et al. (2013) research review of family studies of ADHD shows an association between ADHD and substance use disorder in the family members of children with ADHD. Higher rates of alcoholism were found in the adult siblings of adults with ADHD compared to the siblings of controls. Higher rates of substance use disorder were observed in the relatives of ADHD subjects compared to relatives of comparison subjects without ADHD, suggesting that ADHD and substance use disorder may share familial causes.

Neurocognitive Impairment

Neurocognitive deficits not only interfere with academic achievement. Such deficiencies also result in a disruption of the reward-reinforcement process. Hammond et al. (2014) remind us that:

> Adolescence is a period of dynamic biologic, psychological, and behavioral changes. Adolescence is also associated with an increased risk for substance use and addictive disorders. During adolescence, developmental changes in neural circuitry of reward processing, motivation, cognitive control, and stress may contribute to vulnerability for increased levels of engagement in substance use and nonsubstance addictive behaviors. (p.15)

This is especially complicated for students with ADHD, continue Hammond et al. Their neurocognitive deficits may result in heightened reward sensitivity, which does not affect their peers. This can also relate to their executive functioning skills, leaving them unable to set goals and maintain the perseverance to achieve them, or to delay gratification. This can also result in a need to self-medicate, as many drugs simulate the effects of the kinds of medications used to relieve ADHD symptoms, most often stimulants.

Self-Medication

One theory is that students with ADHD use substances to self-medicate the effects of their ADHD symptoms. That is, they self-medicate to relieve the pain of anxiety or depression or negative feelings.

Trucco et al. (2020) state that self-medication theory points to the similarities in the neurobiological and psychological effects of nicotine and other psychostimulant medications (e.g., Ritalin). They suggest that individuals with ADHD may self-medicate with nicotine to manage their symptoms. Though harmful, they say that nicotine may be useful as a means of self-medication, as it has been found to improve attention in adults with ADHD. They also note that medical marijuana is used in many states as a treatment for anxiety, a common ADHD distress symptom.

Internalizing Problems

Blackman et al. (2005) note that, if left untreated, children with ADHD may develop a dual diagnosis of a mood or anxiety disorder. They assert that children with combined ADHD and depression exhibit more severe impairment in academic and social functioning. The emergence of internalizing problems can lead to turning to tobacco and other substances to cope. Then, the development of ADHD into adolescence, (already an emotionally volatile time) seems to follow a path to early initiation of tobacco use through internalizing problems and peer rejection.

Virtulano et al. note that internalizing problems are directly linked to substance abuse. That ADHD may directly and indirectly (through things such as peer rejection and poor school bonding) result in increased internalizing problems due to an external locus of control, and internalizing problems then may ultimately lead to risk for early substance use as a function of maladaptive coping strategies.

They summarize research on internalizing problems and ADHD:

Based on the biological origins of ADHD, demonstrating that ADHD symptoms emerge in early childhood, internalizing symptoms such as depression tend to develop later, typically during adolescence (Kessler, Berglund, Demler, Jin, & Walters, 2005; Lewinsohn, Clarke, Seeley, & Rohde, 1994). Extending theories of internalizing problems and ADHD to understand this link, children with ADHD demonstrate impairment in self-control (Barkley, 1997) and are more likely to report an external locus of control (Linn & Hodge, 1982). This external locus of control may account for the link between symptoms of ADHD and depressive symptoms based on cognitive theories of depression and anxiety (Arslan, Dilmac, & Hamarta, 2009; McCauley, Mitchell, Burke, & Moss, 1988). More specifically, depressed and anxious children and adolescents often exhibit a cognitive style that attributes positive events to external, unstable, and specific factors, with effective interventions targeting this cognitive style (Garber & Horowitz, 2002; McCauley et al., 1988). This attributional style often manifests among children with symptoms of ADHD (Ostrander & Herman, 2006), suggesting a unifying link between the two conditions. (p. 6)

These maladaptive coping strategies are categorized as either internalizing or externalizing behaviors. Whereas internalizing behaviors are turned inward, externalizing behaviors are expressed outwardly. Both can be factors in substance use.

Externalizing Problems

Early childhood externalizing problems have been linked to both ADHD symptoms and later involvement in substance use (Flory & Lynam, 2003). Externalizing behaviors include hyperactivity itself and many of its associated behaviors: tantrums, obsessive behaviors, compulsive behaviors, and defiance, all behaviors that are disturbing and extremely disruptive to the learning process.

Dishion et al. (1991) believe that children's behavior problems in school (e.g., the impulsivity and inattention associated with ADHD) result in school failure and rejection by conventional peers. These children then seek out deviant peer groups, which promote engagement in deviant behaviors, such as acting out and using substances. Flory et al. (2011) agree that many children with ADHD experience school problems and rejection by peers and then begin to identify with unconventional or deviant peer groups and become involved in deviant activities, including substance use and other delinquent or disruptive behaviors.

Vitulano et al. conclude that students who fail to bond are vulnerable to delinquency, and agree that individuals who fail to thrive in school and become disengaged from prosocial peer groups are more likely to involve themselves with antisocial peers and become socialized to engage in deviant and harmful behavior such as substance use.

Conduct Disorders

As if to add insult to injury to the child diagnosed with ADHD, many also have another diagnosed behavior disorder, either *oppositional defiant disorder (ODD)* or *CD* (see figure 2.2). It is ADHD, plus CD, that is known to have the higher incidence of substance use. Students with ADHD are at increased risk for problem behavior, but ADHD symptoms with a CD are strongly associated with adolescent substance use.

The association between ADHD and cigarette smoking, for example, remains even after controlling for the overlap of ADHD with conduct problems, which are a strong predictor of substance use (Flory et al., 2003). Compared with children with ADHD and no CD/ODD, children with ADHD and CD/ODD were at additional risk only for more frequent adult illicit drug use. Still, there is uncertainty about the role each disorder plays and their possible interactive effects:

> The link between ADHD and substance use is hypothesized to follow a general developmental pathway in which ADHD symptoms emerge initially, followed by less severe behavioral problems and then more severe conduct problems that include substance use (Waschbusch, 2002). Due to overlap with such behavioral problems, there is debate whether the risk for substance use in ADHD is primarily accounted for by other diagnoses such as conduct disorder. In particular, other factors in childhood have been found to predict adolescent substance use independent of ADHD, such as maltreatment (De Sanctis et al., 2008) and conduct disorder (Brook, Brook, Zhang, & Koppel, 2010). Although evidence is mixed on the issue (Lynskey & Hall, 2001; Thompson, Riggs, Mikulich, & Crowley, 1996), ADHD symptoms may in fact account for significant incremental variance in predicting substance use and substance dependence beyond that accounted for by conduct disorder, including tobacco, alcohol, marijuana, and other illicit drug use (Flory, Milich, Lynam, Leukefeld, & Clayton, 2003. (p. 156)

Early Use

Children with ADHD are more likely to report early use of all substances in adolescence than those without ADHD and have faster increases in substance use early in adolescence. As stated, early substance use is known to predict substance use problems later and faster progression for both ADHD and comparison groups.

Molina et al.'s (2018) reviewed research confirms that adolescents with ADHD are more likely than non-diagnosed peers to escalate from experimentation to regular substance use and to escalate more rapidly:

> We previously found that 58% of children with ADHD (vs. 40% of non-ADHD) initiated substance use early (e.g., drinking alcohol at age 14) *and* engaged in

repeated or heavy substance use early (e.g., binge drinking at age 15). Being an *early user* by this inclusive definition predicted faster increases in alcohol, marijuana, cigarettes, and other illicit drugs, and large differences in rates of use by age 25 for adolescents with and without childhood ADHD (p. 9).

Except for cigarette use, they note that substance opportunity and availability may be the dominant factors in early adolescents' experimentation with one substance over another. They observed two-thirds of childhood ADHD early users and 43.9 percent of non-ADHD early users met criteria for early use across multiple substances.

Poor Emotion Regulation

ADHD is often associated with symptoms of *emotional lability* (EL), a term which is used for symptoms such as irritability, hot temper, low frustration tolerance, and sudden unpredictable shifts toward negative emotions such as anger, dysphoria (feeling uneasy or unhappy), and sadness, occurring with an intensity or frequency that is inappropriate in relation to the situational context, age, and developmental stage (Flory et al., 2003).

Severe mood dysregulation (SMD) refers to persistent irritability, hyper-arousal, and emotional over-reactivity. This occurs in many, but not all, children and adolescents with ADHD (Margherio et al., 2014). Such high emotional lability is associated with more severe ADHD symptoms and with a higher prevalence of oppositional behavior, anxiety, affective symptoms, and substance abuse, however. They found that difficulties with emotion regulation are particularly relevant for individuals with ADHD, with twice as many adolescents with ADHD experiencing impairment in emotion regulation compared with controls.

They also found that adolescents with ADHD likely experience difficulties monitoring and controlling shifts in emotion as well as expressing emotion in socially appropriate ways. This greatly affects their social relationships.

Poor Social Skills and Peer Rejection

Vitulano et al. summarize several studies relating to social skills and peer rejection of students with ADHD:

Given the impulsive, disruptive, and distractible behaviors of ADHD, children with ADHD often struggle to form friendships, evidenced by fewer close friendships and greater peer rejection (Bagwell, Molina, Pelham, & Hoza, 2001; Hoza, 2007). For example, children with ADHD are rated lower on social preference, disliked by children of higher status, and over 50% are rejected by peers (Hoza et al., 2005). In turn, peer rejection, peer isolation, and low social competence are risk factors for early substance use (Hawkins et al., 1992; Lochman, Wells, & Murray, 2007). . . . Rejection by peers may result in decreased investment and motivation to pursue and develop adaptive relationships with teachers, parents, and other children due to low perceived social competence (Lochman et al., 2007). . . . Peer rejection was then also associated with internalizing symptoms. Thus, it appears that ADHD symptoms in fourth grade may follow a path to peer rejection in fifth grade and then to internalizing problems, such as depression and anxiety in sixth grade. (pp. 5–9)

Students having difficulties with emotion regulation may have a limited arsenal of coping strategies, compounded by limited social skills, which may result in peer rejection and peer conflict. Then, if rejected, adolescents with ADHD who experience social skill deficits may become involved with deviant peer groups because of rejection and isolation from the conventional peer groups. This deviant peer group may create opportunities for engaging in alcohol use (Marshal, Molina, & Pelham, 2003).

These statistics do not convey the pain that these children must experience, the intense pain of being shunned simply for who they are. It is understandable that, without many coping skills, they may, in desperation, reach out to non-conforming peers to try to fit in somewhere. Many feel they have nowhere else to go, that they cannot go to their parents or families—or their teachers—and some of the research on this bears them out.

Ineffective or Poor Parenting

King et al. (2017) identify studies that found that children and adolescents with ADHD come from families in which they are exposed to higher levels of negative life events, such as exposure to marital conflict, divorce, general family adversity, and parental alcoholism. They found that adolescents not only may report greater exposure to negative life events, but that they may also be more sensitive to their effects, which is then exacerbated by limited or no coping skills.

Family studies of ADHD document an association between ADHD and substance use disorder in family members, with higher rates of the disorder in their relatives, compared to those without ADHD. Researchers have found that ADHD and substance use disorder share familial causes. For example, Biederman et al. (2009) found that patterns of familial risk analysis suggest an association between ADHD and substance use disorder in adolescents consistent with their hypothesis that these disorders are independently transmitted.

Conflict with parents has also been identified as a behavioral characteristic of students with ADHD. Several studies have found that parents of children with ADHD are more likely to utilize negative/ineffective discipline than parents whose children do not have ADHD.

Adolescents with childhood ADHD reported that their parents used lower levels of positive parenting behaviors, including knowledge, consistency, support, and more conflict, and that they engaged in higher levels of problem behaviors, including substance use (alcohol, cigarette, and marijuana use) and delinquency, compared to adolescents without childhood ADHD (Molina & Pelham, 2003).

Walther et al. (2019) found that:

> The lower levels of positive parenting behaviors reported by adolescents with histories of childhood ADHD were consistent with, and expanded upon, prior research reporting higher levels of conflict between children diagnosed with ADHD and their parents (Edwards, Barkley, Laneri, Fletcher, & Metevia, 2001; Fischer, 1990). There are several explanations for these findings. Prior studies have shown that oppositional behaviors characteristic of some adolescents with childhood ADHD may exacerbate negative/controlling parenting behavior (Barkley & Cunningham, 1979; Lang, Pelham, Atkeson, & Murphy, 1999). Oppositionality by some adolescents with childhood ADHD may amplify the normal strain found in parent-adolescent relationships (Elder, Caspi, & Nguyen, 1986). As a result, parents of adolescents with ADHD histories may utilize more negative and fewer positive parenting behaviors. Parents of adolescents with childhood ADHD may also underuse positive parenting strategies due to their own mental health struggles. Parents of children with ADHD have higher rates of antisocial personality disorder, alcoholism, depression, and ADHD. (p. 11)

Other parenting considerations that impact ADHD and substance use disorder include a harsh parenting style, lack of consistency, lack of parent knowledge or parental monitoring of the child's behavior and whereabouts, and poor communication and bonding. These will be discussed in chapter 7.

It is important to emphasize that not all parents of children with ADHD have poor parenting skills, nor that poor parenting causes ADHD. At the same time, responding to behaviors such as *impulsivity*, *defiance*, and being oppositional can put stress on this relationship and may explain much of the findings described here.

Poor Academic Achievement and Poor School Connectedness

Children with ADHD are likely to experience poorer academic performance, which may be a function of associated neurocognitive deficits. Children's behavior problems in school result in school failure as well as painful peer rejection. Both academic success and school connectedness are important for positive outcomes, such as achievement and graduation. Yet many students with ADHD do not feel accepted by and connected with school, which compounds their academic challenges and increases their distress.

Flory et al. (2011) state that in addition to increased conflict in school, students with ADHD symptoms demonstrate less academic engagement compared with their peers and, as such, school adjustment may influence the link between ADHD symptoms and substance use. Flory et al. concluded that both school adjustment aspects (i.e., academic success and school connectedness) are important in explaining the relation between early ADHD symptoms and adolescent cigarette smoking, the drug known to be the gateway to further use.

The Flory et al. research review found that persistent or increasing perceptions of academic failure between ages thirteen and fifteen predicted weekly cigarette use at age fifteen. Students who were more connected with school in the fifth and sixth grades were less likely to start smoking during seventh grade and to ever smoke during adolescence.

A final consideration here is the student with co-occurring ADHD and a CD. These students are much more likely to be rejected by peers and to fail academically as their symptoms get more and more problematic. For example, adolescents with ADHD and a CD are more likely to be suspended or expelled from school, and to experience alcohol and drug abuse (Morgan et al., 2020).

Although much attention has been given to academic underachievement of individuals with ADHD, the social impairment and emotional problems that accompany ADHD appear to be a vitally important area of concern for schools. If socio-emotional difficulties are not addressed in children with ADHD early, they are likely to lead to early substance use—and more. Understanding the risk factors is very important so they can be identified and reduced whenever and wherever possible.

The flip side of that equation is the protective factors. It is just as important to understand them, and the research base behind them, so that school personnel can incorporate as many of them as possible into their classrooms and schools. This can increase the chances that they turn to the professionals who care about them, rather than to substances, when they are in distress.

PROTECTIVE FACTORS FOR STUDENTS WITH ADHD AT RISK FOR SUBSTANCE USE

Five big areas remerge regarding protective factors that protect all students but can be especially helpful for students with ADHD:

1. Executive functioning skills
2. Emotional regulation skills
3. Social skills
4. Assertiveness and refusal skills
5. Parent education

While not expressly targeted for the co-occurring disorders of ADHD and SUD, these areas target risk factors and boost competence of students in these areas. This can increase their chances of drawing on these coping skills and strategies when necessary and reducing their chances of turning to substance use. The following sections summarize what the protective factors are. Appendix A. provides a matrix of evidence-based programs and curricula (i.e. The School Mental Health Matrix), organized by behaviors and disorders and foci, for school teams to review and select based on locally identified needs.

Executive Functioning Skills

As has been demonstrated, ADHD affects a person's ability to self-regulate. The mental processes individuals rely on to self-regulate are called *executive functions*. The executive functions enable a person to control their thoughts, words, actions, and emotions. They also assist them to perceive and manage time, and to direct and manage their behavior over time. Studies on teaching executive functioning to adolescents with ADHD show that they do make a difference for them.

For example, one study demonstrated that even brief interventions could make a difference. Pieler and Winters (2017) examined the role of adolescent decision-making style in response to two different brief interventions, one with adolescents only and one with parents too. Results demonstrated that being taught an adaptive problem-solving style predicted a stronger response overall to both brief intervention models (Pieler and Winters, 2017). Interestingly, adolescents with more impulsive or careless decision-making approaches benefited the most from parental involvement in the intervention.

Emotional Regulation Skills

The best strategies for emotion regulation are proactive and positive since so many of these students experience so much frustration and psychological distress. Breaux (2020) recommends four strategies for teachers and parents: encouraging the student to develop a list of coping strategies; listening and validating their emotions; encouraging the adolescent to engage in healthier habits; and helping them recognize their emotions and stress levels. This chapter's Promising Program focuses on emotional regulation and there are many good ones identified in the matrix in Appendix A.

Social Skills

Interventions that improve social skills and promote social competence may protect against the risk for peer rejection in children with ADHD symptoms. Peer programs that promote friendships and help children develop at least one strong friendship have been useful for ADHD children with social impairments and may be an effective intervention (Hoza et al., 2003). Though some research has shown that social skills training programs have been minimally effective with students with ADHD and substance use, Morris et al. (2020) suggest that these treatments should incorporate a parenting component as well to enhance their effectiveness.

Assertiveness and Refusal Skills

Along with important skills in communication is the need for explicit training in assertiveness and, especially, refusal skills. Even students with good communication skills often have trouble resisting peer pressure. Rizzal et al.

(2021) conducted a study of high school students and peer refusal interventions. Students demonstrated significantly increased substance abuse refusal skills after group therapy and assertiveness training. These skills should be part of interventions for students with ADHD as well.

Parent Training

Molina et al. (2007) say there is recent promising evidence that behavior therapy for childhood ADHD, which includes parent training, leads to lower rates of experimentation with substances in early adolescence. They suggest that parental discipline consistency in adolescence may also have important implications for the management of problematic behavior and substance use for adolescents with ADHD histories.

The emotional quality of the relationship is, of course, of the utmost importance. Walther et al. (2019) reviewed several studies relevant to the quality of the parent–child relationship and substance use and found:

> In addition to parental monitoring and parenting consistency, the emotional quality of the parent-adolescent relationship has often been invoked as important in facilitating healthy adjustment in youth (Conger & Ge, 1999). The extent to which adolescents feel that their parents are available for emotional support and assistance with problem-solving is typically considered as a distinct yet important component of the parent-adolescent relationship (Ackard, Neumark-Sztainer, Story, & Perry, 2006; Letourneau et al., 2001). Studies have shown that adolescent-perceived parental support is associated with lower levels of adolescent substance use and delinquency, even when parental monitoring and use of rules and discipline were controlled (Chassin et al., 2005; Fleming, Kim, Harachi, & Catalano, 2002; Hill, Hawkins, Catalano, Abbott, & Guo, 2005; Tilson, McBride, Lipkus, & Catalano, 2004). (p. 585)

Walther et al. suggest that modifications to existing parent training programs for children with ADHD that incorporate the teaching of developmentally relevant parenting strategies may result in better outcomes for adolescents with ADHD. For example, they say, treatment programs could include strategies that not only utilize increased parental monitoring, but also encourage parent–adolescent communication about friendships, activities, and whereabouts. They also advocate for booster sessions delivered in adolescence as part of training programs delivered in childhood as potentially helpful with this population as well.

Smoking Prevention/Cessation

The need for improved smoking prevention for all students, and especially for those with ADHD, is imperative. According to the CDC, cigarette smoking causes about one of every five deaths in the United States each year. Cigarette smoking is estimated to cause more than 480,000 deaths annually and life expectancy for smokers is at least ten years shorter than for non-smokers. If schools can strongly reinforce an anti-smoking message in addition to teaching coping skills and enhancing school connectedness, they can further reduce use of this drug by students with ADHD.

Medication

Treating students with medication is beyond the scope of this book and beyond the author's expertise. There are many new developments in this area, and many decisions parents and families must make concerning what is best for their child. For example, a meta-analysis of six longitudinal studies investigating substance use disorders during adolescence or adulthood among youth with ADHD was conducted and concluded that there is a nearly two-fold reduction in substance use in those who received stimulants compared with those who did not (Wilens, et al., 2003).

While the decisions about medication are the family's responsibility, educators can be informed when a student is on physician-prescribed medication, understand the possible side effects, and remain in close communication with parents and medical professionals, as needed.

PROMISING PROGRAM

The RELAX (Regulating Emotions Like An eXpert) Intervention was developed to address the high levels of emotion regulation difficulties and family conflict experienced by adolescents with ADHD and their families (Breaux, 2020).

RELAX is an eight-week group-based intervention, says Breaux. Parents and teens meet separately for the first sixty minutes on skill-building activities and meet for the last thirty minutes for a discussion activity, and to problem-solve skill use for their family over the coming week. RELAX seeks to equip adolescents with coping, communication, and conflict management skills. RELAX also helps parents learn how to support their adolescents in using these skills and to utilize helpful emotion socialization practices.

Breaux says that RELAX is unique in its structure of teaching skills to parents the week prior to adolescents to facilitate parental reflection and utilization of skills in their own lives. This helps parents model these skills for adolescents and facilitates parents supporting their adolescents' skill use in the following weeks. This structure is critical given the importance of emotion socialization for emotional development, and the fact that parents of teenagers with ADHD often experience emotion regulation difficulties and high levels of stress themselves.

The program's developers piloted the program with eighteen families in Spring 2019 and was found to result in large improvements in adolescent emotion regulation (i.e., managing negative emotions like anger, sadness, frustration) and communication, and reductions in family conflict. Additionally, parents made large improvements in their ability to support their adolescents during conflict discussions and in their own emotion dysregulation.

They then piloted a telehealth version of the program in 2020. They found attendance was higher for telehealth than in person RELAX groups (95 percent vs. 87 percent), but homework completion was higher for in-person (85 percent vs. 70 percent). Caregiver and adolescent feedback indicated very high rates of satisfaction with RELAX, with no significant differences in caregiver satisfaction and minimal differences in adolescent satisfaction between the in-person and telehealth groups. Similarly, treatment outcomes were similar for in-person and telehealth groups, with some evidence for larger improvement of adolescent ED for telehealth, whereas larger improvement in family conflict emerged for in-person groups. These results suggest that both the in person and telehealth RELAX intervention are feasible, acceptable, and effective treatment options for families of adolescents with ADHD.

CONCLUDING THOUGHTS

The association of ADHD with substance use is worrisome for teachers and parents. It is a warning call to address symptoms and behaviors of ADHD as early as possible to prevent—or interrupt—substance use and its escalation.

Such support of the social and emotional development of students with ADHD, as well as their academic development, is so important for their overall well-being, because when there is this co-occurring disorder present, the problems associated with ADHD are magnified.

Not only do educators have to teach these students, but they must also protect them from their inability to regulate their emotions and cope with stress, from peer rejection, from academic failure, and from turning to substances to escape their pain. Yet they don't have to do this alone, however. While there are some things out of a teacher's control (e.g., decisions about medication, family dysfunction), there are other professionals in the school who can share the load (e.g., social workers, counselors), though at times they are overloaded and overwhelmed too.

But in classrooms, teachers can incorporate more of the strategies Breaux suggests teaching and practicing coping skills, and incorporating executive functioning skills (e.g., critical thinking and problem solving) in both academic and social situations. Teachers can also be vigilant in creating a classroom community where bullying and peer rejection are prohibited, and where social skills are also explicitly taught, modeled, reinforced, and rewarded.

School leadership teams can identify evidence-based curricula targeted to individual school needs for everyone (universal programs), for those at-risk (selective programs), and indicated programs (for those already in-risk). This chapter has presented reasons why educators must be aware of the many dimensions of ADHD and appreciate just how important interventions can be.

Schools and classrooms can engender the sense of belonging, create the comfort—and be the comfort—struggling students need so they know they are worthy, and that they are capable. So they will turn to caring adults when they are distressed, instead of turning to substances.

REFERENCES

Arrazola, R. A., Singh, T., Corey, C. G., Husten, C. G., Neff, L. J., Apelberg, B. J., Bunnell, R. E., Choiniere, C. J., King, B. A., Cox, S., McAfee, T., Caraballo, R. S., & Centers for Disease Control and Prevention (CDC). (2015). Tobacco Use Among Middle and High School Students – United States, 2011–2014. *Morbidity and Mortality Weekly Report*, 64(14), 381–385. PMID: 25879896; PMCID: PMC5779546.

Blackmon, G. L., Ostrander, R., & Herman, K. C. (2005). Children with ADHD and Depression: A Multisource, Multimethod Assessment of Clinical, Social, and Academic Functioning. *Journal of Attention Disorders*, 8, 195–207.

Breaux, R. (2020). Emotion Regulation in Teens with ADHD. Children and Adults with Attention-Deficit/Hyperactivity Disorder (CHADD). Retrieved from: https://chadd.org/adhd-news/adhd-news-caregivers/emotion-regulation-in-teens-with-adhd/

CDC ACE Pyramid. Retrieved from: About the CDC-Kaiser ACE Study | Violence Prevention | Injury Center | CDC.

CDC Facts about ADHD. Retrieved from: Data and Statistics About ADHD | CDC.

Dishion, T. J., Patterson, G. R., Stoolmiller, M., & Skinner, M. L. (1991). Family, School, and Behavioral Antecedents to Early Adolescent Involvement with Antisocial Peers. *Developmental Psychology*, 27, 172–180.

Early Risers Skills for Success Program Program Profile, U.S. National Institute of Justice.crimesolutions.ojp.gov.

Flory, K., Milich, R., Lynam, D. R., Leukefeld, C., & Clayton, R. (2003). Relation between Childhood Disruptive Behavior Disorders and Substance Use and Dependence Symptoms in Young Adulthood: Individuals with Symptoms of Attention-Deficit/Hyperactivity Disorder and Conduct Disorder are Uniquely at Risk. *Psychology of Addictive Behaviors*, 17, 151–158.

Groenman, A. P., Oosterlaan, J., Rommelse, N., Franke, B., Roeyers, H., Oades, R. D., Sergeant, J. A., Buitelaar, J. K., & Faraone, S. V. (2013). Substance Use Disorders in Adolescents with Attention Deficit Hyperactivity Disorder: A 4-year Follow-up Study. *Addiction*, 108(8), 1503–1511. https://doi.org/10.1111/add.12188. Epub 2013 Apr 22. PMID: 23506232.

Hammond, C. J., Mayes, L. C., & Potenza, M. N. (2014). Neurobiology of Adolescent Substance Use and Addictive Behaviors: Treatment Implications. *Adolescent Medicine: State of the Art Reviews*, 25(1), 15–32.

Howard, A. L., Molina, B. S. G., Swanson, J. M., Hinshaw, S. P., Belendiuk, K. A., Harty, S. C., . . . Wigal, T. (2015). Developmental Progression to Early Adult Binge Drinking and Marijuana Use From Worsening Versus Stable Trajectories of Adolescent Attention Deficit/Hyperactivity Disorder and Delinquency. *Addiction*, 110(5), 784–795. PubMed: 25664657

Hoza, B. (2007). Peer Functioning in Children with ADHD. *Journal of Pediatric Psychology*, 32(6), 655–663. PubMed: 17556400

King, K., Vidourek, R., & Merianos, A. (2016). Typical Sources and Locations Where Recent Youth Drinkers Obtain and Consume Alcohol Based on Intensity of Use. *Journal of Substance Use*, 21, 204–209.

Lee, S. S., Humphreys, K. L., Flory, K., Liu, R., & Glass, K. (2011). Prospective Association of Childhood Attention Deficit/Hyperactivity Disorder (ADHD) and Substance Use and Abuse/Dependence: A Meta-analytic Review. *Clinical Psychology Review*, 31(3), 328–341. PubMed: 21382538

Margherio, S. M., Brickner, M. A., Evans, S. W., Sarno Owens, J., DuPaul, G. J., & Allan, N. P. (2020). The Role of Emotion Regulation in Alcohol Use among Adolescents with Attention-deficit/Hyperactivity Disorder. *Psychology of Addictive Behaviors*, 34(7), 772–782. https://doi.org/10.1037/adb0000582

Marshal, M., Molina, B., & Pelham, W. (2003). Childhood ADHD and Adolescent Substance Use: An Examination of Deviant Peer Group Affiliation as a Risk Factor. *Psychology of Addictive Behaviors*, 17, 293–302. https://doi.org/10.1037/0893-164X.17.4.293

Marshal, M. P., & Molina, B. S. (2006). Antisocial Behaviors Moderate the Deviant Peer Pathway to Substance Use in Children with ADHD. *Journal of Clinical Child & Adolescent Psychology*, 35(2), 216–226. https://doi.org/10.1207/s15374424jccp3502_5. PMID: 16597217; PMCID: PMC2680090.

Molina, B. S. G., Howard, A. L., Swanson, J. M., Stehli, A., Mitchell, J. T., Kennedy, T. M., Epstein, J. N., Arnold, L. E., Hechtman, L., Vitiello, B., & Hoza, B. (2018). Substance Use through Adolescence into Early Adulthood after Childhood-diagnosed ADHD: Findings from the MTA Longitudinal Study. *Journal of Child Psychology and Psychiatry*, 59(6), 692–702. https://doi.org/10.1111/jcpp.12855

Molina, B. S., & Pelham, W. E. Jr. (2003). Childhood Predictors of Adolescent Substance Use in a Longitudinal Study of Children with ADHD. *Journal of Abnormal Psychology*, 112(3), 497–507. https://doi.org/10.1037/0021-843x.112.3.497. PMID: 12943028.

Morgan, P. L., Li, H., Cook, M., Farkas, G., Hillemeier, M. M., & Lin, Y. C. (2016). Which Kindergarten Children are at Greatest Risk for Attention-deficit/Hyperactivity and Conduct Disorder Symptomatology as Adolescents? *School Psychology Quarterly: The Official Journal of the Division of School Psychology, American Psychological Association*, 31(1), 58–75. https://doi.org/10.1037/spq0000123

Morris, S., Sheen, J., Ling, M., Foley, D., & Sciberras, E. (2020). Interventions for Adolescents with ADHD to Improve Peer Social Functioning: A Systematic Review and Meta-analysis. *Journal of Attention Disorders*. Advance online publication. https://doi.org/10.1177/1087054720906514

Piehler, T. F., & Winters, K. C. (2017). Decision-making Style and Response to Parental Involvement in Brief Interventions for Adolescent Substance Use. *Journal of Family Psychology*, 31(3), 336–346. https://doi.org/10.1037/fam0000266

RELAX, CALMER (Coping Skills and Learning to Manage Emotions). Retrieved from: https://www.calmerlab.com/the-relax-intervention

Rizzal, A. F., Keliat, B. A., & Wardani, I. Y. (2021). Save the Future: Enhancing Substance Abuse Refusal Skill in Adolescent. *Enfermeria Clinica*, 31, S405–S407. https://doi.org/10.1016/j.enfcli.2020.09.034

SAMSHA. 2017 NSDUH Annual National Report (2018). Retrieved from: Key Substance Use and Mental Health Indicators in the United States: Results from the 2018 National Survey on Drug Use and Health (samhsa.gov)

Sibley, M. H., Pelham, W. E. Jr., Molina, B. S. G., Coxe, S., Kipp, H., Gnagy, E. M., . . . Lahey, B. B. (2014). The Role of Early Childhood ADHD and Subsequent CD in the Initiation and Escalation of Adolescent Cigarette, Alcohol, and Marijuana Use. *Journal of Abnormal Psychology*, 123(2), 362–374. PubMed: 24886010

Sobanski, E., Banaschewski, T., Asherson, P., Buitelaar, J., Chen, W., Franke, B., Holtmann, M., Krumm, B., Sergeant, J., Sonuga-Barke, E., Stringaris, A., Taylor, E., Anney, R., Ebstein, R. P., Gill, M., Miranda, A., Mulas, F., Oades, R. D., Roeyers, H., Rothenberger, A., Steinhausen, H. C., & Faraone, S. V. (2010). Emotional Lability in Children and Adolescents with Attention Deficit/Hyperactivity Disorder (ADHD): Clinical Correlates and Familial Prevalence. *Journal of Child Psychology and Psychiatry*, 51(8), 915–923. https://doi.org/10.1111/j.1469-7610.2010.02217.x. Epub 2010 Feb 1. PMID: 20132417.

Thapar, A., & Stergiakouli, E. (2008). An Overview on the Genetics of ADHD. *Xin li xue bao. Acta psychologica Sinica*, 40(10), 1088–1098. https://doi.org/10.3724/SP.J.1041.2008.01088

Trucco, E. M., Villafuerte, S., Hussong, A., Burmeister, M., & Zucker, R. A. (2018). Biological Underpinnings of an Internalizing Pathway to Alcohol, Cigarette, and Marijuana Use. *Journal of Abnormal Psychology*, 127(1), 79–91. https://doi.org/10.1037/abn0000310

Vitulano, M. L., Fite, P. J., Hopko, D. R., Lochman, J., Wells, K., & Asif, I. (2014). Evaluation of Underlying Mechanisms in the Link between Childhood ADHD Symptoms and Risk for Early Initiation of Substance Use. *Psychology of Addictive Behaviors*, 28(3), 816–827. https://doi.org/10.1037/a0037504. PMID: 25222174.

Walther, C. A., Cheong, J., Molina, B. S., Pelham, W. E., Jr., Wymbs, B. T., Belendiuk, K. A., & Pedersen, S. L. (2012). Substance Use and Delinquency among Adolescents with Childhood ADHD: The Protective Role of Parenting. *Psychology of Addictive Behaviors: Journal of the Society of Psychologists in Addictive Behaviors*, 26(3), 585–598. https://doi.org/10.1037/a0026818

Wilens, T. E., Faraone, S. V., Biederman, J., & Gunawardene, S. (2003). Does Stimulant Therapy of Attention-deficit/Hyperactivity Disorder Beget Later Substance Abuse? A Meta-analytic Review of the Literature. *Pediatrics*, 111(1), 179–185. https://doi.org/10.1542/peds.111.1.179. PMID: 12509574

Chapter 4

Understanding Co-occuring Disorders

Conduct Disorders and Adolescent Substance Use

CONDUCT DISORDER AND COD: DEFINITIONS AND PREVALENCE

Conduct Disorder Definition

About 10 percent of students have a diagnosable conduct disorder (CD). This disorder is characterized by behavior problems, norm, and rule violations, but also greater psychological distress than non-diagnosed peers. Conduct disorders also cause havoc in the classroom. Add in students with other mental health issues, and this is an extremely challenging situation for any teacher, especially a new teacher. It is very difficult not to take defiance or oppositional behavior personally. The impact of such behavior on other students is also a big concern.

Kazdin ct al. (1990) described disruptive behavior disorders (e.g., oppositional defiant disorder, conduct disorder) as among the most prevalent types of mental disorders affecting children and common problems for which parents seek professional help. It was estimated that more money is spent on children's mental health conditions than on any other type of childhood disorder (Soni, 2009).

Conduct disorders involve behavioral problems involving violation of rules, societal norms, and laws. Estimates suggest that around 10 percent of children suffer from oppositional defiant disorder (ODD) and similar numbers from CD (Masroor et al., 2019). Pihet et al. (2012) found that the lifetime prevalence of conduct disorder in the United States is estimated to be 9.5 percent, that is, 12 percent among males and 7.1 percent among females.

Pihet et al. go on to say that the research shows that adolescents diagnosed with conduct disorder have a higher degree of distress and impairment in virtually all domains of living than adolescents with other mental disorders. Pihet et al. reference numerous studies that demonstrate the long-term impact of conduct disorder as a developmental precursor of antisocial behavior and even criminality.

Conduct disorder diagnosed in childhood, they say, acts as a strong predictor of many problems in adolescence and adulthood, including mental illness, substance abuse, legal problems, school drop-out, academic issues, and occupational problems. It is important to understand how conduct disorders can lead to substance use so that strategies and interventions can be put in place to decrease the chances of these co-occurring.

CO-OCCURRING DISORDERS: CD AND SUD

Overview

The research review of Pihet et al. also shows that many children with a conduct disorder may have co-occurring conditions (i.e., existing simultaneously) such as attention-deficit/ hyperactivity disorder (ADHD) at 3–41 percent, depression at 0–46 percent, and anxiety disorder at 0–41 percent. Among youth who met criteria for conduct disorder, they say, 52 percent also met criteria for a substance use disorder. In fact, one class of behavioral problem consistently associated with early onset of SUD is conduct disorder.

These researchers also found that co-occurring disorders are very common. Surveys indicate that about half of those who experience a mental illness during their lives will also experience a substance use disorder and vice versa, they say. Pihet et al. also found that adolescents with substance use disorders also have high rates of co-occurring mental illness.

For example, over 60 percent of adolescents in community-based SUD treatment programs also meet diagnostic criteria for another mental illness. Pihet et al. also found that conduct disorder increases the risk for substance

DSM-V Clinical Model of CD

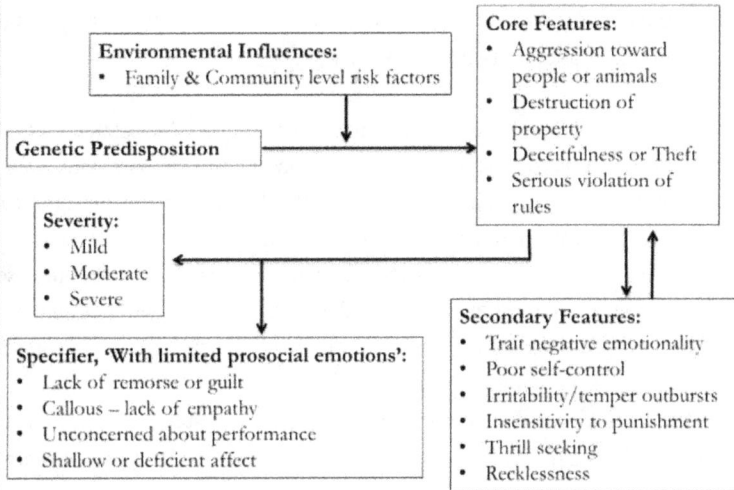

Environmental Influences:
• Family & Community level risk factors

Genetic Predisposition

Severity:
• Mild
• Moderate
• Severe

Specifier, 'With limited prosocial emotions':
• Lack of remorse or guilt
• Callous – lack of empathy
• Unconcerned about performance
• Shallow or deficient affect

Core Features:
• Aggression toward people or animals
• Destruction of property
• Deceitfulness or Theft
• Serious violation of rules

Secondary Features:
• Trait negative emotionality
• Poor self-control
• Irritability/temper outbursts
• Insensitivity to punishment
• Thrill seeking
• Recklessness

Figure 4.1   Danielle Herring's Model of Conduct Disorder. *Source:* https://slideplayer.com/slide/4241401/

use initiation at age fifteen and with a greater relative risk for illicit substances it continues until age eighteen. They also found that 51 percent of youth with pervasive conduct problems (five or more) reported high levels of substance use compared with only 11 percent of youth without pervasive conduct problems.

Hemphala and Tengstrom (2010) point to studies that also conclude that about 60 percent of adolescents with a substance misuse problem have co-occurring mental disorders. They also advise that adolescence is a particularly important time to examine such co-occurring disorders, as many forms of psychopathology and risk behaviors, including delinquency, drug use, and depression, either begin or peak at this stage. Schuckit (2006) notes that these behaviors are associated with a worse prognosis, more severe symptoms, and lower social competence.

As to the reverse, Fisher et al. (2018) study of incarcerated juvenile offenders (presumably with high rates of conduct disorder), demonstrates rates of substance abuse ranging from 50 to 80 percent in males.

Types of Substances Used by Students
with Conduct Disorders

Pihet et al. (2012) concluded that a diagnosis of conduct disorder is an important predictor of substance use disorder, especially for marijuana, alcohol, and tobacco abuse. This can vary by age:

> In a study by Hopfer et al. [[7]] conduct disorder was associated with elevated adjusted hazards for initiation of all substances, with comparatively greater hazard ratios at age 15 . . . At age 21, the adjusted hazard ratios were significant only for cocaine, amphetamines, inhalants, and club drugs [[7]]. A similar pattern was seen in our study for ages 16 to 18 years': cocaine/amphetamine use disorders were prevalent followed by opioid, tobacco, alcohol, and marijuana whereas marijuana-use disorder was seen majorly in adolescents 12 to 15 years (p.436).

The Pihet et al. study found that, among all substance use disorders, marijuana use disorder (23.7percent) was most prevalent in conduct disorder inpatients, followed by tobacco and alcohol use disorders (10.1 percent each). The most common substance to be abused is marijuana followed by tobacco and alcohol abuse. Regarding illicit drug use, Vitulano et al. (2014) say that such use, including prescription misuse, is rare compared with other substances.

Fisher and Brown (2018) noted that conduct problems appear to increase the risk of subsequent marijuana use irrespective of whether they are preceded by adversity in earlier life. They speculated that problem marijuana use might be a later manifestation of a pattern of conduct problems established in early childhood, although it is also associated with disadvantage and maternal substance use.

Barnes et al. (2011) also found that marijuana problems, compared to marijuana use without apparent problems, were associated more strongly with risk factors in earlier life, most notably social disadvantage, maternal substance use, maternal depression, and early-onset persistent conduct problems. Almost a quarter of marijuana problems at age sixteen, they estimate, appeared possibly attributable to early-onset persistent conduct problems.

Gender Considerations

The Pihet et al. (2012) research review indicated that boys are more likely to have childhood-onset conduct disorder than girls because they had a more severe risk profile. Other studies have also concluded that boys are two to three times more likely to be diagnosed with conduct disorder than girls.

Barnes et al. (2011) cite the work of several researchers on gender differences in CD and substance use disorders:

> Tiet et al. [[29]] reported evidence of a gender paradox, such that girls were found to have lower conduct problems overall; however, a greater proportion of females (19%) reported pervasive conduct problems compared with males (9%). Farrell et al. [[13]] found that while females had lower initial rates of substance use, aggression, and delinquency, there were no differences by gender in pattern or rates of change for any of the problem behaviors across middle school. Lillehoj et al. [[18]] found no gender differences in aggression, disobedience, and misconduct among a sample of rural seventh graders; however, males did report higher levels of substance initiation in the seventh grade compared with females. Among both genders, aggression, disobedience, and misconduct predicted initiation of substance use but not change in substance use over time . . . (there were) documented gender differences in early childhood conduct/ behavioral problems with males reporting higher levels than females. [Dodge et al., [10] (p. 168)

They studied an urban minority sample of adolescents and concluded that the lack of gender differences in trajectories of aggression, delinquency, and substance use implies that the developmental progression of engagement in these behaviors during middle school is roughly equivalent for both males and females. Although females and males follow similar patterns of change during middle school regarding aggression, delinquency, and substance use, the greater number of males who follow a trajectory of continued high delinquency may account for the gender difference in average rates of this behavior, they say.

Race/Culture Considerations

The Pihet et al. research review noted Blacks are more likely than Whites to live in lower socioeconomic environments, characterized by greater exposure to aggressive models and higher rates of conduct disorder. They emphasize the fact that Black and minority adolescents are exposed to an additional source of stress: racial discrimination. And, this stress has been linked with both internalizing and externalizing behaviors in adolescents.

Pihet et al. found that White adolescents (aged twelve to fifteen years) have a higher likelihood of conduct disorder-related hospitalization. These inpatients have a higher risk of comorbid substance use disorder as compared to other psychiatric illnesses. They found a high prevalence of marijuana abuse/dependence in African American adolescents, followed by tobacco, as compared to opioids abuse in Whites, followed by tobacco and cocaine and amphetamines. Hispanics adolescents primarily abused alcohol, according to their study.

Morino (2019) found that, in early adolescence, Hispanics self-report higher drug use rates compared to White and African American peers. Among adolescent users, heavy users have more negative behavioral and health consequences. Conduct disorder, higher levels of maternal attachment, lower levels of acculturation, and higher levels of psychological benefits of use were associated with an increased likelihood of heavy illicit drug use in this group.

RISK FACTORS FOR CO-OCCURRING CD AND SUD

There are several factors influencing the development of a conduct order. They include gene and biology, family influences, early use, heavy use, and emotional dysregulation. In Figure 4.1 Herring (2014) presents a visual of the inter-related factors which are associated with conduct disorders. The environment interacts with the genetic predisposition, resulting in the kinds of behaviors characterized by a conduct disorder diagnosis, which can be mild, moderate, or severe.

Overview of Risk Factors

According to Pihet et al. (2012) there are several important risk factors that predict conduct disorder. These include impulsiveness, low IQ and low school achievement, inadequate parental supervision, punitive or erratic parental discipline, cold parental attitude, child physical abuse, parental conflict, disrupted families, antisocial parents, large family size, low family income, antisocial peers, high-delinquency-rate schools, and high-crime neighborhoods.

D'Onofrio et al. (2009) found a causal association between family income and conduct disorder and note that low family income is a critical risk factor for the development of early-onset conduct disorder. Fisher and Brown (2018) agree that risk factors for conduct disorder, particularly early-onset persistent conduct disorder, have been found to include parental substance use and mental health problems, early-life social disadvantage, and family adversity and childhood victimization.

Based on these findings, Fisher and Brown speculate that this association could arise because these factors predispose adolescents to conduct disorder which, in turn, predisposes them to substance use. Still, it might develop through other pathways, including other environmental influences and genetic factors.

Genes and Biology

There are no definite answers as to why some children develop conduct disorder. There are multiple factors involved, including traumatic events, social problems, and biological factors, and many other factors contribute to the development of conduct disorders (Pihet et al.,). They say that children and adolescents with conduct disorder have frontal lobe impairment which may have an underlying genetic basis.

Masroor et al. (2019) reviewed research that finds strong evidence to support persistent antisocial behavior as being a neurodevelopmental disorder that arises due to an interaction between an individual vulnerability, presumably genetic, and environmental adversities. For example, they describe studies that have demonstrated that boys with ODD have similar neuropsychological deficits to those with ADHD.

The 2010 Hemphala et al. research review corroborated this. They say that the extreme risky behaviors seen in many children with conduct disorder might partly result from faulty neural processing of behavior-motivating rewards, behavior-inhibiting punishments, and impaired integration of reward–punishment information in brain regions that determine future behaviors.

Fisher and Brown found evidence that there are neurobiological deficits (e.g., brain dysfunction leading to impaired emotional response) exhibited by those high in conduct disorder characteristics. They say that the core features of conduct disorder are developmental in nature, tending to emerge before the age of ten, and agree that it is likely that environmental factors interact with neurobiological factors to play a role in conduct disorders.

Emotional Dysregulation

Children diagnosed with conduct disorder have a higher degree of distress and impairment in virtually all domains of living than youth with other mental disorders (Angold and Costello, 1993). Fisher et al. (2018) found that conduct disorder is associated with several brain deficits related to emotion dysregulation. Emotional regulation deficits may be exacerbated by high stress levels characteristic of adolescence.

The Child Behavior Checklist (CBCL) is a parent checklist to measure general child and adolescent emotional and behavioral problems. Severe affective and behavioral dysregulation is captured by the CBCL. Such dysregulation affects 1–2 percent of youth in population samples, 6–7 percent in child psychiatric clinical samples, and 13–20 percent of children with attention-deficit/hyperactivity disorder (Malone et al., 2010).

Malone found that young adults with a higher CBCL score in childhood were at increased risk for substance use disorders, suicidality, and poorer overall functioning at age nineteen, even after adjustment for parental education, family income, impairment, and psychiatric disorders at baseline. They say that children with behavioral and affective dysregulation in childhood are at increased risk for substance use, suicidal ideation and suicide attempts, and impairment in young adulthood.

Behavioral Dysregulation

Conduct disorder and drug use may follow a common developmental pattern of externalizing behavior: an externalizing factor accounts for 79 percent and 95 percent of conduct disorder and drug use, respectively (Measelle et al., 2006).

Externalizing Behaviors and Aggression

Barnes et al. (2011) say that adolescents who are engaging in multiple problem behaviors represent a significant subgroup of individuals at higher risk for continued problems in adulthood. Studies which have specifically examined the predictive role of aggression or delinquency on substance use initiation in early adolescence, they say, find higher average levels of aggressive or delinquent behavior associated with higher levels of substance use among both females and males.

Examples of Internalizing Behaviors	Examples of Externalizing Behaviors
Depression	Aggression
Anxiety	Hyperactivity
Low Self Esteem	Tantrums
Withdrawn	Defiance
Shy and Timid	Obsessive Compulsive behaviors
Fears & Phobias	Rule violations

Figure 4.2 Examples of Internalizing and Externalizing Behaviors. *Author created.*

Figure 4.2 presents a comparison between behaviors identified as externalizing and those as internalizing.

When it comes to externalizing behaviors, Malone et al. say that the
CBCL-DP administered during middle childhood predicted considerable
psychosocial impairment in late adolescence. They say that young children
who were impulsive, restless, negativistic, distractible, and labile in their
emotional responses ("uncontrolled temperament") were more likely to be
diagnosed with alcohol dependence and suicidality and were characterized
by high levels of impulsivity in young adulthood.

Tiet et al. (2001) found that a joint trajectory of conduct disorder and
substance use analyses revealed that individuals with patterns of high-stable
aggression and delinquency had high probabilities of increases in substance
use during middle school. They say that, while information about externalizing behaviors does inform risk for future substance use, the reverse association of predicting externalizing behavior based on substance use trajectory
was not as informative.

Adolescents who followed patterns of increasing substance only use during
middle school had virtually equal probabilities of engaging in low, increasing, or high levels of both aggression and delinquency. This, Tiet et al. suggest, provides some evidence that externalizing behaviors may serve as a
pathway to substance use during middle school, whereas the reverse is not
necessarily true.

Impulsivity, Conduct Disorder, Substance Use, and Gambling

According to Holtmann et al. (2011), gambling behaviors and problem gambling in young people are strongly related to other problem behaviors, particularly substance use and conduct disorder. They studied the co-occurrence of

gambling with substance use and conduct disorder in a representative sample of 2,274 youth between ages fourteen and twenty-one years old. They found that problem gambling occurs within a problem-behavior syndrome with other substance use behaviors and conduct disorder.

Petry and Tawfik (2001) interviewed adolescents who were in treatment for marijuana abuse. Twenty-two percent experienced gambling problems. The problem gamblers as compared with non-problem gamblers reported a greater frequency of overall drug and alcohol use, and a greater intensity of marijuana use. Problem gamblers had elevated levels of impulsivity, impulsivity which, they note, often commences in childhood with conduct disorder.

Holtmann et al. (2011) reference a study of seventh- to thirteenth-grade students which found that probable pathological gamblers exhibited significantly higher levels of conduct problems than did other gamblers and non-gamblers. There was a strong effect of male gender in predicting gambling behaviors and gambling problems. Their findings, they say, support the concept that gambling behaviors and gambling problems are part of a more general problem behavior syndrome associated with substance use behaviors and conduct disorder.

Family and Community Dysfunction and Substance Use

Hemphala and Tengstrom (2010) report that parent–child abuse and community violence are independently associated with higher levels of depression, conduct disorder, and drug use. They found that harsh physical punishment and maltreatment, and community violence, were associated with increased odds of conduct disorder and drug use.

Fisher and Brown investigated the role of adversity in early life and of conduct disorder between ages four and thirteen years as risk factors for marijuana use and problem use in boys and girls at age sixteen. They found that maternal smoking and marijuana use, early material disadvantage, and early-onset persistent conduct problems are all important risk factors for adolescent problem marijuana use.

Parental substance use is also a factor. Cerda et al. (2012) studied the maximum number of drinks ever consumed by mothers in a twenty-four-hour period and found this was associated with conduct disorder diagnoses in their children and with disruptive behavior diagnoses in general. They found it was also associated with a variety of substance-related measures including "initiation of substance use, having ever been intoxicated, breadth of substance experimentation, all by age 15, and with substance use disorders and offspring's own maximum drinks consumed in 24 hours, both by the time of the age-17 assessment" (p. 658).

In their other work, they found that the number of drinks either parent has ever consumed in a single twenty-four-hour period is associated with conduct disorder, disruptive behavior disorders, and substance-related problems in their adolescent children: "the maximum number of drinks consumed in a 24-hr period is associated with tolerance and physiological features of alcoholism as well as with genes implicated in alcohol metabolism. It is also likely related to loss of control over drinking, a cardinal feature of alcoholism" (p. 659).

Community factors play a role in conduct disorders as well. Breslau et al. (1995) found that harsh physical punishment and maltreatment ceased to predict conduct disorder and drug use once they included witnessing and victimization. They concluded that community violence may partly influence the relationship between harsh physical punishment and maltreatment and conduct disorder and drug use.

Early Use

Early use comes up repeatedly as a risk factor, no matter the co-occurring disorder studied. The earlier a student starts to use substances, the faster the escalation into abuse and dependence and the greater the chance of debilitating addiction in young adulthood. Costello et al. (1999) found that both depressive symptoms and disruptive behavior disorders (e.g., conduct disorder) were associated with a higher rate and earlier onset of substance use. Severe addiction in adulthood may be a consequence of early initiation into substance use that later escalates into heavy use among adolescents with conduct disorders.

Heavy Use

Malone et al. (2010) found that conduct disorder is associated with heavy illicit drug use and not just experimental use. Their literature review found that psychiatric symptoms (e.g., ADHD, conduct disorder, and depression) are major factors in the transition from lighter drug and alcohol use to heavier use. Adolescents with co-occurring conduct disorder and substance use disorder who are heavy users experience many problems (e.g., academic, health, behavioral, relationships).

Heavy drug and alcohol users experience more problems with physical and mental health (including suicidal ideation), academic concerns, legal involvement, financial hardship, delinquency, violence, physical injury, interpersonal problems, and risky sexual behavior (Morino, 2019). Greenblatt (2000) found that heavy alcohol users are more likely to report academic problems, engage in suicidal behaviors, engage in aggressive and delinquent behaviors, and drive under the influence.

PROTECTIVE FACTORS

Adolescents who are engaging in multiple problem behaviors represent a significant subgroup of individuals at higher risk for continued problems in adulthood. Educators can be part of changing that trajectory. There is a range of treatment options available. The choice of which one to use depends, among other things, on the nature, severity, and duration of the problems.

Pihet et al. claim that several interventions have proven effective in treating early emerging conduct problems with a significant decrease in their effectiveness in older children and adolescents. Thus, intervening early in the developmental trajectory of childhood-onset conduct problems is an essential goal for preventing later severe aggression and antisocial behavior. Interventions need to be comprehensive and target multiple risk factors.

Early Intervention

Fisher and Brown (2018) assert that, given the severity of behavioral problems that are often associated with conduct disorders, it may be important for programs designed to address them and their precursors to be more targeted, instead of universal, in nature. They say that by identifying a subset of children who demonstrate early emotional, behavioral, or environmental risk of developing problematic behavior by adolescence, prevention efforts may be more effective, whether they are being implemented within the context of the home or classroom.

Hemphala and Tengstrom (2010) advise that treatment of adolescents with a substance misuse problem needs to consider co-occurring mental disorders as well as behavioral traits, which can affect treatment response and outcome. Specific treatment programs for adolescents with such traits can address many aspects, for example, anger management, social skills, resolving mental problems, family relationships, and substance abuse. Again, interventions need to be strategic and targeted to unique problems.

Fisher and Brown advocate that a more contextualized training, focusing on emotional regulation of minor delinquent acts (i.e., learning not to steal or break small things when upset) and for cognitive flexibility on major delinquent ones (i.e., learning more ways of looking at the situation) may help improve efficacy. They point out that most of the existing intervention programs focus on social skills and have proven moderately effective in reducing delinquent behavior. They suggest that these might be enriched by the contextualized training on coping and emotional regulation skills.

Barnes et al. (2011) conclude that early intervention aimed at reducing engagement in aggressive behavior in late childhood and minimizing engagement in delinquent behavior in early adolescence may reduce substance use initiation in early and mid-adolescence. Barnes et al. remind us of the general lack of gender differences in trajectories of aggression, delinquency, and substance use during middle school and say this has strong implications for prevention programming. It is important to emphasize that prevention of aggressive, delinquent, and substance-using behaviors at this early age is not just limited to males.

Parent/Family Intervention

To reduce the risk of conduct disorder, parents can learn positive parenting techniques. This can help to create a closer parent–child relationship, claim Pihet et al. (2010) and also create a safe and stable home life for the child. Early detection and intervention into negative family and social experiences may be helpful in disrupting the development of experiences that may lead to more disruptive and aggressive behaviors as seen in conduct disorder (Frick, 2012).

By targeting home chaos through home-based intervention, efforts aimed at helping families to make their homes organized and safe environments for children and to develop predictable and calm family routines may concurrently reduce children's risk of developing problematic behavior characteristics (Fisher and Brown, 2018). The home context, particularly regarding the influence of parenting behaviors on child social-emotional and behavior problems, has been shown to be a successful avenue for intervention.

Home-based therapy can be useful for children with conduct disorder as it provides children, family, and therapists with information, resources, opportunities, and good access, which are not always available in customary clinical or school settings (Masroor et al., 2019). They suggest that these should include group-based parenting programs and child-focused social and cognitive problem-solving programs for younger children with less complex problems—combined parent and child training programs for those with more complex needs and multimodal interventions for adolescents with conduct disorder.

Pharmacological Intervention

Masroor et al. (2019) claim that there are positive effects seen for some medications in reducing unwanted problematic behaviors that do not cause sedation or cognitive slowing. They also note, however, that there is very little good quality evidence to support the efficacy, effectiveness, and safety of medication treatments for conduct disorder currently.

School Culture/Connectedness

Fisher and Brown (2018) found that delinquency and home chaos in childhood were related to problematic behavior in adolescence and that exposure to higher-quality classroom climates across childhood can act as a buffer. Previous research has demonstrated that classroom climate quality may influence several social-emotional and behavioral issues. And many evidence-based school interventions, highlighted in the matrix in Appendix A. (The School Mental Health Matrix), focus on social-emotional and behavioral outcomes proven to effectively target and minimize problem behavior.

PROMISING PROGRAM: EARLY RISERS SKILLS FOR SUCCESS

Program Goals

The Early Risers "Skills for Success" Program is a comprehensive preventive intervention that targets elementary school children (ages six to ten) who are at high risk for early development of conduct problems, including substance use, (i.e., who display early aggressive, disruptive, or non-conformist behaviors). The Early Risers Program aims to prevent high-risk children's further development of problem behaviors by improving their social and academic skills and intervening in their family environment. Early aggression in children can lead to a progressive stacking of disruptive behavior and failed skill acquisition, which in turn can result in significant issues with school, family, and friends—including academic failure, alienation from family members, peer rejection, and more serious conduct problems. This developmental pathway of antisocial behavior has several theoretical labels (e.g., early starter model of antisocial behavior, life-course persistent antisocial behavior, the aggressive–versatile pathway). The goal of Early Risers is to alter the developmental trajectory of early aggressive, high-risk children onto a more adaptive developmental pathway.

Program Theory

Intervention components of Early Risers integrate social learning, social development, and cognitive–behavioral models. The program also draws on developmental theory and comprehensive parenting interventions to preempt problem and delinquent behavior in young children exhibiting early aggression, which can progress into more serious conduct problems. The program targets four salient competence domains related to an adaptive developmental pathway: (1) academic competence; (2) behavioral self-regulation; (3) social competence; and (4) parent investment in his/her child. Deficits in these domains can increase a child's risk for future antisocial behaviors. Enhancing these domains can serve as a protection against future risk. The enhanced competence gained through the program leads to the development of positive self-image, independent decision making, healthy problem solving, assertive communication, and constructive coping. Once acquired, these attributes and skills collectively enable youths to resist personal and social forces that encourage early substance use and potential abuse and dependency.

Program Components

Early Risers is a multicomponent, high-intensity, competency-enhancement program based on the premise that early, comprehensive, and sustained intervention is necessary to target multiple risk and protective factors. Early Risers uses a full-strength intervention model with two complementary components, CORE and FLEX. The interventions are:

- Parent education and skills training
- Proactive parent–school consultation

- Child social skills training and strategic peer involvement
- Reading/educational enrichment activities
- Family support, consultation, and brief interventions to cope with stress
- Contingency management of aggressive, disruptive, and noncompliant behavior

The CORE component is delivered during six weeks of summer school sessions and includes ongoing teacher consultation and student mentoring during the school day as well as a biweekly family program that consists of parent education, skills training, and child social skills training groups.

CONCLUDING THOUGHTS

The most striking takeaway after reviewing this literature is the distress and pain so many children with conduct disorder must feel. They can seem arrogant and belligerent and defiant at times that educators can forget that they are just children crying out for help. The promise of this research is that there are very specific protective factors that can be incorporated, and strengthened or improved, that can make a difference for children with conduct disorders—and their teachers.

And as the Early Risers program description states, such interventions can decrease the chances that children with conduct disorder will turn to substance use to self-medicate the pain away. The increased competence and confidence and enhanced self-concept nurtured in such programs can help reduce psychological distress. By providing an array of coping skills and strategies, these students can draw on more effective tools to meet their needs and improve their relationships and overall success in school.

For it is by getting to the underlying issues that enables professionals to better help these students. This chapter not only reviewed the risks, but as with the other co-occurring disorders covered here, delves into the protective factors that can address some of these behavioral concerns. By analyzing them, students can be identified and provided with coping skills that, hopefully, they can fall back on to better regulate their emotions and behavior rather than acting out or turning to substances.

Educators can look to these promising, evidence-based practices and programs as exemplars of strategies and approaches that can be adopted and adapted as local needs dictate. For children struggling with severe behavior disorders, such practices and programs can be the difference between a life of confidence and competence, or one of dysregulation and distress.

REFERENCES

Angold, A., & Costello, E. J. (1993). Depressive Comorbidity in Children and Adolescents: Empirical, Theoretical, and Methodological Issues. *The American Journal of Psychiatry*, 150, 1779–1791.

Barnes, G. M., Welte, J. W., Hoffman, J. H., & Tidwell, M. O. (2011). The Co-occurrence of Gambling with Substance Use and Conduct Disorder among Youth in the United States. *American Journal on Addictions*, 20(2), 166–173. https://doi.org/10.1111/j.1521-0391.2010.00116.x

Behavior Disorders, Externalizing and Internalizing Behaviors, Retrieved from: Behavior Disorders - Guidebook (weebly.com).

Breslau, N., Davis, G. C., & Andreski, P. (1995). Risk factors for PTSD-related Traumatic Events: A Prospective Analysis. *American Journal of Psychiatry*, 152, 529–535.

Cerdá, M., Tracy, M., Sánchez, B. N., & Galea, S. (2011). Comorbidity among Depression, Conduct Disorder, and Drug use from Adolescence to Young Adulthood: Examining the Role of Violence Exposures. *Journal of Traumatic Stress*, 24(6), 651–659. https://doi.org/10.1002/jts.20696

Costello, E. J., Erkanli, A., Federman, E., & Angold, A. (1999). Development of Psychiatric Comorbidity with Substance Abuse in Adolescents: Effects of Timing and Sex. *Journal of Clinical Child Psychology*, 28(3), 298–311.

D'Onofrio, B. M., Goodnight, J. A., Van Hulle, C. A., Rodgers, J. L., Rathouz, P. J., Waldman, I. D., & Lahey, B. B. (2009). A Quasi-experimental Analysis of the Association between Family Income and Offspring Conduct Problems. *Journal of Abnormal Child Psychology*, 37, 415–429. https://doi.org/10.1007/s10802-008-9280-2

Fisher, J. H., & Brown, J. L. (2018). A Prospective, Longitudinal Examination of the Influence of Childhood Home and School Contexts on Psychopathic Characteristics in Adolescence. *Journal of Youth & Adolescence*, 47(10), 2041–2059. https://doi.org/10.1007/s10964-018-0861-2

Frick, P. J. (2012). Developmental Pathways to Conduct Disorder: Implications for Future Directions in Research, Assessment, and Treatment. *Journal of Clinical Child & Adolescent Psychology*, 41, 378–389. https://doi.org/10.1080/15374416.2012.664815. 22475202

Getz, J., & Bray, J. H. (2005). Predicting Heavy Alcohol Use among Adolescents. *American Journal of Orthopsychiatry*, 75(1), 102–116. https://doi.org/10.1037 /0002-9432.75.1.102

Greenblatt, J. C. (2000). *Patterns of Alcohol Use Among Adolescents and Associations with Emotional and Behavioral Problems*. Substance Abuse and Mental Health Services Administration (DHHS/PHS) OAS Working Paper. Rockville, MD: Office of Applied Studies.

Hemphälä, M., & Tengström, A. (2010). Associations between Psychopathic Traits and Mental Disorders among Adolescents with Substance Use Problems. *British Journal of Clinical Psychology*, 49(1), 109–122. https://doi.org/10.1348 /014466509X439216

Herrera, A., Benjet, C., Méndez, E., Casanova, L., & Medina-Mora, M. (2017). How Mental Health Interviews Conducted Alone, in the Presence of an Adult, a Child or Both Affects Adolescents' Reporting of Psychological Symptoms and Risky Behaviors. *Journal of Youth & Adolescence*, 46(2), 417–428. https://doi.org/10 .1007/s10964-016-0418-1

Herring, D. (2015). Model of Conduct Disorders. University of Central Florida. Presentation.

Holtmann, M., Buchmann, A. F., Esser, G., Schmidt, M. H., Banaschewski, T., & Laucht, M. (2011). The Child Behavior Checklist-Dysregulation Profile Predicts Substance Use, Suicidality, and Functional Impairment: A Longitudinal Analysis. *Journal of Child Psychology & Psychiatry*, 52(2), 139–147. https://doi.org/10.1111 /j.1469-7610.2010.02309.x

Howard, R., McCarthy, L., Huband, N., & Duggan, C. (2013). Re-offending in Forensic Patients Released from Secure Care: The Role of Antisocial/borderline Personality Disorder Co-morbidity, Substance Dependence and Severe Childhood Conduct Disorder. *Criminal Behaviour & Mental Health*, 23(3), 191–202. https:// doi.org/10.1002/cbm.1852

Howard, A. L., Molina, B. S. G., Swanson, J. M., Hinshaw, S. P., Belendiuk, K. A., Harty, S. C., . . . Wigal, T. (2015). Developmental Progression to Early Adult Binge Drinking and Marijuana Use from Worsening versus Stable Trajectories of Adolescent Attention Deficit/Hyperactivity Disorder and Delinquency. *Addiction*, 110(5), 784–795. PubMed: 25664657

Kazdin, A. E., Bass, D., Ayers, W. A., & Rodgers, A. (1990). Empirical and Clinical Focus of Child and Adolescent Psychotherapy Research. *Journal of Consulting and Clinical Psychology*, 58(6), 729, 740. https://doi.org/10.1037/0022-006X.58.6.729

Malone, S. M., McGue, M., & Iacono, W. G. (2010). Mothers' Maximum Drinks Ever Consumed in 24 Hours Predicts Mental Health Problems in Adolescent Offspring. *Journal of Child Psychology and Psychiatry*, 51(9), 1067–1075.

Masroor, A., Patel, R. S., Bhimanadham, N. N., Raveendran, S., Ahmad, N., Queeneth, U., Pankaj, A., & Mansuri, Z. (2019). Conduct Disorder-Related Hospitalization and Substance Use Disorders in American Teens. *Behavioral Sciences* (2076-328X), 9(7), 73. https://doi.org/10.3390/bs9070073

Measelle, J. R., Slice, E., & Hogansen, J. M. (2006). Developmental Trajectories of Co-occurring Depressive, Eating, Antisocial and Substance Abuse Problems in Female Adolescents. *Journal of Abnormal Psychology*, 115, 524–538. https://doi.org/10.1037/0021-843X.115.3.524

Morino, Y. (2019). Ideas of the Change Process: Family and Therapist Perspectives on Systemic Psychotherapy for Children with Conduct Disorder. *Journal of Family Therapy*, 41(1), 29–53. https://doi.org/10.1111/1467-6427.12202

Pacek, L. R., Malcolm, R. J., & Martins, S. S. (2012). Race/Ethnicity Differences between Alcohol, Marijuana, and Co-occurring Alcohol and Marijuana Use Disorders and their Association with Public Health and Social Problems using a National Sample. *The American Journal on Addictions*, 21, 435–444. https://doi.org/10.1111/j.1521-0391.2012.00249.x

Petry, N. M., & Tawfik, Z. (2001). Comparison of Problem-gambling and Non-problem-gambling Youths Seeking Treatment for Marijuana Abuse. *Journal of the American Academy of Child and Adolescent Psychiatry*, 40, 1324–1331.

Pihet, S., Combremont, M., Suter, M., & Stephan, P. (2012). Cognitive and Emotional Deficits Associated with Minor and Serious Delinquency in High-Risk Adolescents. *Psychiatry, Psychology & Law*, 19(3), 427–438. https://doi.org/10.1080/13218719.2011.598634

Schuckit, M. A. (2006). Comorbidity between Substance Use Disorders and Psychiatric Conditions. *Addiction*, 101 (Suppl. 1), 76–88. https://doi.org/10.10.1111/j.1360-0443.2006. 01592.x

Soni, A. (2009). *The Five Most Costly Conditions, 1996 and 2006: Estimates for the US Civilian Non-institutionalized Population*. Statistical Brief 248, 2009, Rockville, MD: Agency for Healthcare Research and Quality.

Tiet, Q. Q., Wasserman, G. A., Loeber, R., McReynolds, L. S., & Miller, L. S. (2001). Developmental and Sex Differences in Types of Conduct Problems. *Journal of Child and Family* Studies, 10, 181–197.

Vitulano, M. L., Fite, P. J., Hopko, D. R., Lochman, J., Wells, K., & Asif, I. (2014). Evaluation of Underlying Mechanisms in the Link Between Childhood ADHD Symptoms and Risk for Early Initiation of Substance Use. *Psychology of Addictive Behaviors*, 28(3), 816–827. https://doi.org/10.1037/a0037504. PMID: 25222174.

Winters, K. C., & Arria, A. (2011). Adolescent Brain Development and Drugs. *The Prevention Researcher*, 18(2), 21–24.

Chapter 5

Understanding Co-occurring Disorders

Depression/Anxiety and Adolescent Substance Use

ANXIETY AND DEPRESSION:
DEFINITIONS, PREVALENCE

While the externalizing behaviors of behavior and conduct disorders can be so obvious, and so frustrating, educators can often overlook our students with internalizing disorders because they are not obvious behavior problems. They are the quiet ones, the well-behaved ones, the ones staring off into space, shutting the world out—and inwardly crying out for help just the same.

The extent of child suffering is huge when all kinds of mental health disorders are included, including substance use and its associated co-occurring disorders. This suffering plays out daily in the classroom, so understanding that all behavior is purposeful is critical.

This chapter explores what we know about the trifecta of the most common of co-occurring disorders: anxiety and substance use disorder; depression and substance use disorder; and a combination of anxiety and depression and substance use disorder. Figure 5.1 illustrates the extent and rate of depression, anxiety, and behavior disorders by age range according to the Center for Disease Control (CDC).

Russell and Odgers (2020) remind us that adolescence is a period of heightened vulnerability for the onset and escalation of mental health problems such as depression, anxiety, and inattention/impulsivity and experimentation. Costello et al. (2011) note that about one adolescent in five has a psychiatric disorder, and that from childhood to adolescence there is an increase in rates of depression, panic disorder, agoraphobia, and substance use disorders.

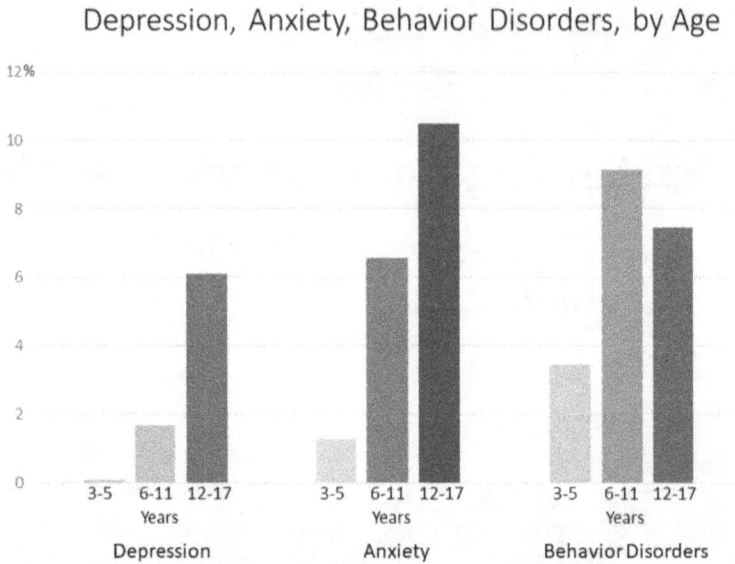

Depression, Anxiety, Behavior Disorders, by Age

Figure 5.1   Rates of Depression, Anxiety, and Behavior Disorders by Age. *"Data and Statistics on Children's Mental Health". Content source: National Center on Birth Defects and Developmental Disabilities, Centers for Disease Control and Prevention.* https://www.cdc.gov/childrensmentalhealth/data.html.

Finch et al. (2020) find that mental health disorders affect 10–20 percent of children and adolescents worldwide making them, they say, among the most prevalent and debilitating health conditions affecting children and adolescents today. They warn that early onset of anxiety is often a precursor to co-occurring anxiety disorders, mood disorders, or substance disorders, highlighting the need for better detection and early intervention.

Anxiety disorders are the most common mental health disorders experienced by children and adolescents (Crouch et al., 2019), with a median age of onset of about eleven. The period of greatest vulnerability is ages fourteen to seventeen (Essau et al., 2020). And anxiety and depression tend to predict one another from childhood/adolescence to adulthood (Copeland et al., 2013).

While externalizing behaviors or symptoms represent those impulsive in nature, internalizing symptoms include those associated with depression (i.e., characterized by feelings of sadness, little interest or pleasure in doing things, and/or a range of other symptoms) or anxiety (i.e., characterized by feelings of tension, worried thoughts, and/or physiological symptoms) (Essau et al., 2020).

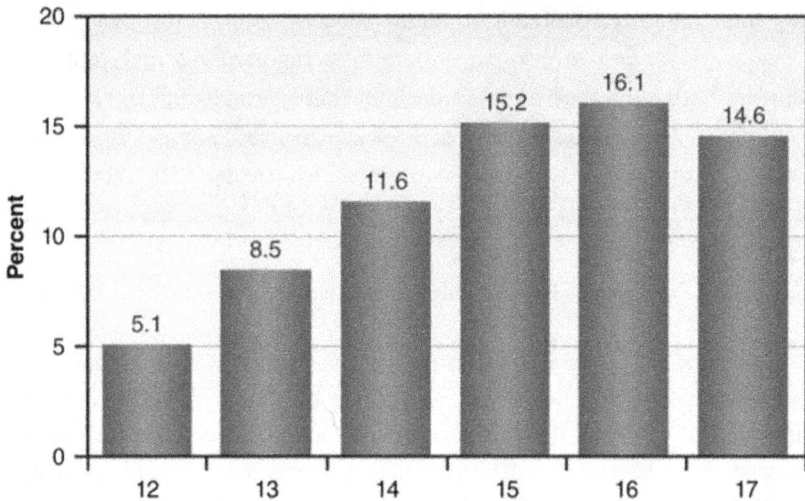

Figure 5.2   Major Depressive Episode in the Past Year among Girls Aged Twelve to Seventeen: 2008 to 2010. *"Depression Triples between the Ages of 12 and 15 among Adolescent Girls." In Data Spotlight: National Survey on Drug Use and Health. (July 19, 2012).* https://www.samhsa.gov/data/sites/default/files/NSDUH-SP77-AdolescentGirls Depression-2012/CBHSQ-NSDUH-Spotlight-077-AdolescentGirlsDepression-2012.htm.

Recent years have seen an increase in such internalizing disorders among adolescents. For example, figure 5.2 provides a stark look at the threefold increase of a major depressive disorder in girls ages twelve to fifteen in a just a two-year period, between 2008 and 2010, from 5.1 percent to 15.2 percent.

ANXIETY AND/OR DEPRESSION AND SUBSTANCE USE

Extent of Co-occurring SUD and Anxiety and/or Depression

Marmorstein et al. (2010) report that there is a great deal of research supporting the fact that internalizing disorders (depression and anxiety) and substance use disorders (abuse and dependence) often co-occur. And while externalizing disorders such as conduct disorder and ADHD are the most frequently found co-occurring psychiatric disorders among young people with substance use problems, this is followed by internalizing disorders such as depression or dysthymia and anxiety (Couwenbergh et al., 2006).

Horigan et al. (2013) found similar results: as many as 75 percent of adolescents with substance use disorders have a mental health problem.

They found that externalizing problems such as conduct disorder, ADHD, and oppositional defiant disorder are the most reported and investigated co-occurring with substance use disorder, but that internalizing problems such as anxiety disorders, depression, and substance use disorder are also very common, with rates of depression with substance use disorders ranging from 11 percent to 32 percent and anxiety disorders with substance use disorders ranging from 7 percent to 40 percent.

Horigan et al. discuss the possible causes of these co-occurring disorders:

> Several models have been proposed for the development of co-occurring mental health and SUD (substance use disorder) in adolescence. Reviews of these describe: (a) common factor development in which shared common factors predispose adolescents to both mental health problems and SUDs; (b) secondary SUDs; (c) secondary mental/psychiatric disorder; and (d) bidirectional models. (p. 292)

A co-occurring disorder is also associated with a greater likelihood of recurrence, longer episodes, suicide attempts, increased utilization of mental health services, and functional problems (Gallerani et al., 2010). Adolescents identified as having a co-occurring disorder and in treatment have been found to have very high rates of anxiety, depression, and worse outcomes that those only diagnosed with having a substance use disorder. They describe the interaction of these disorders:

> Depression and anxiety are among the most commonly co-occurring conditions. They also found that, "controlling for other comorbidities, anxiety significantly predicted depression, depression significantly predicted anxiety, ADHD significantly predicted oppositional defiant disorder, and anxiety significantly predicted substance use disorders." In a follow-up of a clinical sample, [24] reported that two-thirds of children with comorbid depression and anxiety disorders experienced the anxiety disorder prior to the depression. Similarly, the Oregon Adolescent Depression Project ([36]) showed that anxiety, externalizing, and substance use disorders all preceded depression. Additionally, [41] found that among offspring of depressed parents, 28.6% of those with an initial diagnosis of conduct disorder developed depression over the next two years (p. 243).

Other researchers have come to similar conclusions. Chan et al. (2008) reported that, among a sample of treatment-seeking substance users, 78–90 percent had either an internalizing or externalizing disorder, and 42–61 percent presented with symptoms of both.

Richert and Dahlberg (2020) agree that those with this co-occurring disorder experience more severe problems. They have more extensive drug problems, higher levels of social problems, and criminality, as well as worse treatment outcomes and greater risk of relapse, compared with young people with substance use problems alone. On the other hand, they note, there are also studies demonstrating that a relatively large proportion of adolescents with substance use problems do not report any mental disorders or symptoms at initiation of treatment.

While there was little in the literature on race, substance use, and anxiety and/or depression, one study, that by Goldstick et al. (2018), found that being African American was associated with a lower likelihood of membership in groups reporting higher levels of symptoms, including the substance use rates, except for marijuana use in males. This finding, they say,

> may indicate greater resiliency among African American youth and is consistent with prior research indicating African Americans have lower levels of lifetime depression ([29]), and lower rates of alcohol use ([8]) than their white counterparts. In addition, relative to the group with only mental health symptoms, those with comorbid symptoms and drinking were more likely to be male, which is consistent with a prior paper from these data showing males had more severe marijuana use trajectories ([37]). (p. 664)

Psychological Distress

Wu et al. (2018) describe psychological distress variables as strong risk factors of substance use and related disorders among adolescents. They say that anxiety and depression are also potential risk factors. Their work with non-engaged youth found that they were vulnerable to develop anxiety and depression as their negative life experiences such as school dropout, unemployment, and associated problems created stress. Non-engaged youth in their study reported loneliness, also considered a risk factor of substance use among youths.

Wu et al. found three psychological distress variables (i.e., depression, anxiety, and stress) positively associated with both ever using substances and with the intention to use such substances in the next twelve months. (Loneliness was associated only with intention to use psychoactive substances.) Anxiety negatively affected the association between resilience and ever using of psychoactive substances, whereas depression negatively affected the association between resilience and behavioral intention.

Other Potential Causes of These Co-occurring Disorders

Richert and Dahlberg tell us that there are various theories about the causal relationship between mental health problems and drug problems. While they note that some problems usually precede drug and alcohol problems with the drugs serving a self-medicating function, the link between mental health problems and drug use cannot be explained solely based on self-medication because youth give varying reasons for use.

They also found the opposite as well, that drug and alcohol use increases the risk of mental health problems. Mental health problems and substance abuse problems may also intertwine and develop simultaneously over time. Their conclusion is that the relationship between these disorders and substance use is strong and extremely complex.

McKenzie et al. (2010) point to additional possibilities. Symptoms of depression and anxiety and nicotine dependence, for example, may share causal influences, such as predisposing biological or genetic factors. They say that the extent of heritability of substance use appears to depend upon substance type. They point to the association between nicotine dependence and genes underlying the reward system of the brain. They also say it is possible that genetic and/or biological predispositions may interact with a variety of psychosocial, behavioral, and contextual risk factors.

Marmorstein et al. (2010) agree and found support for a common genetic tendency for both internalizing disorders (perhaps particularly major depressive disorder) and substance use disorders. They also say that the available evidence seems to indicate that there may be differences by type of symptom, age of participant, and what measures of symptoms are used. The bulk of the studies of internalizing problems of preadolescents through early adolescents they examined support the notion that they increase risk for initial use of substances.

There may be differences according to type of the internalizing symptom and type of substance. Their study of adolescent girls found the following:

> The effects of the first use of substances depended on the type of substance, the
> type of internalizing symptoms, and the internalizing symptom trajectory that

the girl was on. Trajectory group differences were found such that (a) initial use of marijuana was related to increases in depressive symptoms among girls experiencing high levels of depressive symptoms, (b) initial use of alcohol was related to increases in social anxiety among girls experiencing increasing levels of social anxiety but decreasing levels of social anxiety among girls experiencing decreasing levels of social anxiety, (c) initial use of cigarettes was related to increases in social anxiety among girls experiencing decreasing social anxiety but decreases in social anxiety among girls experiencing increasing levels of social anxiety, and (d) initial use of marijuana was related to decreases in social anxiety among girls experiencing increasing levels of social anxiety. In addition, the initial use of alcohol or cigarettes was associated with increases in depressive symptoms for girls overall, and the initial use of cigarettes was associated with increases in generalized anxiety symptoms overall. (p. 555)

Gender Considerations

In examining gender implications related to mental health issues, Richert and Dahlberg (2020) found that although the list of problems is ranked similarly by gender, the percentage of girls with various mental health problems is consistently higher than boys. Their study findings show substantial gender differences, with a larger percentage of girls reporting both mental health problems and receiving psychiatric care and prescription medications for psychiatric disorders.

Experiences of traumatic events, violence, and physical abuse, which they said were more common among the girls in their study, is one possible explanation for the higher level of female mental health problems. It is also probable, they speculate, that some girls begin to use drugs or alcohol to alleviate or manage such painful experiences and the stress they cause. The girls in their study also generally showed somewhat earlier onset of drug use and more frequent use.

Essau et al. (2020) found that, compared to males, females have steeper increases in depressive symptoms to age twenty, after which levels of depression first plateau and then start to show a decrease for both males and females. They also discovered that females have an earlier age of peak of depressive symptoms than males (13.5 years and 16.4 years, respectively). Those with serious symptoms tended to be female, with low self-concept, low socioeconomic status, poor interpersonal relations, and chronic health conditions, with few coping skills and few friends.

The Marmorstein et al. study of gender, depression, and marijuana use found that when it came to initial use:

> For girls on a "high depressive symptom" trajectory, initial use of marijuana was related to further increases in depressive symptoms. Initial uses of alcohol and cigarettes were associated with overall increases in depressive symptoms, and the initial use of cigarettes was associated with an overall increase in generalized anxiety symptoms. Initial use of all substances was related to change in social anxiety, but the direction of change varied by trajectory group and substance. Links between initial use and internalizing symptoms depended on the type of substance, type of internalizing symptom, and trajectory group. (p.545)

Among boys, Marmorstein et al. found both generalized and social anxiety predicted first use of alcohol and tobacco, whereas only generalized anxiety predicted first use of marijuana. Among ninth- and tenth-grade students, depressed mood was positively related to alcohol use initiation two years later.

They found that higher levels of both types of anxiety were associated with increased risk for initial use of alcohol, cigarettes, and marijuana during the subsequent year; in addition, generalized anxiety predicted increased risk for initial use of marijuana. Therefore, in both studies, increased social anxiety was sometimes associated with increased risk for first use of substances. However, "only an overall link between generalized anxiety and initial use of cigarettes was found for girls in the present study, whereas links for alcohol and marijuana were also found for boys" (p. 556).

They concluded that girls with high levels of depressive symptoms who try or start using marijuana should be considered at high risk for escalation of depressive symptoms. Specifically, young girls who try or start using alcohol or cigarettes should be considered at risk for increased depressive symptoms, and young girls who try or start using cigarettes should also be considered at risk for increased generalized anxiety symptoms.

Galleroni et al. (2010) also examined gender and co-occurring disorders. They found that the odds that girls with prior substance use disorders having a depressive disorder subsequently were three times those of girls with no prior substance use disorders. They found that, controlling for prior anxiety and risk, the odds of girls having been diagnosed with an anxiety disorder were twice those of boys; the odds of girls having been diagnosed with a depressive disorder were 1.5 times those of boys; the odds of boys having been diagnosed with an externalizing disorder were almost twice those of girls.

Several interesting findings emerged regarding sex differences. Gallerani et al. found:

> First, the relation between anxiety and depression differed for males and females. Whereas for girls the rates of depression were high regardless of prior anxiety, the odds of boys with prior subthreshold anxiety disorders having subsequent subthreshold depression were one and a half times those of boys without prior subthreshold anxiety. These findings highlight the pernicious effects of anxiety symptoms in boys. Perhaps for boys, having anxiety is more debilitating in a culture where boys are socialized to be 'tough.' For anxious boys, social support and acceptance may be less forthcoming, thereby leading to feelings of rejection and depression. (p. 248)

RISK FACTORS

In addition to genes and biology, risk factors for co-occurring disorders include poverty, community stress, trauma (which was discussed in chapter 2), early use and use of multiple substances, and even the type of substance used.

Environmental Stress

Cumulative environmental risk is greater among low- versus high-income youth, and cumulative stressors influence the association between social status disparities and mental health problems, including psychological distress and self-regulation difficulties (Dilworth et al., 2007). Goldstick et al. (2018) found that community violence exposure was highest among those with high depression or anxiety symptom. Those with high alcohol use and depression or anxiety disorders reported the most delinquent peer affiliations and the highest rates of severe violence over time.

Community violence exposure as an important correlate of depression/anxiety symptoms in this population, they say, and negative peer associations are key factors. Their identified "high drinking/high mental health concerns" group studied reported more friends engaging in delinquent behaviors than all other groups. Peer associations distinguished between those who had anxiety/ depression symptoms versus those who had both symptoms and high-severity alcohol use, indicating that those with anxiety/depression symptoms may be particularly susceptible to negative peer influences.

Poly Drug Use

Regarding the use of multiple substances (i.e., poly use), Richert and Dahlberg (2020) found anxiety problems appear to be clearly linked to poly drug use and frequent drug use, but not to early onset of use. Young people with experiences of physical and sexual abuse also reported high rates of poly drug use, initiated substance use earlier than their peers and gave more reasons for using, including for coping with painful emotions. Post-Traumatic Stress Disorder (PSTD), which can be a result of traumatic experiences such as abuse, has also been shown to increase the risk of developing substance use problems (Harrison et al., 1997).

Type of Substance

Marijuana

While many believe that marijuana is relatively harmless, there are associations between the psychoactive drug and anxiety and depression. Anxiety problems in adolescence have been shown to predict alcohol use problems in young adulthood. Regarding marijuana, the opposite appears to be true: marijuana use in adolescence can increase the risk of anxiety and depression later in life (Richert and Dahlberg, 2020).

For example, in their research review, they found that weekly or more frequent marijuana use in teenagers predicted an approximately twofold increase in risk for later depression and anxiety. They also found early onset of marijuana use to be associated with higher rates of later substance use, juvenile offending, mental health problems, unemployment, and school dropout.

Knopf (2019) found that regular use of marijuana during adolescence was associated with diminished scholastic achievement, liability to addiction, earlier onset of psychosis, and neuropsychological decline. Their meta-analysis found that adolescent marijuana users had more than three times the risk than non-users of attempting suicide in young adulthood. The increased risk for developing depression was 1.37 and the risk for suicidal ideation (i.e., thoughts) was 1.50.

For girls, Marmorstein et al. (2010) found that the initial use of marijuana was particularly associated with increased depressive symptoms among girls who already had stable high levels of depressive symptoms. They suggest that those who already have high levels of depressive symptoms may be most vulnerable. Alternatively, those who already have high levels of depressive symptoms may be the ones to most likely to try marijuana, which may further increase their vulnerability to depressive symptoms.

Tobacco and Nicotine

Mammorstein et al. also found that the initial uses of alcohol and cigarettes are associated with overall increases in depressive symptoms, and that initial use of cigarettes is associated with an overall increase in generalized anxiety symptoms. The Essau et al. (2020) research review found that the use of tobacco was more strongly associated with the internalizing symptoms of depression and anxiety. Greater anxiety symptoms also predicted greater symptoms of nicotine dependence. Depressive symptoms were also marginally predictive of greater nicotine dependence.

McKenzie et al. (2010) found that, among teen smokers, symptoms of depression and anxiety in adolescence significantly altered the course of smoking and predicted progression to nicotine dependence. Adolescents who smoked less than daily and who experienced high levels of symptoms of depression and anxiety, they say, had a more than threefold risk of nicotine dependence in young adulthood compared to less than daily smoking peers, who had low levels of symptoms of depression and anxiety.

Adolescent smokers with high levels of symptoms of depression and anxiety remain at high risk of progression to nicotine dependence. Adolescent daily smokers who reported high levels of symptoms of depression and anxiety had an almost twofold risk of nicotine dependence in young adulthood, compared to daily smoking peers with low levels of symptoms of depression and anxiety. Heavy tobacco use may also cause cognitive and/or affective impairment.

Self-harm and Suicidality

Suicide is the third leading cause of death between ages ten and twenty-four. Self-harm and suicidal thoughts and behavior are associated with the internalizing disorders such as anxiety and depression. Add in substance use, with its associated diminishment of self-control, and you have another lethal combination.

The relationship between substance use and suicide is well established (Moon et al., 2020). They continue:

> Poorolajal et al. ([46]) conducted a meta-analysis and found a significant association between substance use and suicide behavior: suicidal ideation OR 2.04 (95% CI: 1.59, 2.50; I 2 = 88.8%, 16 studies); suicide attempt OR 2.49 (95% CI: 2.00, 2.98; I 2 = 94.3%, 24 studies) and suicide death OR 1.49 (95% CI: 0.97, 2.00; I 2 = 82.7%, 7 studies). Substance use disorders, and alcohol use disorders in particular, can increase the risk of attempting suicide. (Erskine et al. [16])

Guerriero et al. (2017) reported on a study that found that 7.3 percent of respondents reported at least one episode of self-harm and those rates were three times higher for females than males. Almost half reported repeated self-harm in the form of cutting. Anxiety, depression, and substance abuse were linked to self-harm as well, particularly repeated self-harm. Other studies reviewed by Guerriero et al. found that 13.5 percent of females and 4.3 percent of males had self-harmed on at least one occasion. The most common means were self-cutting and overdoses, with half the adolescents harming themselves more than once.

Carballo et al. (2020) reviewed the research on these issues and found three main factors that appear to increase the risk of suicidality:

- Psychological factors (depression, anxiety, previous suicide attempt, drug and alcohol use, and other comorbid psychiatric disorders).
- stressful life events (family problems and peer conflicts); and
- personality traits (such as neuroticism and impulsivity). (p. 759)

They found that the incidence of suicide attempts peaks during the mid-adolescent years, and suicide mortality, which increases with age steadily through the teenage years. Young people with suicidal behavior had significant psychiatric problems, mainly depressive disorders, and substance abuse disorders.

They conclude that:

> Drug and/or alcohol misuse may also increase the risk for suicide attempts and intoxication may even trigger the suicidal act in vulnerable individuals by increasing impulsiveness, enhancing depressive thoughts and suicidal ideation, limiting cognitive functions and ability to see alternative coping strategies, and reducing barriers to self-inflicted harm [[53]]. . . . . . , common neurobiological vulnerability has been described in depression, impulsivity and drug and/or alcohol use disorders such as a greater serotonergic impairment [[53]], which may help explain their frequent co-association and also their relationship with suicidal behavior (p. 774).

According to the CDC, in addition to anxiety, stress, and depression, other warning signs or risk factors—beyond verbalized suicidal ideation—include feeling like a burden, being isolated, increased anxiety, feeling trapped or in unbearable pain, increased substance use, looking for access to lethal means, increased anger or rage, extreme mood swings, expressing hopelessness, sleeping too little or too much, and making plans for suicide.

Another important finding from this work, which has tremendous implications for schools, is a very low rate of help-seeking behavior for both self-harm thoughts and episodes. Adolescent self-harm also is associated with risk of suicide in adulthood. It is so important for educators to be aware of the signs and risk factors for suicide, and to make connections with students so they will *talk* to us when they are experiencing such psychological distress.

PROTECTIVE FACTORS

The first step, obviously, is to identify the students who are experiencing anxiety or depression, and well as those that are experiencing co-occurring anxiety or depression and substance use disorder. Vigilant observation, referral, and screening students for these disorders is a start, followed by counseling and providing coping skills, support, and substance use treatment.

Screening

Richert and Dahlberg (2020) point to the vital importance of screening, and screening for mental health problems when treating young people with drug use problems. They describe the importance of exploring the specific roles or functions that drug use have for young people, especially how these functions may relate to traumatic events and different mental health problems.

The American Academy of Pediatrics recommends that pediatricians routinely screen and evaluate children for substance use and offer interventions or referrals. Just as educators, they describe barriers to this work due to lack of training and lack of time. Babajide et al. concur and advocate for screening and treatment being conducted in primary care facilities to reduce the stigma associated with getting such mental health treatment. They say that the support of a treatment team may also aid in helping a young adult better understand his or her need for mental health treatment.

SBIRT is an important screening tool gaining greater and greater acceptance and use in a variety of settings, including schools and medical facilities. SBIRT (Screening, Brief Intervention, and Referral to Treatment) is a comprehensive, integrated, public health approach to the delivery of early intervention and treatment services for persons with substance use disorders, as well as those who are at risk of developing these disorders (SAMSHA). Advantages of SBIRT include:

- Screening quickly assesses the severity of substance use and identifies the appropriate level of treatment.
- Brief intervention focuses on increasing insight and awareness regarding substance use and motivation toward behavioral change.
- Referral to treatment provides those identified as needing more extensive treatment with access to specialty care.

Crouch et al. (2019) discussed how parents do not often know how to identify what is happening with their distressed children. They recommend that providing families and professionals working with families with information and guidance on identifying anxiety difficulties in children would address key recognition barriers. They found that school staff recognizing and acting on a child's anxiety difficulties played a helpful role in parental help-seeking. This includes providing children support within the school, as well as being referred to and accessing specialist mental health services.

Focus on Well-Being and Coping Skills

Recently we have seen more of an emphasis on student social and emotional development in schools. This is a crucially important emphasis that requires commitment and resources. Schools need support in the form of more school mental health professionals (i.e., social workers, counselors, psychologists) who can provide professional expertise on such issues. Just adding additional responsibilities on to already overloaded school-level clinicians, as happens all too frequently, is a guarantee of poor—or no—implementation.

Focusing on student well-being and coping skills is not only important for student (and staff well-being), but it can also help educators advance the mission of educating the next generation. The link between well-being and student achievement is likely to be one of the most important prerequisites to improving the academic performance (Finch et al., 2020).

Wu et al. (2020) advocate for resilience training as one solution. They cite research, for example, that shows that resilience is protective against risk behaviors and substance use among adolescents. They also found resilience to be negatively associated with both substance use and psychological distress, the distress that drives many young people to use substances. Finch et al. (2018) agree but say that this must go beyond resilience training alone.

They studied a program called HERO, teaching Hope, Efficacy, Resilience, and Optimism, and found that:

> (1) significant and positive associations were found between all HERO constructs and flourishing (H1); (2) all HERO constructs were significantly negatively associated with anxiety, and depression (H2); and (3) PsyCap (HERO construct combined) significantly predicted flourishing (H3a), significantly predicted anxiety and depression (H3b), and had greater predictive power than the individual HERO constructs (H3c). The significant contribution of this study was the finding that the combined PsyCap constructs of hope, efficacy, resilience and optimism accounted for more of the variance in flourishing, anxiety, and depression than each construct alone. (p.1033)

They concluded that the current middle school interventions aimed at increasing student well-being via resilience programs alone may not be as effective as programs that target both efficacy and optimism. They found optimism was the strongest predictor of all outcomes, including the amount of flourishing, anxiety, and depression.

This chapter's Promising Program, called FRIENDS, incorporates resiliency training and problem solving to reduce anxiety.

Drug Education and Treatment for Students with SUD

Horigan et al. (2013) observe that adolescents with co-occurring substance use and mental health problems are a population at a very high risk for co-occurring problems into adulthood, making early treatment important for preventing later escalation. They suggest that interventions for substance use disorders may be helpful in reducing internalizing disorders in adolescents. Their reviews found significant reduction of anxiety and depressive symptoms and significant reductions in probable anxiety and depression diagnoses were observed at treatment follow-up.

It used to be that treatment of these co-occurring disorders occurred separately. Advances in the fields have led to treating them simultaneously for better results. Horigan et al. (2013) say it is possible that interventions for one disorder may help reduce the incidence of another disorder, either by changing a common risk factor (family environment) or by reducing a maintaining disorder (anxiety fostering substance abuse). The effects of depression treatment that carry over to anxiety symptoms often helps alleviate the substance use disorder as well, they found.

School staff are not being asked here to be substance use counselors or provide addiction treatment. But school mental health professionals can identify community resources and have referrals available for students and families. Even having such a list of community resources to offer students and their families is a lot more than many schools have now.

Community Support

As discussed, there is more of an emphasis on student social and emotional development in schools today. This is a crucially important emphasis that requires commitment and resources. Schools need support in the form of more resources such as school mental health professionals (i.e., social workers, counselors, and psychologists) who can provide professional expertise on such issues.

Community support is also necessary to address the stress and exposure to violence that many students experience in their communities. Goldstick et al.

(2018) who studied high-risk youth advocate for substance use interventions including content related to mental health and community violence exposure. Understanding such dynamics, they say, may aid in the prevention of not only alcohol use and mental health symptoms, but also in other negative co-occurring outcomes.

Community support is also essential in providing the necessary resources for prevention and intervention beyond the schoolhouse. Most communities have very few agencies or facilities that provide treatment for adolescent with co-occurring disorders. In addition to direct services, communities also need to support adolescents with opportunities for meaningful recreation, employment, and other initiatives so adolescents have alternatives to turning to substance use. Chapter 9 will further address additional community responsibilities and responses for substance use prevention and intervention.

PROMISING PROGRAM: FRIENDS

FRIENDS Program

FRIENDS is a cognitive behavioral program that is an adaptation of the Australian Coping Cat workbook. FRIENDS has been recognized by the World Health Organization as the only evidence-based program effective in reducing anxiety as a universal and targeted intervention. Originally developed in Australia by Professor Paula Barrett, Webster, and Turner (2000), FRIENDS is a school-based, preventative program. The name of the program is an acronym for central components of the intervention:

F = FEELINGS
R = REMEMBER TO RELAX. HAVE QUIET TIME.
I = I CAN DO IT! I CAN TRY MY BEST!
E = EXPLORE SOLUTIONS AND COPING STEP PLANS.
N = NOW REWARD YOURSELF! YOU'VE DONE YOUR BEST!
D = DON'T FORGET TO PRACTICE!
S = SMILE! STAY CALM, AND TALK TO YOUR SUPPORT NETWORKS!

The program utilizes peer learning, experimental learning, and family-directed problem solving. The objective is to have the child understand the psychological cues for their anxiety and use positive reinforcement to change behavior in response to those cues. Building a peer network for socialization and support is also part of the program.

Parents are an integral part of this learning and support system and are taught reinforcement strategies, tangible rewards, and cognitive techniques to challenge unhelpful thoughts, and communication and problem-solving skills. This involves a collaborative team approach between the therapist, parents, and child.

A controlled study of the FRIENDS program is underway, but positive outcomes for other models that the FRIENDS program is based on have been found in several studies. One found 88 percent of children were drug free in this family model compared to 61 percent in the CBT only and 30 percent of the waitlist. Twelve-month follow-up results were maintained.

The program is a ten-to-twelve-week resilience intervention that can be delivered to whole classes, or as a targeted intervention for children with anxiety disorders or those identified as at risk. After running the intervention, expected outcomes include:

- significant reductions in symptoms of anxiety and depression for up to 80 percent of participants.
- developing coping and resilience strategies to help deal with stress and worries.
- developing emotional and social skills.
- supporting positive engagement with learning.

CONCLUDING THOUGHTS

Just as was seen with ADHD and conduct disorders, students with anxiety and/or depression are in a lot of pain. Yet they don't often reach out and share their pain. Schools can, and must, put more emphasis on student mental health. It only makes sense that when they get help for psychological distress, students will do better in other areas of their lives, including academics.

The welcome and rather new emphasis in schools on incorporating student social and emotional development provides a way to connect on this level. Teacher guides to the coping and emotional regulation skills and strategies in many of these evidenced based programs provide direction to educators in these areas that they may not be as familiar with.

Addressing student psychological well-being by systematically incorporating these skills and strategies into everyday schooling can result in a reduction of many of the risky behaviors described here: substance use, risky sex, dangerous driving, suicide.

Students need to be able to talk to caring adults about what is going on in their lives. Doing everything possible to make every single child feel welcome and protected is essential. Preventing bullying and harassment is part of that. And part of these efforts means addressing the stigma of having issues with mental health. Many students won't get help, or even admit they have a problem, due to this stigma. Protecting their confidentiality is important too.

Relationships are what it's all about. The only way to know what is going on with students is if they tell a trusted adult. The only way they will confide is if they trust—trust that adults care as much about what's going on with them as they do about their homework. Then, and only then, will they reach out. Then, at least armed with greater knowledge of the effects of student psychological distress, that caring adult can begin to help them.

REFERENCES

Anthenelli, R. M., & Schuckit, M. A. (1993). Affective and Anxiety Disorders and Alcohol and Drug Dependence: Diagnosis and Treatment. *Journal of Addictive Diseases*, 12, 73–87.

Babajide, A., Ortin, A., Wei, C., Mufson, L., & Duarte, C. S. (2020). Transition Cliffs for Young Adults with Anxiety and Depression: Is Integrated Mental Health Care a Solution? *Journal of Behavioral Health Services & Research*, 47(2), 275–292. https://doi.org/10.1007/s11414-019-09670-8

Carballo, J. J., Llorente, C., Kehrmann, L., Flamarique, I., Zuddas, A., Purper-Ouakil, D., Hoekstra, P. J., Coghill, D., Schulze, U. M. E., Dittmann, R. W., Buitelaar, J. K., Castro-Fornieles, J., Lievesley, K., Santosh, P., Arango, C., the STOP Consortium, Sutcliffe, A., Curran, S., Selema, L., & Flanagan, R. (2020). Psychosocial Risk Factors for Suicidality in Children and Adolescents. *European Child & Adolescent Psychiatry*, 29(6), 759–776. https://doi.org/10.1007/s00787-018-01270-9

Cerdá, M., Prins, S. J., Galea, S., Howe, C. J., & Pardini, D. (2016). When Psychopathology Matters Most: Identifying Sensitive Periods When Within-person Changes in Conduct, Affective and Anxiety Problems are Associated with Male Adolescent Substance Use. *Addiction*, 111(5), 924–935. https://doi.org/10.1111/add.13304

CDC Data and Statistics on Children's Mental Health. Retrieved from: Data and Statistics on Children's Mental Health | CDC.

Chan, Y. F., Dennis, M. L., & Funk, R. R. (2008). Prevalence and Comorbidity of Major Internalizing and Externalizing Problems among Adolescents and Adults Presenting to Substance Abuse Treatment. *Journal of Substance Abuse Treatment*, 34(1), 14–24. https://doi.org/10.1016/j.jsat.2006.12.031

Copeland, W. E., Adair, C. E., Smetanin, P., Stiff, D., Briante, C., Colman, I., Fergusson, D., Horwood, J., Poulton, R., Costello, E. J., & Angold, A. (2013). Diagnostic Transitions from Childhood to Adolescence to Early Adulthood. *Journal of Child Psychology and Psychiatry*, 54(7), 791–799.

Costello, E. J., Copeland, W., & Angold, A. (2011). Trends in Psychopathology across the Adolescent Years: What Changes When Children become Adolescents, and When Adolescents become Adults? *Journal of Child Psychology and Psychiatry*, 52(10), 1015–1025.

Couwenbergh, C., van den Brink, W., Zwart, K., et al. (2006). Comorbid Psychopathology in Adolescents and Young Adults Treated for Substance Use Disorders: A Review. *European Child & Adolescent Psychiatry*, 15, 319–328.

Crouch, L., Reardon, T., Farrington, A., Glover, F., & Creswell, C. (2019). "Just Keep Pushing": Parents' Experiences of Accessing Child and Adolescent Mental Health Services for Child Anxiety Problems. *Child: Care, Health & Development*, 45(4), 491–499. https://doi.org/10.1111/cch.12672

Dilworth-Bart, J. E., Khurshid, A., & Vandell, D. L. (2007). Do Maternal Stress and Home Environment Mediate the Relation between Early Income-to-need and 54-months Attentional Abilities? *Infant and Child Development: An International Journal of Research and Practice*, 16(5), 525–552. https://doi.org/10.1002/(ISSN)1522-7219

Essau, C. A., Torre, L. A., Lewinsohn, P. M., Rohde, P., & de la Torre-Luque, A. (2020). Patterns, Predictors, and Outcome of the Trajectories of Depressive Symptoms from Adolescence to Adulthood. *Depression & Anxiety* (1091-4269), 37(6), 565–575. https://doi.org/10.1002/da.23034

FRIENDS: The Psychology Tree, http://thepsychologytree.com/friends.

Finch, J., Farrell, L. J., & Waters, A. M. (2020). Searching for the HERO in Youth: Does Psychological Capital (PsyCap) Predict Mental Health Symptoms and Subjective Wellbeing in Australian School-Aged Children and Adolescents? *Child Psychiatry & Human Development*, 51(6), 1025–1036. https://doi.org/10.1007/s10578-020-01023-3

Fosco, G. M., Mak, H. W., Ramos, A., LoBraico, E., & Lippold, M. (2019). Exploring the Promise of Assessing Dynamic Characteristics of the Family for Predicting

Adolescent Risk Outcomes. *Journal of Child Psychology & Psychiatry*, 60(8), 848–856. https://doi.org/10.1111/jcpp.13052

Gallerani, C. M., Garber, J., & Martin, N. C. (2010). The Temporal Relation between Depression and Comorbid Psychopathology in Adolescents at Varied Risk for Depression. *Journal of Child Psychology and Psychiatry*, 51(3), 242–249.

Goldstick, J. E., Bohnert, K. M., Davis, A. K., Bonar, E. E., Carter, P. M., Walton, M. A., & Cunningham, R. M. (2018). Dual Trajectories of Depression/Anxiety Symptoms and Alcohol Use, and their Implications for Violence Outcomes Among Drug-Using Urban Youth. *Alcohol & Alcoholism*, 53(6), 659–666. https://doi.org /10.1093/alcalc/agy036

Guerreiro, D. F., Sampaio, D., Figueira, M. L., & Madge, N. (2017). Self-Harm in Adolescents: A Self-Report Survey in Schools from Lisbon, Portugal. *Archives of Suicide Research*, 21(1), 83–99. https://doi.org/10.1080/13811118.2015.1004480

Harrison, P. A., Fulkerson, J. A., & Beebe, T. J. (1997). Multiple Substance Use Among Adolescent Physical and Sexual Abuse Victims. *Child Abuse & Neglect*, 21(6), 529–539.

Horigian, V. E., Weems, C. F., Robbins, M. S., Feaster, D. J., Ucha, J., Miller, M., & Werstlein, R. (2013). Reductions in Anxiety and Depression Symptoms in Youth Receiving Substance Use Treatment. *American Journal on Addictions*, 22(4), 329–337. https://doi.org/10.1111/j.1521- 0391.2013.12031.x

Hussong, A. M., Ennet, S. T., Cox, M. J., & Haroon, M. (2017). A Systematic Review of the Unique Prospective Association of Negative Affect Symptoms and Adolescent Substance Use Controlling for Externalizing Symptoms. *Psychology of Addictive Behaviors*, 31(2), 137–147.

Knopf, A. (2019). Teen Marijuana Use Increases Risk of Suicidality and Depression during Young Adulthood. *Brown University Child & Adolescent Behavior Letter*, 35(5), 3–4. https://doi.org/10.1002/cbl.30378

Marmorstein, N. R., White, H., Chung, T., Hipwell, A., Stouthamer-Loeber, M., & Loeber, R. (2010). Associations between First Use of Substances and Change in Internalizing Symptoms among Girls: Differences by Symptom Trajectory and Substance Use Type. *Journal of Clinical Child and Adolescent Psychology*, 39(4), 545–558.

Mars, B., Heron, J., Klonsky, E. D., Moran, P., O'Connor, R. C., Tilling, K., Wilkinson, P., & Gunnell, D. (2019). What Distinguishes Adolescents with Suicidal thoughts from Those Who Have Attempted Suicide? A Population-based Birth Cohort Study. *Journal of Child Psychology & Psychiatry*, 60(1), 91–99. https://doi .org/10.1111/jcpp.12878

McKenzie, M., Olsson, C. A., Jorm, A. F., Romaniuk, H., & Patton, G. C. (2010). Association of Adolescent Symptoms of Depression and Anxiety with Daily

Smoking and Nicotine Dependence in Young Adulthood: Findings from a 10-year Longitudinal Study. *Addiction*, 105(9), 1652–1659. https://doi.org/10.1111/j.1360 -0443.2010.03002.x

Moon, S. S., Kim, Y. J., & Parrish, D. (2020). Understanding the Linkages between Parental Monitoring, School Academic Engagement, Substance Use, and Suicide among Adolescents in U.S. *Child & Youth Care Forum*, 49(6), 953–968.

Richert, T., Anderberg, M., & Dahlberg, M. (2020). Mental Health Problems among Young People in Substance Abuse Treatment in Sweden. *Substance Abuse Treatment, Prevention & Policy*, 15(1), 1–10. https://doi.org/10.1186/s13011-020 -00282-6

Russell, M. A., & Odgers, C. L. (2020). Adolescents' Subjective Social Status Predicts Day-to-Day Mental Health and Future Substance Use. *Journal of Adolescent Resilience*, 232–254.

SAMSHA. (2012). Depression Triples between the Ages of 12 and 15 among Adolescent Girls. Retrieved from: CBHSQ Data Spotlight: Depression Triples between the Ages of 12 and 15 among Adolescent Girls Natioanl Survey on Drug Use and Health (samhsa.gov).

Shope, J. T., Raghunathan, T. E., & Patil, S. M. (2003). Examining Trajectories of Adolescent Risk Factors as Predictors of Subsequent High-risk Driving Behavior. *Journal of Adolescent Health*, 32(3), 214– 24. https://doi.org/10.1016/S1054-139X (02)00424-X

Smyth, B. P., Ducray, K., & Cullen, W. (2018). Changes in Psychological Well-being among Heroin- dependent Adolescents during Psychologically Supported Opiate Substitution Treatment. *Early Intervention in Psychiatry*, 12(3), 417–425. https:// doi.org/10.1111/eip.12318

Wu, A. M. S., Lau, J. T. F., Mo, P. K. H., & Lau, M. M. C. (2018). Psychological Distress and Resilience as Risk and Protective Factors of Psychoactive Substance Use among Chinese Nonengaged Youth. *Journal of Community & Applied Social Psychology*, 28(2), 49–64. https://doi.org/10.1002/casp.2340

Yau, J.-T. J., & Nager, A. L. (2021). Adolescent and Young Adult Stress and Coping During COVID-19: The Utility of a Pediatric Emergency Department Screener. *International Journal of Emergency Medicine*, 14(1), 1–6. https://doi.org/10.1186 /s12245-021-00359-4

Chapter 6

Understanding the Role of the Family and Adolescent Substance Use

THE ADOLESCENT AND THE FAMILY

Role of the Family

Even though parents often feel that they are losing their influence over their adolescent children, in reality, these childeren still need their parents a lot. Due to their developmental levels, they want independence and freedom, but they also need structure and support, though they don't always show this. Parents are tempted to let go of the reins, letting go too much, too soon, can have negative consequences. Schools can help families navigate these challenging waters.

Relationships change as peers and friends do hold more and more sway over adolescents. The Cordova et al. (2014) research review found that from early to late adolescence, one's orientation toward family lessens relative to peer groups and other influences outside the family system. These changes can transform how family members interact and their roles consequently affecting family functioning. McLaughlin et al. (2016) found that, although peers are a central influence on young people's attitudes and behaviors, they do not negate the influence of parents, particularly where the parent–child relationship is a positive one.

Strong family cohesion is defined by Lac et al. (2009) as strong emotional bonds or closeness between family members. Members of cohesive families, they say, have similar goals, enjoy spending time together, and value interdependence and the exchange of emotional and instrumental support; therefore, they may be less likely to seek support from people outside the family, including peers who engage in risky and dangerous behaviors.

And Piehler and Winters (2017) advise that, despite the potential for the development of psychological adjustment problems, adolescence is also a window of opportunity for prevention of such problems and promotion of well-being. They say that families continue to serve as important developmental contexts during adolescence, and positive family relationships can help foster healthy psychological adjustment. The challenge, say Tur et al. (2019), is for parents to adapt to their adolescents' new independence needs while continuing to play a fundamental role as a source of support and care in their lives.

Parenting Styles

There has been much research done on parenting styles and their impact on adolescent behavior, with different styles having drastically different behavior outcomes. This work developed from Baumrind who proposed two distinct dimensions of parenting: warmth/ responsiveness and control/demandingness. Mac (2019) notes that Baumrind's original schema defined three parenting styles: authoritative (high in both warmth and control); authoritarian (high in control but low in warmth); and permissive (low in control).

Tur-Pocar et al. (2019) identify the ability to provide a warm, supportive response to meet the needs of the child lies at one end of the first dimension, and control with demandingness, or rigidity at the other end. They note that research has widely shown the positive influence of affect- and communication-based parenting, which fosters trust and two-way communication, on children's development.

Piehler and Winter found that parenting style is related to the extent of peer influence in adolescent decision-making, noting that adolescents with parents characterized by an authoritative parenting style (as opposed to permissive and authoritarian styles) tend to reference their parents, as opposed to their peers, in their decision-making more than adolescents with parents characterized by other parenting styles. And that is a very good thing when it comes to making decisions about using substances.

Parental Knowledge

Rothenberg et al. (2020) studied the concept of parental knowledge, which, they say, is one of the specific parenting practices that has been studied extensively and strongly linked to adolescent adjustment. This is more than actual monitoring of the adolescent's behavior. It means the level of knowledge that parents have about their child's behavior. They found that it was parental knowledge, and not parental monitoring, that was significantly related to problematic behavior in adolescence.

Parental involvement/monitoring was strongly inversely linked to adolescents' relationships with deviant peers (Su and Supple, 2018). Higher levels of parental involvement/monitoring are associated with a lower level of association with peers who get into trouble. Su and Supple say that while previous studies have found that positive parental practices can serve as buffers to adverse adolescent outcomes, their findings indicated that even the child's *perception* of the parents' involvement and knowledge of activities can mitigate the influence of peers who engage in deviant behaviors.

Conversely, the lack of involvement by parents may be associated with feelings of alienation, which facilitates their desire to find support and acceptance elsewhere.

THE FAMILY AND SUBSTANCE USE

The Critical Developmental Period of Adolescence

When an adolescent does turn to outside influences (e.g., peers, internet) and decides to try a substance, it can change everything in a family. Mak (2019) notes that substance use exacts very heavy personal costs on both the adolescents involved and their families. Referencing the "critical period" hypothesis, Mak suggests that there is a developmental period in the early teens during which individuals are particularly sensitive to the effects of substance use. Those using substances at this age may be at substantially elevated risk of substance use disorder, or substance-related harm, in later life.

Cordova et al., for example, point to research indicating that the transition from eighth grade to tenth grade is a particularly vulnerable period for increased risk of adolescent substance use and misuse. Educators and parents both need this kind critical information to really help kids struggling with the potentially life-altering decisions they face.

Genetics, Environment, and Family History Influences

According to the National Institute on Drug Abuse (NIDA), genes account for between 40 and 60 percent of the cause of addiction. Researchers believe that genes may be responsible for a predisposition to addiction. Then, due to interaction with stress, abuse, trauma, or other life events, genes and environment interact, increasing the risk of addiction. This report also notes that adolescents and people with mental health disorders are at greater risk of drug use and addiction than others. Figure 6.1 illustrates the possible influences and interactions believed to contribute to addiction.

Brown et al. (2020) studied young college students and looked at their scores on something called the Transmissible Liability Index (TLI), an instrument measuring the generational transmission of addiction. They found TLI scores were associated with increased family history of substance use, alcohol use, and internalizing problems, as well as earlier age of onset of drinking.

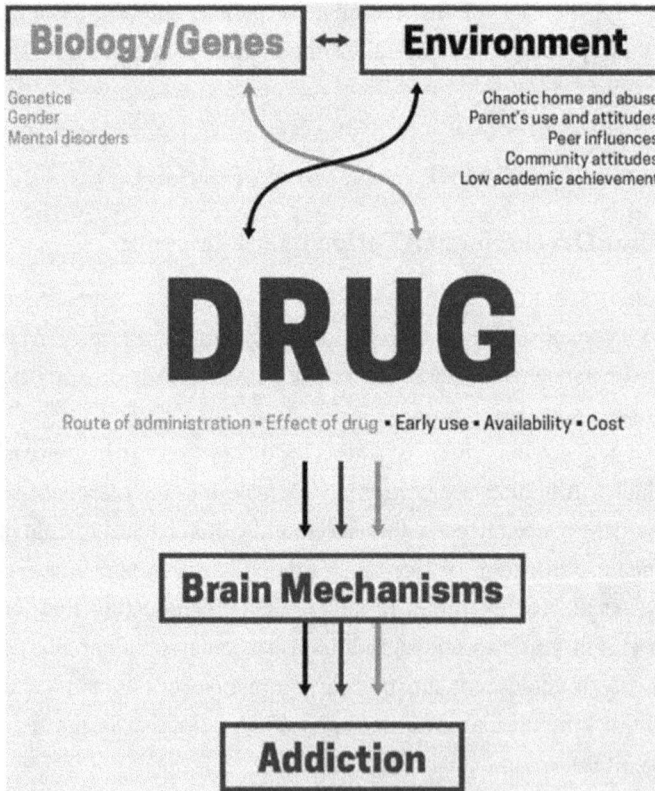

Figure 6.1   Drug Misuse and Addiction. *"Drugs, Brains, and Behavior: The Science of Addiction." National Institute on Drug Abuse; National Institutes of Health; U.S. Department of Health and Human Services. (July 2020).* https://nida.nih.gov/publications /drugs-brains-behavior-science-addiction/drug-misuse-addiction.

A family history of internalizing behavior, drinking, and illicit substance use reflects generalized risk for a broad set of behaviors associated with risk for alcohol initiation and use during the transition from high school to college.

The Brown et al. literature review found studies showing that

> students with a family history (FH) of alcohol and substance problems have previously been shown to exhibit higher levels of impulsivity, as well as (1) an increased risk for initiating alcohol use during college, (2) higher levels of alcohol consumption, and (3) a greater number of endorsed alcohol use disorder (AUD) criteria.[7] Likewise, a family history of internalizing problems (FH-IP) has also been shown to be a transmissible component of liability to substance use disorders (SUDs). Several cross-sectional and longitudinal studies have reported associations between FH of depression, [8] anxiety, [9] and AUDs [10] with the presence of the same pathological outcome in the offspring. Furthermore, FH of AUDs and anxiety disorders have been shown to influence the risk of developing either condition. (p. 2)

They found factors, including childhood and adolescent behavioral and developmental problems, known to have strong genetic influences, and suggested that there is a shared genetic liability between internalizing problems and alcohol use.

Maternal depression is also a known factor correlated to adolescent substance use (Sang et al., 2019). Sang et al. evaluated the relationship between childhood exposure to maternal depression and adolescent engagement in health risk behaviors, and found that adolescents exposed to maternal depressive symptoms during middle childhood were more likely to use substances at an earlier age. They concluded that maternal depression, potentially a genetic and/or environmental influence, increases the risk of substance use for adolescents.

Parenting and Substance Use

The family system is critical to the development of substance use and misuse in adolescents (Cordova et al., 2014). Poorly functioning family systems could result in adolescents feeling unsupported by family, as well as feeling disengaged or even alienated from family members, leading them to turn outward.

Mak says that the evidence is unequivocal: that parental warmth, as opposed to control, protects against substance use problems in adulthood. He found that it is the authoritarian and neglectful styles which are associated with elevated risks of later substance use. Mak also suggests that while it is reasonable to believe that parenting style affects substance use, it is also likely that parenting style is itself influenced by adolescents' prior substance use.

Plummer Lee et al. (2019) say negative parenting behaviors often associate with negative child outcomes such as higher anxiety, somatic symptoms, and increased substance use. Tur-Porcar et al. found evidence that substance use and parents' neglect are greater in middle adolescence than in early adolescence; that support and family communication and perceived academic self-efficacy are lower; and that substance use is positively related to parents' neglect, psychological control, and rejection.

Parental knowledge plays a key role as well as parental monitoring. Rothenberg et al. (2020) say that the degree to which parents know about their children's activities and friendships is one of the major risk or protective factors for substance use in adolescence. Interestingly, they found significant differences in the level of parental knowledge perceived by parents and adolescents: parents perceive higher levels of knowledge regarding their child's whereabouts, activities, and friendships than their children.

Race and Culture

Cordova et al. (2014) have reported on racial and ethnic disparities in adolescent substance use and misuse, which result in a myriad of health and social consequences that disproportionally affect racial/ethnic minority urban populations. This includes the risk of sexually transmitted infections, intentional and unintentional injury, physical and social development, and incarceration. The following section summarizes studies on families and substance use, in racial or ethnic minority groups.

Asians

Su et al. (2018) explored higher intergenerational cultural dissonance (ICD), the difference in the acculturation experience between youth from immigrant families and their parents or caregivers. They found ICD levels significantly predicted increased family conflict, which in turn was associated with reduced parental involvement/monitoring, increased association with deviant peers, and a subsequently higher risk of alcohol use. Differences in cultural identity can cause increased miscommunication, they say, and family conflict can impact parental involvement and monitoring.

Hispanics

For Hispanic youth, Su et al. found that ICD was associated with increased family tension and decreased parental involvement among Latino youth, which led to an increased risk for substance use. This finding is also consistent with previous ICD studies, say Su et al., that analyzed parenting domains, in which ICD led to unsupportive parenting practices, reduced parent–child bonding, and limited monitoring from parents during a critical time for initiation of risk behaviors.

The Lac et al. (2011) research review confirms that Latino adolescents face numerous challenges that increase their risk of drug use, including acculturative stress, ethnic discrimination, socioeconomic stress, and lack of educational and vocational opportunities. They found that parental monitoring, but not parent–child communication, predicted fewer deviant behaviors. Other studies find that both parental monitoring and close family relationships concurrently predicted decreased consumption of marijuana.

African Americans

Cordova et al. note that the patterns of substance use and misuse are known to be different among African American adolescents, who historically report less alcohol use, but greater marijuana use, than non-Hispanic Whites and Hispanics. They say that due to the historical legacy of racism and discrimination, family structures and resources of African American families can be quite different than for non-Hispanic Whites, and are often characterized by lower access to financial, educational, and other social material resources.

Despite this, they found that most of their research sample of urban youth, identified as at increased risk of high school dropout, reported experiencing high levels of family functioning (67.1 percent) and parent support (59.3 percent). Thus, they say, despite the potential additional community-level risk factors that may negatively affect urban youth substance use and misuse, their participants benefited from the promotive effects of a positive family environment.

Taylor et al. (2012) found that there were no differences between African Americans and Whites regarding reported levels of family communication around the harms of substance use. The adolescents in their study reported similarities in the receipt of harm communication messages. African Americans in their study reported more peer substance involvement than Whites, however, which, they said, suggests that despite meaningful harm communication and family sanctions, they still had associations with substance-involved peers.

Sang et al. (2019) reviewed research on African American family styles and substance abuse and found that, relative to White parents, African American parents have more proactive parenting styles and antidrug use attitudes and that African American adolescents, whose parents communicate with them about substance use, are less susceptible to using them.

Gender Considerations

Sang et al. also examined research on gender and substance use. Their review found that female adolescents may be more vulnerable to substance use compared to their male counterparts. Females tend to have a stronger emotional response to stressful events due to increases in cortisol (i.e., stress-related hormone), and they may experience more psychological distress than males. Adolescent girls' risks for substance use are also heightened for low-income minorities, who are exposed to other environmental stressors, such as neighborhood risk factors, financial challenges, and racism, they concluded.

Lac et al. studied family factors and marijuana use among 1,369 Latino adolescents. They found that girls reported higher levels of parental monitoring, parental communication than boys, but no gender differences in family cohesiveness. Parent–child communication and family cohesion in ninth grade were each predictive of lower levels of marijuana consumption in eleventh grade. Higher levels of parent–child communication predicted lower marijuana use among boys, whereas girls' use was always low regardless of parent–child communication levels.

These authors speculate that Latino adolescent boys may be given more autonomy by their parents and may have more opportunities to experiment with risky behaviors without adult supervision. Adolescent girls, they suggest, may be socialized to spend more time at home and may be strongly discouraged from participating in rebellious behaviors such as drug use.

Lac and Crano (2009) conducted a meta-analysis involving over 35,000 participants across 17 studies. They confirmed the link between parental monitoring and lower rates of marijuana use. They also observed that, while girls' marijuana use was low regardless of their levels of parent–child communication, boys showed significantly higher levels of marijuana use only when parent–child communication was poor.

Piehler and Winter et al. (2017) looked at parent–youth connectedness, depression, and adjustment problems. They found that, for depressive symptoms, there were no differences in the protective effects of parent–youth intimacy between girls and boys. There also were no gender differences in the link between father–youth intimacy and self-esteem across age. These findings, they say, suggest that parent–youth intimacy is protective for both girls and boys. The lack of it is a risk factor.

RISK FACTORS

Family Dysfunction

Family dysfunction can include everything from chronic conflict and disorganization to parental substance use. Things like a lack of rules around substance use, permissiveness toward substance use, and acceptance of alcoholic drink consumption in a family setting (at meals and with friends) increases use in late adolescence and young adulthood (Tur-Porcar et al., 2019). Conflict also plays a role. Sang et al. point out association between high levels of family conflict and high levels of adolescent substance use. More frequent, intense, and prolonged exposure to interparental conflict negatively relates to children's well-being.

One measure of family dysfunction is parental incarceration. Roettger et al. say that paternal incarceration is significantly associated with drug use among U.S. males and females, even after controlling for family background, parental, and individual characteristics. They report that 13 percent of young adults in the United States report a biological father having been incarcerated:

[T]he number of children with an incarcerated father has increased dramatically. In 2006, nearly 7.5 million children were estimated to have a parent either incarcerated or on probation/parole [3]. Wildeman [4] estimates that by age 14, 4 percent of white children and 25 percent of African American children will have had a parent in prison; moreover, 13 percent of young adults in the United States report that their father had spent time in jail or prison. [5], [6] (p. 122)

In their research review, Roettger et al. (2011) found associations between parental incarceration and increased levels of delinquency, mental health problems, homelessness, decreased civic participation, and internalizing and externalizing symptoms. Parental imprisonment increases the odds of drug use by a factor of 3.7 in adulthood, suggesting that parental incarceration is associated with use of drugs across the life-course.

They conclude that "in a society where drug users make up one-fourth of incarcerated prisoners [52] and 60% of inmates report regular drug use prior to incarceration [53], the early onset and heightened risk of drug use also increases the likelihood of an intergenerational transmission of incarceration between fathers and their children" (p. 130).

Parental Substance Use

Bandura's social learning model applies when it comes to this risk factor: the role that social learning processes play in parental modeling of behaviors and attitudes regarding substance use with their adolescents. As parents are their child's first teachers, so their behaviors have a tremendous influence on them, influence as seen with the incarceration example, that can last a lifetime. The child wants to grow up and be just like mom and dad. Figure 6.2 illustrates the number of children affected by parental substance use by age.

Rothenberg et al. (2020) reviewed research on parental marijuana use. They found that a history of parent marijuana or substance use is associated with less effective parenting practices. Rothenberg et al. say that children from families with a parental substance use disorder have greater stress, and that unmanaged stress can make it more likely that these adolescents engage in marijuana use. They also found that adolescents from substance-using families are at greater risk for the development of impulsive, sensation-seeking behaviors that lead to their own substance use.

Becker and Curry (2014) cite research findings that indicate that adolescents who reside with a parent or guardian who engages in heavy or problematic drinking are at increased risk for heavy alcohol consumption. The link between parent and adolescent drinking may be partially explained by

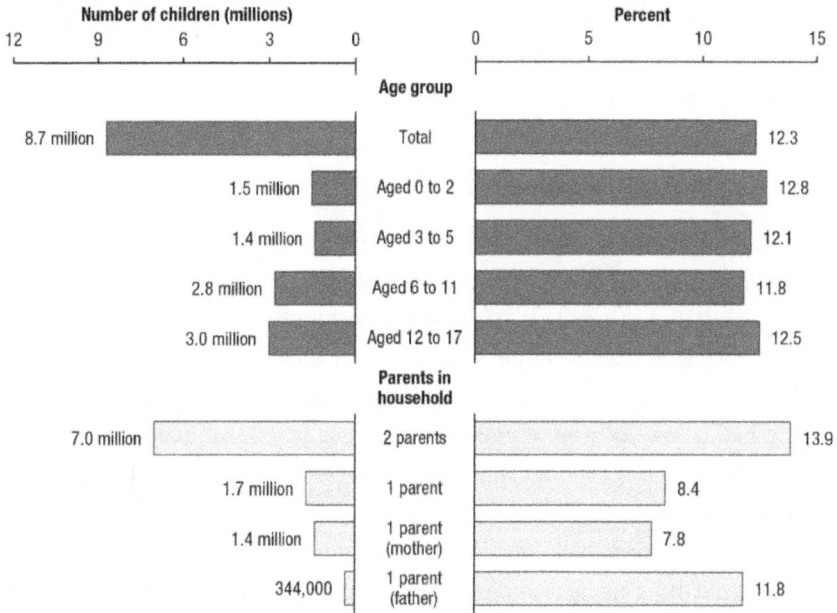

Figure 6.2 Number and Percentage of Children Aged Seventeen or Younger Living with at least One Parent with a Past Year Illicit Drug Use Disorder, by Age Group and Household Composition: Annual Average, 2009 to 2014. *Lipari, R.N. and Van Horn, S.L.* Children living with parents who have a substance use disorder. *The CBHSQ Report: August 24, 2017. Center for Behavioral Health Statistics and Quality, Substance Abuse and Mental Health Services Administration, Rockville, MD.* https://www.samhsa.gov/data /sites/default/files/report_3223/ShortReport-3223.html.

familial risk, they found, with findings indicating children of parents who abuse alcohol are at increased risk to also experience alcohol misuse in the future.

Becker and Curry suggest that a more indirect association may occur through negative parenting behaviors, such as low parental monitoring, authoritarian parenting style, lack of positive parent–child relationship, low warmth, low positive involvement, negative or ineffective discipline, and lack of parental monitoring, all of which are conducive to adolescent alcohol consumption.

Social learning applies to substance use and driving as well. Dora Laskey et al. (2020) researched adolescent driving after drinking. They found that negative parental influences—including exposure to parental substance use and/or drug-related illegal activity—were associated with increased the risk of youth driving after drinking. They found that parents' alcohol intoxication and history of alcohol use disorder treatment increase the risk of youth driving after drinking, a potentially disastrous combination.

Lack of Communication and Connection

A dysfunctional family situation, possibly rife with conflict, is not conducive to good parent–child communication or feelings of connection, warmth, and bonding—all the things that can protect children from adverse situations. Parenting style relates to communication and connectedness. In their work on the culture gap, Su et al. found that adolescents who perceived that their fathers had a low level of acculturation (i.e., a low identification with U.S. cultural norms) also reported that their fathers were more likely to have an authoritarian parenting style.

In their literature review, they found that *authoritarian* parenting styles are characterized by placing a high value on obedience to parenting authority, punitive punishments in cases of disobedience, and emphasis on hard work and tradition, compared to *authoritative* parenting, which includes greater emphasis on communication and child independence. Then, *authoritarian* parenting was also associated with an increased risk for adolescent depressive symptomatology and low self-esteem compared to adolescents who reported their fathers had a more *authoritative* parenting style.

Su et al. concluded that higher levels of ICD result in less openness and communication between adolescents and their families. The adolescents lose a key source of support that would otherwise be able to help them navigate difficult circumstances, leading to depression symptoms of hopelessness and helplessness. Alcohol use may then follow depression as a means for coping or regulating negative moods, they found.

Family Socioeconomic Status and Substance Use

Buu et al. (2009) also indicated that low socioeconomic status (SES) during childhood was linked to an increased risk of nicotine and marijuana use during emerging adulthood. Experiencing family economic constraints (or problems) in youth may put these young people at greater risk of experiencing poorer well-being and increased substance use in emerging adulthood (Plummer Lee, 2000).

For example, Plummer Lee et al. conducted a study of well-being and smoking among emerging adults and found that economic problems (or distress) experienced during childhood were linked with poor emotional and social well-being and a greater likelihood of cigarette smoking. These individuals experienced behavioral problems early on, experienced more family economic problems in their youth, and had parents inclined to exhibit more psychological control.

This group was also more likely to come from families with more financial stress and more parent–child conflict, which related to the child's behavioral problems. They concluded that it is likely that such individuals attempt to cope with their cumulative family stress and current poorer well-being with substance use behaviors.

PROTECTIVE FACTORS

Positive Parenting and Family Relations

This research on parenting and family factors that correlate with low, or no, substance use covers a variety of variables and terms from cohesion to warmth to bonding to acceptance and monitoring and communication, and more. Many of the protective factors are the opposites of the risk factors. The family may prevent, intervene with, and interrupt substance use through either promoting risk and/or promoting protection and resilience. And schools can help families help their distressed children.

Table 6.1 presents a summary of some of major findings around positive parenting practices as protective factors known to prevent substance use.

Communication and Connectedness

Positive parent–adolescent communication has been found to predict engagement in health-promoting behaviors and resistance to peer pressure to engage in negative health-endangering behaviors. Communication between parents and adolescents reduces the risk for substance use. Communication is significantly lower the more adolescents perceive parental sanctions for use (Taylor et al., 2012).

A meta-analysis on communication and substance abuse (Carver et al., 2017) determined that open communication occurs within the context of high connectedness between parents and children. Parent–child connectedness (described as

Table 6.1 Summary of Findings on Parents/Family Influences on Adolescent Substance Use

Source	Findings
Lac et al. (2009)	Found parent–child **attachment** was identified as an important factor in protecting adolescents from substance use in addition to effective parenting particularly an **authoritative style** supplemented with parental monitoring and strong parent-child communication to encourage child disclosure: found parental **monitoring,** parental **communication,** and **family cohesion** each emerged as protective factors, even after controlling for the risk factors of peer marijuana norms, past marijuana use, and demographic covariates. Found that family cohesion yielded the strongest protective effect, suggesting that the feelings of connectedness and enjoyment of spending time with family might represent a greater desire to be around parents and therefore fewer opportunities to affiliate with delinquent others.
McLaughlin et al. (2016)	Found evidence indicates **authoritative parenting styles** and **parental monitoring** can protect young people from substance use.
Hernandez et al. (2010)	Found **parental monitoring** and **parental warmth and support** are protective factors against adolescent substance use.
Taylor et al. (2012)	Found that the perception of **family caring** (e.g., support, warmth, encouragement) appears to be related to adolescent substance use: adolescents who **feel supported** by caregivers may be more likely to identify with them and thus listen to their communications about appropriate behaviors.
Cordova et al. (2014)	Found family promotive factors protect against urban adolescent substance use and misuse; adolescents experiencing a high level of family support and responsiveness to their emotional and social needs may result in increased **communication** and **clear expectations** about health risk behaviors which, in turn, has been shown to have promotive effects on engagement in substance use and misuse.
Plummer Lee et al. (2018)	Found that **parental acceptance** and **psychological control** in childhood and adolescence predicted all aspects of well-being during the transition to adulthood; that more parental acceptance and less psychological control predicted positive well-being and less likelihood of substance use.
Mak (2019)	Found that **warmth** is associated with reduced risks of problem substance use in adulthood, via reduced risks of early initiation and a lower risk of depression; parental control also has a protective effect via reduced risks of early initiation.

(Continued)

Table 6.1   Summary of Findings on Parents/Family Influences on Adolescent Substance Use *(Continued)*

Source	Findings
Piehler and Winters (2017)	Found that father–youth **intimacy** appeared to be consistently protective against low self-esteem; that the protective effects of parent–youth intimacy are present by early adolescence and vary across age; that parent-youth intimacy (i.e., emotional closeness, warmth, acceptance, and support) is protective against a range of adolescent psychological adjustment problems.

feelings of closeness, warmth, love, and satisfaction) and communication are potential protective factors against substance use in adolescence. They found that communication about health risks is associated with lower levels of substance use, while more frequent conversations, those about parents' own use, and permissive messages are associated with higher levels of use.

Carver et al. found that when conversations are open and involve discussions rather than lectures, adolescents feel more comfortable and report lower rates of substance use. Their review found that high-quality communication is associated with lower rates of smoking, more negative attitudes, about use and higher ability to refuse cigarette use, as well as lower rates of alcohol use and higher self-efficacy to refuse.

They conclude that:

> This review of the literature provides important evidence that parent-child connectedness (PCC), general communication and particular types of substance-use specific communication can be protective against alcohol, tobacco and drug use in adolescence. Parents should be encouraged to have open, credible, high-quality conversations with their adolescents about substance use, which are facilitated by high quality general communication and high levels of PCC. High quality conversations should be "constructive and respectful" (de Leeuw et al., 2010, p. 1003), in which parents and adolescents feel comfortable and understood and that their opinions matter and are being taken seriously. Parents should be encouraged to talk about health risks and potential consequences of use when communicating about substance use. (p. 130)

Parent Education/Prevention and Intervention

When it comes to selecting or designing specific educational, prevention, or intervention programs, there are as many recommendations as there are topics for positive family functioning. Peihler and Winters (2017) recommend targeting parent–youth intimacy for potentially positive results for multiple adjustment problems. In cases in which the target population is predominantly experiencing a specific adjustment problem, they say it may be particularly impactful to boost parent–youth intimacy at the age at which the association between parent–youth intimacy and that adjustment problem is strongest.

Piehler and Winters reference research comparing brief interventions for adolescent substance use, with and without parental involvement. They found that youth with a higher severity of symptoms get more benefit from parental involvement, and that adolescents with more impulsive or careless decision-making styles benefited the most from parental involvement. These adolescents, they say, may require a higher dose or more intensive intervention, with parent involvement, to improve their skills and reduce their alcohol use when compared to youth without such decision-making deficits.

McLaughlin et al. (2016) recommend that parenting programs may benefit families via components on authoritative styles, parental monitoring, communication, nurturing attachments, and parent–child conflict. They suggest effective strategies to implement these in the home (e.g., granting autonomy, setting safe boundaries, discussing outcomes, nurturing confidence) as important. Components on monitoring they note could highlight the importance of identifying changes in child behavior, encouraging child disclosure, and countering the negative influence of the peer group.

Lac and Crano (2009) strongly advocate for culturally relevant programs that teach parenting skills and knowledge that can prevent substance use and high-risk behaviors. Parents and adolescents may need to learn more effective techniques for promoting open communication about controversial topics such as drug use, they found.

Prevention and intervention programs that focus on enhancing adolescents' sense of belonging and increasing parental monitoring and supervision may be beneficial (Hernandez et al., 2010). Tur-Porcar (2019) suggests that education for families can provide tools for active and effective communication that help foster the autonomy of their children and on consistently applied disciplinary standards shown to decrease substance use.

How Schools Can Help Families

School-based initiatives can offer parents relevant experiences, services, and referrals to help them help their children build coping skills and reduce the likelihood of turning to substances. Schools already provide parent and family education on a variety of issues and topics. This research offers a road map for examining current practices and identifying gaps in current parent education, incorporating findings into existing programs, and adding programs, as necessary.

Crouch et al. (2019) discuss the challenges parents face when grappling with the question of student substance use. They found that parents experience challenges identifying their child's mental health difficulties, and that parents often delay seeking help because they were unsure whether their child needed support or not.

They emphasized the extent of parental effort and persistence required throughout the help-seeking process. "It was also clear that uncertainty and concerns surrounding key elements of the help-seeking process, including where and when to seek help, what to expect from services, and possible negative consequences for their child, presented hurdles for families" (p.498). Knowledgeable school personnel can help parents navigate the help-seeking process with support, encouragement, resources, and referrals, as needed.

PROMISING PROGRAM

According to the Washington State Healthcare Authority, Family Effectiveness Training (FET) is a family-based program for Hispanics that targets family factors known to place children at risk. FET helps Hispanic immigrant families with children ages six to twelve, particularly when the child is exhibiting behavior problems, associating with deviant peers, or experiencing parent–child communication problems. The goal of FET is to strengthen families by increasing their ability to adapt to new situations, particularly developmental and cultural challenges the family will face.

The program consists of three components: Family Development, Bicultural Effectiveness Training, and Brief Strategic Family Therapy. FET uses two primary strategies to initiate change: (1) didactic lessons and participatory activities that help parents master effective family management skills and

(2) organized discussions in which the therapist/facilitator intervenes to correct dysfunctional communications between or among family members. The training sessions last for thirteen weeks, are one-and-a-half to two hours long, and are tailored to each individual family's needs.

Program evaluation showed FET helped Hispanic/Latino immigrant families with six- to -twelve-year-old children, particularly in cases where the child is exhibiting behavior problems, associating with deviant peers, or experiencing parent–child communication problems.

Youths who received FET had significantly fewer behavioral, personality, and inadequacy problems and reported greater improvement in their feelings about themselves at the termination of treatment, compared with the control group. FET significantly improved the family structure, functioning, resonance, developmental stage, and conflict resolution.

Findings included: 35 percent reduction in children's disruptive behaviors; 66 percent reduction in children's associations with antisocial peers; 34 percent reduction in children's irresponsible behaviors; 14 percent improvement in children's self-concept; and 75 percent improvement in family functioning.

CONCLUDING THOUGHTS

Today there are many students who show up to school under the influence. Severe behavior problems with students who may or may not have used substances are typically handed off to the dean of discipline. If a student is found with drugs, the school-based police get involved. If not, parents are called, suspensions are doled out, and when they return, nothing changes.

There is usually no counseling for these students. Many of their parents don't know how to access mental health support for them either, because they too, usually do not recognize, or understand, or want to face, what might be going on with their child.

What could help? An early, concerned phone call from a school counselor or teacher, explaining what they were seeing with the student. A caring word that there was help available. A parent workshop on early recognition of adolescent substance use and how to have "that conversation" with their student. A list of resources that details where to go for professional help.

Most schools don't currently offer such things. That needs to change. The research presented in this chapter highlights vitally important information that can help schools help so many their families help their children. One teacher or staff member cannot provide these things alone, but a team within a school can. More on this will be covered in Chapter 8. Taking this issue on, identifying local needs, and starting somewhere is the necessary first step.

REFERENCES

Becker, S. J., & Curry, J. F. (2014). Testing the Effects of Peer Socialization Versus Selection on Alcohol and Marijuana Use Among Treated Adolescents. *Substance Use & Misuse*, 49(3), 234–242. https://doi.org/10.3109/10826084.2013.824479

Brown, A. L., España, R. A., Benca-Bachman, C. E., Welsh, J. W., & Palmer, R. H. (2020). Adolescent Behavioral Characteristics Mediate Familial Effects on Alcohol Use and Problems in College-Bound Students. *Substance Abuse: Research & Treatment*, 1–10. https://doi.org/10.1177/1178221820970925

Buu, A., Dipiazza, C., Wang, J., Puttler, L. I., Fitzgerald, H. E., & Zucker, R. A. (2009). Parent, Family, and Neighborhood Effects on the Development of Child Substance Use and Other Psychopathology from Preschool to the Start of Adulthood. *Journals of Studies on Alcohol and Drugs*, 70, 489, 498. https://doi.org/10.15288/jsad.2009.70.489

Carver, H., Elliott, L., Kennedy, C., & Hanley, J. (2017). Parent-child Connectedness and Communication in Relation to Alcohol, Tobacco, and Drug Use in Adolescence: An Integrative Review of the Literature. *Drugs: Education, Prevention, and Policy* [online], 24(2), 119–133. https://doi.org/10.1080/09687637.2016.1221060

Cordova, D., Heinze, J., Mistry, R., Hsieh, H.-F., Stoddard, S., Salas-Wright, C. P., & Zimmerman, M. A. (2014). Family Functioning and Parent Support Trajectories and Substance Use and Misuse among Minority Urban Adolescents: A Latent Class Growth Analysis. *Substance Use & Misuse*, 49(14), 1908–1919. https://doi.org/10.3109/10826084.2014.935792

Crouch, L., Reardon, T., Farrington, A., Glover, F., & Creswell, C. (2019). "Just Keep Pushing": Parents' Experiences of Accessing Child and Adolescent Mental Health Services for Child Anxiety Problems. *Child: Care, Health & Development*, 45(4), 491–499. https://doi.org/10.1111/cch.12672

Cutrín, O., Kulis, S. S., Ayers, S. L., Jager, J., & Marsiglia, F. F. (2021). Perception of Parental Knowledge by Parents and Adolescents: Unique Effects on Recent Substance Use in a Latinx Sample. *Journal of Latinx Psychology*, 9(3), 189–203. https://doi.org/10.1037/lat0000155

Dora-Laskey, A. D., Goldstick, J. E., Buckley, L., Bonar, E. E., Zimmerman, M. A., Walton, M. A., Cunningham, R. M., & Carter, P. M. (2020). Trajectories of

Driving after Drinking among Marijuana Using Youth in the Emergency Department: Substance Use, Mental Health, and Peer and Parental Influences. *Substance Use & Misuse*, 55(2), 175–187. https://doi.org/10.1080/10826084.2019.1660675

DrugAbuse.gov. National Institute on Drig Abuse, Washington D.C. Retrieved from: Drug Misuse and Addiction | National Institute on Drug Abuse (NIDA).

Family Effectiveness Training, theathenaforum.org/family_effectiveness_training, Washington State Healthcare Authority, Olympia WA.

Hernandez, L., Eaton, C., Fairlie, A., Chun, T., & Spirito, A. (2010). Ethnic Group Differences in Substance Use, Depression, Peer Relationships, and Parenting Among Adolescents Receiving Brief Alcohol Counseling. *Journal of Ethnicity in Substance Abuse*, 9(1), 14–27. https://doi.org/10.1080/15332640903538874

Hochgraf, A. K., Fosco, G. M., Lanza, S. T., & McHale, S. M. (2021). Developmental Timing of Parent–youth Intimacy as a Protective Factor for Adolescent Adjustment Problems. *Journal of Family Psychology*, 35(7), 916–926. https://doi.org/10.1037/fam0000864

Lac, A., & Crano, W. D. (2009). Monitoring Matters: Meta-analytic Review Reveals the Reliable Linkage of Parental Monitoring with Adolescent Marijuana Use. *Perspectives on Psychological Science*, 4, 578–586.

Lac, A., Unger, J. B., Basáñez, T., Ritt-Olson, A., Soto, D. W., & Baezconde-Garbanati, L. (2011). Marijuana Use Among Latino Adolescents: Gender Differences in Protective Familial Factors. *Substance Use & Misuse*, 46(5), 644–655. https://doi.org/10.3109/10826084.2010.528121

Lipari, R. N., & Van Horn, S. L. (2017). *Children Living with Parents Who Have a Substance Use Disorder*. The CBHSQ Report: August 24, 2017. Center for Behavioral Health Statistics and Quality, Substance Abuse and Mental Health Services Administration, Rockville, MD.

Mak, H. W., & Iacovou, M. (2019). Dimensions of the Parent-Child Relationship: Effects on Substance Use in Adolescence and Adulthood. *Substance Use & Misuse*, 54(5), 724–736. https://doi.org/10.1080/10826084.2018.1536718. Epub 2018 Nov 20. PMID: 30457893.

McLaughlin, A., Campbell, A., & McColgan, M. (2016). Adolescent Substance Use in the Context of the Family: A Qualitative Study of Young People's Views on Parent-Child Attachments, Parenting Style, and Parental Substance Use. *Substance Use & Misuse*, 51(14), 1846–1855. https://doi.org/10.1080/10826084.2016.1197941

NIDA (National Institute on Drug Abuse). Drugs, Brains and Behavior: The Science of Addiction. Retrieved from: Drug Misuse and Addiction | National Institute on Drug Abuse (NIDA).

Piehler, T. F., & Winters, K. C. (2017). Decision-making Style and Response to Parental Involvement in Brief Interventions for Adolescent Substance Use. *Journal of Family Psychology*, 31(3), 336–346. https://doi.org/10.1037/fam0000266

Plummer Lee, C., Beckert, T., & Marsee, I. (2018). Well-being and Substance Use in Emerging Adulthood: The Role of Individual and Family Factors in Childhood and Adolescence. *Journal of Child & Family Studies*, 27(12), 3853–3865. https://doi.org/10.1007/s10826-018-1227-9

Roettger, M. E., Swisher, R. R., Kuhl, D. C., & Chavez, J. (2011). Paternal Incarceration and Trajectories of Marijuana and Other Illegal Drug Use from Adolescence into Young Adulthood: Evidence from Longitudinal Panels of Males and Females in the United States. *Addiction*, 106(1), 121–132. https://doi.org/10.1111/j.1360 -0443.2010.03110.x

Rothenberg, W. A., Sternberg, A., Blake, A., Waddell, J., Chassin, L., & Hussong, A. (2020). Identifying Adolescent Protective Factors that Disrupt the Intergenerational Transmission of Marijuana Use and Disorder. *Psychology of Addictive Behaviors*, 34(8), 864–876. https://doi.org/10.1037/adb0000511.supp (Supplemental)

Sang, J., Cederbaum, J. A., Ko, A. C., & Hurlburt, M. S. (2019). Maternal Depressive Symptoms, Adolescent Daughters' Substance Use, and Father Residence in Minority Families. *Substance Use & Misuse*, 54(11), 1774–1786. https://doi.org/10.1080 /10826084.2019.1610446

Su, J., Supple, A. J., & Kuo, S. I.-C. (2018). The Role of Individual and Contextual Factors in Differentiating Substance Use Profiles among Adolescents. *Substance Use & Misuse*, 53(5), 734–743. https://doi.org/10.1080/10826084.2017.1363237

Taylor, M., Merritt, S., & Brown, C. (2012). Perceptions of Family Caring and Its Impact on Peer Associations and Drug Involvement Among Rural Dwelling African American and White Adolescents. *Journal of Ethnicity in Substance Abuse*, 11(3), 242–261. https://doi.org/10.1080/15332640.2012.701567

Tur-Porcar, A. M., Jiménez-Martínez, J., & Mestre-Escrivá, V. (2019). Substance Use in Early and Middle Adolescence. The Role of Academic Efficacy and Parenting. *Psychosocial Intervention*, 28(3), 139–145. https://doi.org/10.5093/pi2019a11

Chapter 7

Understanding the Role of Peers and Adolescent Substance Use

PEERS AND ADOLESCENT DEVELOPMENT

Socialization and Peer Relationships

Friends play such powerful roles in students' lives. Good friends are there in good times and in bad. They can be a huge support when an adolescent is going through a hard time. Often the friends made as teenagers become lifelong friends.

But what about friends who engage in risky behaviors such as substance use? What kind of support does an adolescent get from this kind of friend? When they are in psychological distress, how does such a friend respond? With empathy and support? Or with an offer of a substance?

And how does a vulnerable adolescent respond? Is the adolescent able to withstand such an offer from a good friend? Can he or she withstand the peer pressure? Is this a friend they want to please or not offend? Do they think that if this good friend is doing that stuff, it must be okay? And how do kids gravitate to the friends who engage in risky behavior? Is it accidental or purposeful?

Socialization and peer relationships are so vital for everyone as the COVID-19 has made painfully clear. Friends are especially important for adolescent development. Hoeben et al. (2021) describe the process as part of the adolescent's move toward autonomy and adulthood, which contributes positively to emotional and social development. But Becker et al. (2019) say that adolescents are particularly susceptible to peer influences given their developmental stage and this importance of peer networks in adolescent life.

Taylor et al. (2012) observe that although the family is the initial social-izing influence, when an adolescent enters and progresses through school, the peer group begins to exert an increased degree of influence. They say that the mechanism of influence for family and peers may be similar, and occurs through the communication of attitudes, values, and beliefs about substance use, as well as the modeling of use or abstinence behaviors.

Adolescent peer groups share similar norms, values, attitudes, and behav-iors. The peer group culture, especially among adolescents, is an important factor in one's identity. Educators know that peers influence each other over everything from clothes to music to the in-and-out groups and more. When these behaviors are positive and prosocial, such as playing sports, academic excellence, say Acosta et al. (2015), and not smoking or taking drugs, peer modeling is encouraged. However, when these behaviors are negative and anti-social, peer modeling is not only discouraged but can be dangerous.

Social Learning and Social Support

Smith et al. (2020) describe social support as interpersonal relationships that influence the way in which we live. They are also a protective factor against an extensive range of risk behaviors. Supportive social relationships have a major influence on health and well-being. Thus, they found that social support acts as a protective factor for various psychological difficulties. Their research review also found that adolescents and young adults, who identify their peers as being more supportive, felt less stress during bad times due to being less apprehensive and worried about their own position within the group.

Several theories have been proposed to explain the effects of peer and social relationships on individuals' attitudes about each other. According to Albert Bandura's well-known Social Learning Theory, discussed in chapter 6, indi-viduals develop behaviors by modeling them after their peers, family mem-bers, media, and other social sources. Smith et al. (2020) suggest that because adolescents spend more time with their peers than with their parents, the more adolescents are exposed to peers, the higher the odds of imitating them.

A couple of theories explain this influence. Social Identity Theory sug-gests that individuals, in general, choose groups that are in accordance with their self-concept (Khasmohammadi et al., 2020). All groups have their own specific identities. The theory suggests that behavioral norms are transferred through social contacts, with parents and peers being the main sources. The

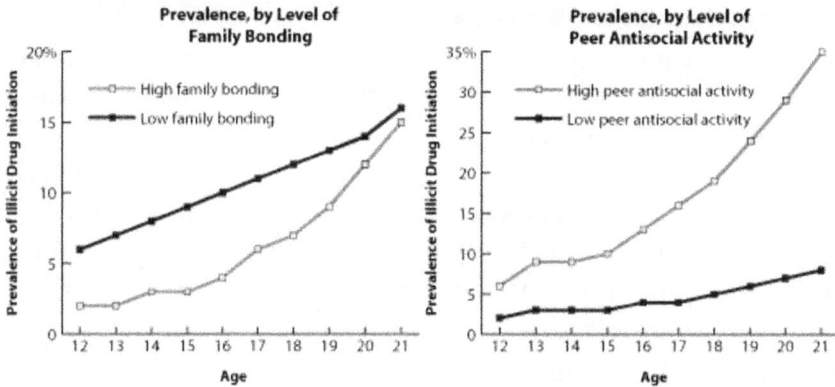

Figure 7.1   Family Bonding and Peer Antisocial Activity Impact Drug Initiation Among Adolescents. *NIDA. (2003, August 1). "Relationships Matter: Impact of Parental, Peer Factors on Teen, Young Adult Substance Abuse." Retrieved from* https://archives.drugabuse.gov/news-events/nida-notes/2003/08/relationships-matter-impact-parental-peer-factors-teen-young-adult-substance-abuse *on 2022, June 17*

combination of social and individual factors increases the probability of engaging in risky behavior. Social Network Theory, described by Kobus (2003), focuses on interdependence in social systems (e.g., school and peers) and suggests that individuals interact with and influence each other in a social system based on attitudes, behavior, and decision making.

Taylor et al. (2012) describe the health belief theory, which was developed to explain and predict health behaviors and provides a framework to view the impact of parental and peer messages on decision making and behavior. The model suggests that:

> In the pre-behavioral decision-making process, individuals assess their suscep-
> tibility to negative outcomes, the severity of these outcomes, and the overall
> threat that such outcomes will actually result from the behavior. Furthermore,
> after behaviors are initiated, a similar process occurs regarding their mainte-
> nance or discontinuation. Implicit in the health belief model is that parental and
> peer messages about use affect the decision-making process. (p. 244)

PEERS AND SUBSTANCE USE

Adolescent Socialization and Risk-Taking

Becker and Curry (2014) reviewed several studies suggesting that peer drinking behaviors may be a more influential predictor of use than family drinking behaviors. They found that both peer alcohol use and sibling alcohol use are strong and comparable predictors of adolescent drinking. They note that peer influences are among the strongest and most consistent factors associated with adolescent substance use.

The Dora-Laskey et al. (2020) literature review found social influences are strong predictors of risk-taking behaviors among youth, such as experimenting with substances. When driving their peers, for example, they found that teenagers are more likely to drink, drive faster, and engage in other risky behaviors, making teenagers the only group whose fatal crash risk increases in the presence of passengers.

Acosta et al. (2015) found that adolescents are strongly influenced by their peers on a variety of dimensions, from physical activity to educational and occupational aspirations to risk-taking and alcohol use. Acosta et al. also say that individuals take more risks and are more likely to think about the benefits, rather than the consequences of these risks, when in a peer group. They describe studies that have shown that adolescent substance use is strongly influenced by peers, but it is even more so among peers who are also substance users.

So, the question is, do adolescents socialize and then get exposed to substance use? Or do they pick friends for that very purpose?

Selection and Socialization

Taylor et al. (2012) found a two-way relationship between individual substance use and that of peers and friends. They say individual use predicts having a higher number of substance-using peers and vice versa. Substance-using adolescents have peers who also use substances and are more likely to support norms for drug use, which perpetuates its continuation. Taylor et al. also found that the role of peers predicts subsequent involvement in adolescent substance use.

Van Ryzin and Dishion (2014) suggest that youth with a history of problem behavior and peer rejection self-organize into deviant peer groups in early adolescence. Their results suggest that the development of substance dependence may have a significant social component that is a function of the how important substance use is in the social interactions of deviant peer groups. These groups establish social norms, expectations, and practices centered on substance use and other deviant behavior, which appear to amplify the risk created by early use and leave youth uniquely vulnerable to later dependence.

Peers can be extremely influential when an adolescent tries to stop using substances and gets treatment for a substance use disorder. Nash et al. (2015) note that the most common context for major relapse of adolescents returning to school after treatment is the presence of substance-using older siblings or friends. And the average length of time before such a teen is offered drugs upon return from treatment is one day (Sanders, 2020).

Peer Friendships

Mason et al. (2017) found that perceived closeness to friends as a measure of friendship quality is associated with substance use. They cite research that says that friendship is enhanced when peers share substances, which seems to be a powerful force playing out in such use. This was especially common for alcohol and marijuana use. They suggest it is important to study how different aspects of friends' behaviors may predict the use of different substances.

Mason et al. looked at the specific behaviors of high-risk friends and feelings of closeness and substance use. They found that selection (i.e., purposely selecting friends who use) of friends who use was stronger with alcohol use, so peer behaviors had little effect. They found that marijuana use was more sensitive to peer influence. They concluded that peer closeness with friends who offer substances significantly increases the risk of tobacco and marijuana use. Closeness, which represents friendship quality and trust, may provide further understanding into the mechanisms of peer behaviors and substance use.

Race and Culture Considerations

Early research by Vega et al. (1996) compared the prevalence of substance use risk factors among non-Hispanic, Cuban, other Hispanic, and African American adolescent males. They found no differences between these ethnic/racial groups in the cumulative prevalence of risk factors, such as family substance use, psychosocial adjustment, peer substance use and approval of substance use, and deviant behaviors.

Su and Supple (2016) who studied substance use and the intergenerational cultural dissonance (ICD) found ICD to be associated with a range of adverse outcomes among youth from immigrant families. They found that a lack of parental involvement could lead to lower parental knowledge of a child's behavior and that this lack of involvement and knowledge can provide increased opportunity for an adolescent to establish relationships with deviant peers.

Association with deviant peers, they said, was the closest factor in predicting problem behaviors among the adolescents they studied. ICD among Vietnamese families was a significant predictor of adolescent substance use, a relationship that was impacted by peer substance use, for example. Among Cambodian adolescents, peer behavior is also strongly associated with adolescent alcohol use.

Taylor et al. (2012) found that African American adolescents typically have lower overall substance use rates compared with other adolescents. Compared with White adolescents, they say, African American adolescents are less likely to have ever smoked cigarettes, or initiate or alcohol use, though African American adolescents appear to be more likely to initiate marijuana use than Whites. And as previously reported, African American adolescents reported more substance-involved peers. This did not universally translate into their own individual substance use.

There are also comparisons between urban and rural adolescent substance use. Taylor found that substance use rates of rural adolescents are not all that different from their urban counterparts, and, for some substances, are higher (e.g., alcohol, cigarettes, and methamphetamine) They point to recent Monitoring the Future (MTF) data that suggest that although adolescent substance use has declined somewhat in urban areas, a similar shift has not happened within non-urban locations.

Gender Influences

Regarding peers, substance use, and gender, Acosta et al. (2015) found that girls are more highly influenced by their best friends than boys. Adolescents in same-sex friendships have equal influence on each other when it comes to alcohol consumption. However, in mixed-sex friendships, they note female adolescents are more influenced by males, but do not have the same influence on their male friends' alcohol use behavior. They did find that substance use among female adolescents is highly associated with having deviant peers and with low parental involvement and monitoring.

Acosta et al. studied peer leader substance use and found such use played an important role in substance use among male and female adolescents. Although peer leader substance use was associated with increase odds of drug use among male students, the opposite effect was seen among female students. They found that among female students, peer leader substance use decreased the odds of cigarette and marijuana use. Female students that had peer leaders who used cigarettes and marijuana, had a decreased odds of using cigarette and marijuana themselves.

They speculated that male and female react differently to group norms, and they also behave differently in their peer groups. They found that in early teenage years, peer social groups became more segregated, with girls tending to have larger groups than boys. Girls also have more exclusive friendships than boys, keeping their friendship groups the same size, while boys tend to expand their friendship groups. Position in the group was associated with acceptance among the boys, and boys were more concerned with their status, while girls cared more for attributes that were important to the relationships within the networks.

Males, say Acosta et al., tend to be more concerned with attributes that promote their status in the network while females are more concerned with quality of the relationship. Males may elevate their status within the peer group by behaving mischievously or, in the case of high-risk adolescent males, using hard drugs. However, among females, they concluded, there is no need to feel accepted and important in the peer group through misconduct, and thus their use did not increase with peer leader use.

RISK FACTORS

Peers and Psychological Distress

Self-medication has been discussed in relation to adolescent emotional regulation, or lack thereof. Shadur et al. (2015) describe self-medication as a process in which substance use is triggered by elevated negative emotion and the use of drugs becomes a learned behavior to regulate emotion. They explored the role of negative affect levels, and greater within-day mood fluctuations, which may prompt drug use. They suggest that drug effects that may be more reinforcing for those with dysregulated mood and poor emotional regulation.

Shadur et al. also say that most substance use in adolescence does not represent self-medication, but that there are vulnerable subgroups at increased risk. They found that self-medication emerges in adolescence for youth in particular contexts. They also found that cross-sectional associations between negative affect and drug use are stronger for adolescents whose friendships are characterized by fewer positive friendship qualities and greater peer substance use.

They also found that, for adolescents with volatile mood and poor emotion regulation, the peer context may predict self-medication. Those with low peer social support and greater negative affect may seek drugs to cope. Additionally, Bandura's social learning theory suggests that exposure to peer drug use may provide adolescents prone to negative affect with an environment conducive to self-medication:

> We found that within person effects of self medication differed depending on the type of negative affect and whether the daily affective experience was chronic or fluctuating. Consistent with our hypotheses, greater daily variability in worry was a strong predictor of increased daily substance use risk, whereas daily maximum levels of worry were a weaker predictor of use...these results suggest that overall high levels of sadness and worry both predict increased risk for drug use perhaps for a variety of reasons, but unique feelings of worry drive adolescent self medication. (within person effects) (p. 578)

Although peer drug use did not impact self-medication risk, peer social support did buffer risk for substance use related to greater variability in worry, but not sadness. Shadur et al. concluded that adolescents with less supportive friendships and greater negative affect may engage in self-medication to cope.

Early Use

Van Ryzin et al. (2014) found that early substance use predicted both an increase in use across time as well as a tendency for youth to self-organize into peer groups that engaged in deviant behavior. They say that early substance use has two consequences: first, adolescents are trained to use substances on a regular basis; and second, use of substances provides a venue for social engagement with a particular group. Self-organization into deviant peer groups appears to be a key mechanism in the progression from early use to later dependence across a variety of substances.

Sibling Use

Becker and Curry (2014) explored family influences and determined that sibling and peer substance use significantly predict adolescent drinking frequency, above and beyond parent alcohol use. Peer substance use predicted high-volume drinking, whereas only sibling alcohol use predicted drinking quantity. These findings, they say, suggest the importance of shared environmental and genetic components of sibling and adolescent alcohol consumption.

Unstructured Time and Peer Pressure

Hoeben et al. (2021) studied unstructured socializing, situations in which peers are present, authority figures are absent, and there is a lack of structured activity. They found that involvement in unstructured socializing is related to increased risks for delinquency and substance use. The presence of peers makes deviant acts rewarding because peers can serve as an appreciative audience. They note that reinforcement of substance use behaviors occurs when peers increase the risk for delinquency or substance use by signaling approval for such behavior.

Hoeben et al. speculate that deviant peers will reinforce acts in which they have engaged because others' refusal to engage in those behaviors would be indirect disapproval of their behavior. They say adolescents may engage in behaviors that are instigated, reinforced, or provoked by peers for the following reasons: (1) out of fear of ridicule, (2) due to status competition, or (3) from a desire to remain loyal to their friends.

Perceptions/Comparisons of Peer/Self Use

Adolescents often wildly overestimate the level of substance use of their peers. Brown et al. (2020) say this can lead to a more normative view of peer substance use and a greater likelihood of substance use. Debnum et al. (2018) agree, finding that youth misperceive drug use by their peers and misperceive the harms of use. They suggest that the perception that others are engaging in a risk behavior increases the intention of the individual to do the same. Underestimating the harms of substances also makes it more likely that they engage in substance use.

Perkins (2012) describes the widespread overestimation of peer substance misuse. He found that students typically perceive the norms for drinking among peers to be substantially greater than is the case, leading them to believe that others are using as much or more than they are, further justifying their own use. Mason et al. (2017) describe this as the false consensus effect, believing that one's peers engage in behavior like one's own, which can greatly influence use, even if those friends do no use or use infrequently.

Hannigan (2012) notes that there is also substantial under-reporting of self-use. Study results of analysis of adolescent hair samples tested for cocaine and opiates showed that the adolescent was fifty-two times more likely to be positive for cocaine (33.7 percent) than was indicated by self-reported frequency/recency of cocaine use. No teen reported opiate use, but 6.6 percent of samples were positive. They concluded that the best self-reports greatly underestimate the prevalence of substance use by youth.

High-Risk Behavior and Peers

Acosta et al. say that, of the many risky behaviors exhibited by "high-risk" youth, substance abuse ranks as one of the most prevalent and serious. Due to the nature of their peer group and environmental surroundings, they note, high-risk adolescents are at an increased risk of being substance abusers and suffering the life-long consequences of substance abuse. Smith et al. (2020) found that the engagement of adolescents in detrimental behaviors including unsafe sex, excessive drug and alcohol use, heightened risk-taking, and delinquent acts under peer support will inevitably negatively affect their psychological health.

High-risk youths generally are individuals who come from disadvantaged socioeconomic groups, children of substance users, risk-takers, those suffering academic problems, or targets of drug promotion by the tobacco and alcohol industries (Sussman et al., 2004). Acosta et al. cite the literature describing "high risk" as referring to adolescents who are at risk of being substance abusers due to the large proportion of substance use within their peer group and overall surroundings.

Process Addictions and Peer Support

Smith et al. (2020) point to studies exploring excessive adolescent Internet use and gambling which are rapidly expanding concerns regarding impact on mental health. They say that the fact that addiction can occur in various forms creates another challenge in supporting adolescent well-being. An individual can become addicted to a variety of objects and activities. The increasing number of adolescents engaged on either Internet addiction or gambling is of concern, they warn.

Research on these "process addictions," (which also include eating disorders, sex addiction, among others) suggests that perceived peer support plays a significant role in adolescents' psychological well-being. Behavioral addictions are like substance addictions in that they consist of maladaptive patterns of behavior such as loss of control over and preoccupation with the behavior. For example, Smith et al.'s analysis shows a significant indirect effect of compulsive Internet use and *problem gambling* on psychological well-being through perceived peer support resulting in many harmful, often lifelong, patterns of behavior .

On the other hand, Acosta et al. found that Internet surfing and engaging in gambling activities excessively were displayed by adolescents with no access to an immediate peer group to socialize with. In addition, they say, the need to receive support from peer groups is prevented among young people who engage excessively in these addictive behaviors and these behaviors replace missing social relationships to some extent. Consequently, this may also lead to lower psychological well-being and higher psychological distress.

PROTECTIVE FACTORS

Peer Support/Peer Leadership

Smith et al. (2020) report that the social support of friends, family, and others decreases psychological stress in individuals. They maintain that positive social support (i.e., peer support) can reduce the prevalence of addiction among adolescents. They concluded that perceived support from peers is significant to adolescents and leads to meaningful mental health outcomes. Providing guidance and support in social groups of young people can be potentially very effective in addiction prevention and recovery.

Knopf (2016) documented one organization based on a "youth-led, adult-guided" model. "This can't be done by a purely adult-led model," says the director of this organization based on peer leadership:

> Youth are the experts of what's going on in their schools and lives and when
> they see peer pressure having an effect, youth can tell adults the best way to

reach out . . . youth have the expertise and knowledge, and when you give them the opportunity to make the change themselves, it's empowering. We try to direct them away from scare tactics, because they don't work . . . Instead, adolescents in this program are given skills that help them be mature and reinforce them in being a positive influence in their communities. (p.2.)

Because peer-to-peer social support facilitates abstinence and recovery, the Federal government has issued calls for recovery support projects designed and delivered by peer leaders, say Nash et al. (2015). A vision of student leadership on this issue of student substance use is a new and important focus. Who better for our adolescents to listen to in order to prevent substance use than other students, those who are seen as influencers and leaders?

Prevention Strategies

Van Ryzin and Dishion (2014) maintain there is a lot of room for improvement in current prevention strategies. Such improvement, they say, could include an emphasis on identifying and intervening in early substance use before it can become an organizing factor in friendship selection and interaction. Shadur et al. (2015) recommend the identification of risk factors as critical targets for prevention. They propose an emphasis on supportive friendships which may buffer risk.

Becker and Curry (2014) concur stating that interventions focused on encouraging supportive friendships and on emotion regulation strategies may help minimize risk for adolescent use. They also advise that understanding influences and predictors of adolescent substance use is necessary for devising prevention efforts. Their findings also highlight the importance of assessing and targeting sibling and peer substance use in intervention and prevention programs. Prevention programs will be further discussed in chapter 10.

Peer Refusal Strategies

Peer refusal strategies are now common elements in evidence-based prevention and intervention approaches. This chapter describes how strong the influence of peers is and the reasons they have difficulty resisting peer invitations to engage in potentially harmful behavior. Helping adolescents understand these harms is not enough. They need explicit instruction, practice, and reinforcement in peer refusal skills and strategies to be able to respond in the moment to peer offers, and to make good decisions about where to be and whom to be with.

Other specific and targeted interventions are important. Dora-Lackey et al. (2020) conducted research on adolescent driving after drinking, including peer influence. They concluded that brief interventions for alcohol use have been shown to reduce alcohol consumption and driving after drinking, including driving with peers, among adolescents. Programs targeting risky drinking have shown reductions in both short-term alcohol consumption and alcohol consequences including driving after drinking.

Acosta et al. also emphasize the importance of targeting substance use prevention programs for high-risk adolescents, keeping in mind the importance of peer influence and how it may have different effects on male and female adolescents. They suggest that an intervention tailored specifically to the two genders might be a more successful approach.

PROMISING PROGRAM: ALTERNATIVE PEER GROUPS

Nash et al. (2015) describe the fact that an alarming percentage of treated adolescents continue to use substances at high rates after treatment, with first-year relapse rates ranging from 55 percent to 89 percent. They note that

Figure 7.2   Elements of an Alternative Peer Group (APG). *Source:* http://www.aapg -recovery.com/

adolescents make riskier decisions when with their peers than adults do and describe an approach for students who are trying to remain substance free called an APG (alternative peer group).

Based on the principle of positive social influence, the APG model integrates a group of recovering peers who value sobriety into a process of recovery, based on peer support. APGs are often incorporated as after-school organizations or clubs. They consist of group social support and frequent supervised fun social activities that lead to friendship bonds with peers who model attitudes and behaviors of recovery. APGs strive to attract reluctant teens to engage in recovery because they perceive sobriety to be more rewarding than alcohol or drug use.

Collier et al. (2014) explain the importance of utilizing the social influence of similar-aged peer support to increase positive outcomes for youth in recovery. The foundation of the APG is the social component: the social functions include after-school hangouts, sober social weekend activities, and retreats. The hallmark of this model is the basic assumption that peer relationships, much like the ones that initiate and support drug and alcohol use, are necessary to facilitate recovery.

The APG model provides a new group of friends that provide alternative attitudes, values, judgments, processes, and behavior that support the change necessary to recover from substance abuse disorders, Collier at al note. It includes mutual support group meetings, counseling (individual, family, and group), multifamily group, and psychosocial education for youth and parents. Other elements included are: increasing prosocial leisure habits, offering sufficient intensity and duration of contact, a focus on relapse prevention, and providing problem-solving skills training.

Collier et al. found that adolescents enrolled in an APG perceive greater attachment to and experience improved communication and trust with their parents compared with control group participants. Parents report that the program helped improve their relationships with their children and other family members. They report that they learn how to set effective boundaries and support their adolescents in recovery.

APG peer relationships are exceptionally enduring, supportive, and superior to relationships observed in their same-age peers who had no need of recovery, say Collier et al. One study revealed two-year sobriety rates near 90 percent for teens who completed an intensive APG program and attended a recovery high school. Adolescents with more time in the APG who have achieved such change model healthy, sober behaviors and exert positive peer pressure on newcomers who might eventually become new leaders themselves.

A valuable peer social network develops as these recovering youth build relationships within the APG and, ultimately, venture outside the peer group.

CONCLUDING THOUGHTS

Mark Sanders, a nationally recognized addiction expert, spoke at a Chicago State University conference in March 2020. He said that the time it takes for a teen returning to school from substance use treatment to be offered drugs is one day. One day. A shocking number. Can a newly sober adolescent withstand the pressure—and the allure?

Sanders's words highlight how lonely such a child is when they do return after getting help for substance use. They are advised to stay away from their using friends. The non-using kids shun the "druggie," and they are alone. The temptation to return to the familiar and welcoming friend group can be too much.

That is why the APG is such an important concept, and one that could be easily incorporated in a school's list of student organizations. This group could meet weekly, offer a combination of skill development (e.g., stress management, refusal skill training) and *a lot* of fun, social activities to keep the adolescents interested and coming back.

The small handful of Chicago high schools are making APGs happen, starting with a small $5,000 mini-grant from a nonprofit organization called Sreenity Academy Chicago as seed money. School staff interested in running with the idea get a team together, identify students who would be a good fit, and invite them to join, with parental permission. Such teams also incorporate parent education.

It is possible to make space for these children; safe spaces where they feel welcome, where they can build friendships with other students while trying to stay away from substances, and where they can continue to receive the necessary support to sustain their recoveries. A place where they belong. This is possible.

REFERENCES

Acosta, S. L., Hospital, M. M., Graziano, J. N., Morris, S., & Wagner, E. F. (2015). Pathways to Drinking Among Hispanic/Latino Adolescents: Perceived

Discrimination, Ethnic Identity, and Peer Affiliations. *Journal of Ethnicity in Substance Abuse*, 14(3), 270–286. https://doi.org/10.1080/15332640.2014.993787

Association of Alternative Peers Groups, Model of APGs. Retrieved from: www.aapg -recovery.com

Becker, S. J., & Curry, J. F. (2014). Testing the Effects of Peer Socialization Versus Selection on Alcohol and Marijuana Use Among Treated Adolescents. *Substance Use & Misuse*, 49(3), 234–242. https://doi.org/10.3109/10826084.2013.824479

Becker, S. J., Marceau, K., Hernandez, L., & Spirito, A. (2019). Is it Selection or Socialization? Disentangling Peer Influences on Heavy Drinking and Marijuana Use Among Adolescents Whose Parents Received Brief Interventions. *Substance Abuse: Research & Treatment*, 13, N.PAG. https://doi.org/10.1177 /1178221819852644

Berndt, T., & Keefe, K. (1996). Friends' Influence on Adolescents' Adjustment to School. *Child Development*, 66, 1312–1329.

Brown, A. L., España, R. A., Benca-Bachman, C. E., Welsh, J. W., & Palmer, R. H. (2020). Adolescent Behavioral Characteristics Mediate Familial Effects on Alcohol Use and Problems in College-Bound Students. *Substance Abuse: Research & Treatment*, 1–10. https://doi.org/10.1177/1178221820970925

Collier, C., Hilliker, R., & Onwuegbuzie, A. (2014). Alternative Peer Group: A Model for Youth Recovery. *Journal of Groups in Addiction & Recovery*, 9(1), 40–53. https://doi.org/10.1080/1556035X.2013.836899

Debnam, K. J., Saha, S., & Bradshaw, C. P. (2018). Synthetic and Other Drug Use among High School Students: The Role of Perceived Prevalence, Access, and Harms. *Substance Use & Misuse*, 53(12), 2069–2076. https://doi.org/10.1080 /10826084.2018.1455699

Defoe, I. N., Khurana, A., Betancourt, L. M., Hurt, H., & Romer, D. (2019). Disentangling Longitudinal Relations between Youth Marijuana Use, Peer Marijuana Use, and Conduct Problems: Developmental Cascading Links to Marijuana Use Disorder. *Addiction*, 114(3), 485–493. https://doi.org/10.1111/add.14456

Dora-Laskey, A. D., Goldstick, J. E., Buckley, L., Bonar, E. E., Zimmerman, M. A., Walton, M. A., Cunningham, R. M., & Carter, P. M. (2020). Trajectories of Driving after Drinking among Marijuana Using Youth in the Emergency Department: Substance Use, Mental Health, and Peer and Parental Influences. *Substance Use & Misuse*, 55(2), 175–187. https://doi.org/10.1080/10826084.2019.1660675

Hannigan, J. H., & Delaney, B. V. (2012). Faithful Friends: Teen Reporters of Peer Substance Use. *Addiction*, 107(5), 889–890. https://doi.org/10.1111/j.1360-0443 .2012.03790.x

Hernandez, L., Eaton, C., Fairlie, A., Chun, T., & Spirito, A. (2010). Ethnic Group Differences in Substance Use, Depression, Peer Relationships, and Parenting

Among Adolescents Receiving Brief Alcohol Counseling. *Journal of Ethnicity in Substance Abuse*, 9(1), 14–27. https://doi.org/10.1080/15332640903538874

Hoeben, E. M., Osgood, D. W., Siennick, S. E., & Weerman, F. M. (2021). Hanging Out with the Wrong Crowd? The Role of Unstructured Socializing in Adolescents' Specialization in Delinquency and Substance Use. *Journal of Quantitative Criminology*, 37(1), 141–177. https://doi.org/10.1007/s10940-019-09447-4

Khasmohammadi, M., Ghazizadeh Ehsaei, S., Vanderplasschen, W., Dortaj, F., Farahbakhsh, K., Keshavarz Afshar, H., Jahanbakhshi, Z., Mohsenzadeh, F., Mohd Noah, S., Sulaiman, T., Brady, C., & Hormozi, A. Kalantar. (2020). The Impact of Addictive Behaviors on Adolescents Psychological Well-Being: The Mediating Effect of Perceived Peer Support. *Journal of Genetic Psychology*, 181(2/3), 39–53. https://doi.org/10.1080/00221325.2019.1700896

Knopf, A. (2016). Youth Trained in Primary Drug Prevention on a Peer Level. *Brown University Child & Adolescent Behavior Letter*, 32, 1–2. https://doi.org/10.1002/cbl.30112

Kobus, K. (2003). Peers and Adolescent Smoking. *Addiction*, 98, 37–55. https://doi.org/10.1046/j.1360- 0443.98.s1.4.x

Mason, M. J., Zaharakis, N. M., Rusby, J. C., Westling, E., Light, J. M., Mennis, J., & Flay, B. R. (2017). A Longitudinal Study Predicting Adolescent Tobacco, Alcohol, and Marijuana Use by Behavioral Characteristics of Close Friends. *Psychology of Addictive Behaviors*, 31(6), 712–720. https://doi.org/10.1037/adb0000299

Nash, A., Marcus, M., Engebretson, J., & Bukstein, O. (2015). Recovery From Adolescent Substance Use Disorder: Young People in Recovery Describe the Process and Keys to Success in an Alternative Peer Group. *Journal of Groups in Addiction & Recovery*, 10(4), 290–312. https://doi.org/10.1080/1556035X.2015.1089805

NIDA. (2003, August 1). Relationships Matter: Impact of Parental, Peer Factors on Teen, Young Adult Substance Abuse. Retrieved from https://archives.drugabuse.gov/news-events/nida-notes/2003/08/relationships-matter-impact-parental-peer-factors-teen-young-adult-substance-abuse on 2021, December 15.

Perkins, H. W. (2012). Misperceptions of Peer Substance Use among Youth Are Real. *Addiction*, 107(5), 888–889. https://doi.org/10.1111/j.1360-0443.2012.03782.x

Shadur, J. M., Hussong, A. M., & Haroon, M. (2015). Negative Affect Variability and Adolescent Self-medication: The Role of the Peer Context. *Drug & Alcohol Review*, 34(6), 571–580. https://doi.org/10.1111/dar.12260

Smith, N. Z., Vasquez, P. J., Emelogu, N. A., Hayes, A. E., Engebretson, J., & Nash, A. J. (2020). The Good, the Bad, and Recovery: Adolescents Describe the Advantages and Disadvantages of Alternative Peer Groups. *Substance Abuse: Research & Treatment*, 14, 1–9. https://doi.org/10.1177/1178221820909354

Su, J., & Supple, A. (2014). Parental, Peer, School, and Neighborhood Influences on Adolescent Substance Use: Direct and Indirect Effects and Ethnic Variations. *Journal of Ethnicity in Substance Abuse*, 13(3), 227–246. https://doi.org/10.1080/15332640.2013.847393

Su, J., & Supple, A. J. (2016). School Substance Use Norms and Racial Composition Moderate Parental and Peer Influences on Adolescent Substance Use. *American Journal of Community Psychology*, 57(3/4), 280–290. https://doi.org/10.1002/ajcp.12043

Sussman, S., Earleywine, M., Wills, T., Cody, C., Biglan, T., & Dent, C. (2004). The Motivation, Skills, and Decision-making Model of "Drug Abuse" Prevention. *Substance Use & Misuse*, 39(10–12), 1972–2016.

Taylor, M., Merritt, S., & Brown, C. (2012). Perceptions of Family Caring and Its Impact on Peer Associations and Drug Involvement Among Rural Dwelling African American and White Adolescents. *Journal of Ethnicity in Substance Abuse*, 11(3), 242–261. https://doi.org/10.1080/15332640.2012.701567

Van Ryzin, M. J., & Dishion, T. J. (2014). Adolescent Deviant Peer Clustering as an Amplifying Mechanism Underlying the Progression from Early Substance Use to Late Adolescent Dependence. *Journal of Child Psychology & Psychiatry*, 55(10), 1153–1161. https://doi.org/10.1111/jcpp.12211

Vega, W. A., Zimmerman, R. S., Warheit, G. J., Apospori, E., & Gil, A. G. (1993). Risk Factors for Early Adolescent Drug Use in Four Ethnic and Racial Group. *American Journal of Public Health*, 83, 185–189.

Chapter 8

Understanding the Role of the School in Addressing Student Substance Use

SCHOOL ROLES AND RESPONSIBILITIES

Society places a tremendous responsibility on our schools. Educators are charged with accomplishing so many things along with providing a quality education, and often without the resources to do so. Between federal, state, and local requirements, schools and educators have been tasked with everything from nutrition to law enforcement to child protection and more.

Adding more responsibility for the prevention and intervention of substance use seems like yet another unfunded mandate to educators. Yet, if educators do not attend to this very important issue, identified as a major public health issue, schools are, in fact, prevented from achieving their primary mission if substance use continues to go largely unaddressed.

This chapter addresses these issues, both presenting many evidence-based strategies that can be incorporated now into school life, and others that will take initiative and leadership, and, of course, some commitment of resources.

Schools have been identified as a vitally important place to provide health information, screening, prevention, and intervention because they are one of the few places in society that sees children on a regular basis. For example, too many children from high-poverty situations do not regularly see a pediatrician, but they regularly see their teachers. Teachers are in a very important position to establish and maintain the trust of children, which is essential if they are to confide in us when they or their family members are experiencing serious problems.

The American Medical Association (2007) suggests that schools are appropriate settings for substance use prevention programs for three reasons: (1)

prevention must focus on children before their beliefs and expectations about substance abuse are established; (2) schools offer the most systematic way of reaching young people; and (3) schools can promote a broad spectrum of drug-related educational policies.

Jaynes et al. (2014) observe that teachers, who are the major reporters of child abuse, are already an integral part of the child welfare intervention system. Their research reviews find that school staff are tasked with the early identification of anxiety disorders, conduct disorder, and other types of mental health problems in children and adolescent, "making them indispensable to the mental health treatment system. In this vein, schools have a role in mediating young people's early experiences with alcohol and illicit substances, and in helping to reduce the risk that adolescents will develop substance abuse problems" (p. 35).

More recently, schools have begun to embrace a focus on social-emotional learning, recognizing how vitally important this focus on the whole child is to their success in learning. This emphasis, much of it mandated by state or local requirements, is an important one. It sets the stage for schools evaluating what they are currently doing for students with trauma and co-occurring disorders. Armed with important information on the links between trauma, co-occurring disorders, and other behavior disorders with substance abuse, these efforts at incorporating and infusing social-emotional learning can be even more effective.

SCHOOLS AND SUBSTANCE USE

The Reality of Student Substance Use and Schools

As reported here, the number of students affected by substance use, either their own or their family members, is substantial. There are real societal costs in both addressing and not addressing this issue. In the *Malignant Neglect: Substance Abuse and America's Schools Report (2001)* the authors estimated that each year substance abuse costs our schools at least $41 billion in truancy, special education and disciplinary programs, disruption, teacher turnover, and property damage. Though somewhat dated, it is packed with pertinent analyses and solid recommendations that still ring true today.

The report's authors said that "parents, teachers, school administrators and even students themselves, have looked the other way, hoping that a curriculum program or zero-tolerance policy would take care of the problem, or that in any case experimentation with drugs was a relatively benign rite of passage."

Below are other key findings from this report:

> More than half of all teens and 60 percent of high school teens--9.5 million high school students and almost five million middle school students--report that drugs are used, kept or sold at their schools.
>
> The $41 billion each year coping with the problem of substance abuse in our schools represents 10 percent of federal, state, local and private spending on elementary and secondary education.
>
> Students who attend schools where substances are used, kept, and sold are nearly three times more likely to smoke, drink or use illicit drugs as students whose schools are substance free.
>
> Illegal drug use is three times likelier to be found in schools where students smoke and drink on school grounds.
>
> Zero-tolerance policies and drug testing in schools may help identify students in trouble, but often are used merely to identify children for expulsion. (p. 2)

The *Malignant Neglect* report also found that efforts to achieve the National Goal of drug-free schools failed, primarily for two reasons. The reasons include the fact that primary prevention efforts of schools—mainly curricular programs—can target only a few of the many risk factors in a child's life. No single curriculum, however well-designed and implemented, can ever be sufficient to address the array of personal, genetic, psychological, family, and social risk factors of teen substance use.

They also found then that too few programs were based on sound evidence of effectiveness and there was little overall coordination of stakeholders to work in concert to reinforce their positive effects. According to current Chicago teachers attending conferences on this issue, most of their schools don't have any substance abuse prevention programs, not to mention any that are evidence-based. Perhaps this is due to attitudes about whether this is the responsibility of the school at all, or denial that this crisis is real.

Perceptions/Attitudes about School's Role

The *Malignant Neglect* report found that school staff face overcrowded classes, limited resources, and uninvolved parents. Substance use is viewed often as just one more problem for which they are unprepared and unqualified to cope, the authors say. Staff may view students with substance problems as disruptive to their classroom and tend to ignore or seek to get rid of them. Even those who do attempt to help often face big roadblocks, the report notes, particularly because of the dearth of quality and affordable treatment programs available for youth in any given community.

There is some very interesting data comparing perceptions of the extent of the problem among teachers and staff, school administrators, and students. This data reveals wide disparities in the views between the adults and the students about what is really going on in school. For example, the Report found:

> Remarkable differences exist between students' and school personnel's percep-
> tions of student drug use. When asked if their school grounds were drug free,
> 11 percent of principals and 35 percent of teachers said that they were not,
> compared to 66 percent of students. While only five percent of principals report
> that students drink on school grounds, 33 percent of students say that drinking
> occurs at school...parents, teachers and policymakers too often accept facts
> such as these as indicators of benign rites of passage of teens to adulthood. (p.4)

Curricular Limitations

The *Malignant Neglect* report found many programs, in the minority of schools that did have some, were of inherently limited value. While they may be helpful in developing the students' perception of risk and perhaps in enhancing the will and skills to say no, they say that a few classroom hours on substance abuse is likely to be of marginal impact in the context of the other influences on student behavior.

While some curricula show promise, they found their effectiveness is inherently limited because the risk factors for student substance use—and the motivations for student drug use—are not restricted to students' knowledge about the effects of the various drugs or their skills to resist pressures to use drugs.

Almost everyone has heard of or has been involved in some way, as a student or schools staff member, in the D.A.R.E program. Malignant notes that D.A.R.E. programs have been implemented in schools in 50 to 80 percent of U.S. school districts, but that independent evaluations reveal little, if any, effect in reducing substance use. Independent evaluations find that students in Project D.A.R.E. show no greater improvements in the measured outcomes (e.g., actual drug use, attitudes about drug use, and self-esteem) than those not receiving the program. There have been some recent revisions to the program, however, that have tried to address these findings.

Policies and Practices/Zero Tolerance

The *Malignant Neglect* report's authors also critiqued school zero tolerance policies. They say that rigidly applied zero tolerance policies may be a double-edged sword in efforts to reduce substance use. These policies may discourage teachers, parents, and other students from reporting instances of student substance use. They note that punishments related to zero tolerance policies may not remedy the problem but merely transfer it. Private school students go to public schools. Students from public schools often are sent to alternative schools with other substance-using students.

Zero tolerance policies are coupled with law enforcement, as students are turned over to the police if found with drugs on school property. These policies then become part of the now infamous school-to-prison pipeline. The focus is punishment, not help for them. In 2001, *Malignant Neglect* report authors note that only 36 percent of public schools and 14.4 percent of private schools said they offer some form of substance abuse counseling and only 9.5 percent of the nation's public school districts employ any type of student assistance program.

As noted in earlier chapters, even school staff with roles involving student counseling (e.g., school psychologists, guidance counselors) report that they have had little or no professional training in effectively dealing with substance use. Commitment of funds, resources, and staffing are all needed to provide the training, and the professional personnel, to support a meaningful, coordinated safety net of support.

School Culture, Race, and Substance Use

Fisher et al. (2019) investigated the relationship between the percentage of White or Black students in a school and substance use and found that this relationship was strongly influenced by school substance use attitudes. Their research review indicates that schools in which most of the student body is Black have the lowest substance use rates, while schools in which White students are the majority have the highest drinking rates.

They also found differences when it came to which substance was being considered: students in schools with higher percentages of White students had less harmful views of alcohol and higher levels of alcohol use. Similarly, students in schools with higher percentages of Black students had less harmful views of marijuana and higher reported levels of marijuana use.

Interestingly, they found that the relationship between school racial composition, substance use attitudes, and substance use was not impacted by student race: Black and White students alike, regardless of the school racial composition, were similarly impacted by the social norms related to substance use. In other words, they generally conformed to the norms of their school, regardless of their race.

Fisher et al. concluded that norms for social behaviors, including substance use, are learned predominately in the context of the norms of the culture. They said this study provides evidence that the relationship between school racial composition and substance use behavior operates in part through the transmission of cultural norms related to attitudes toward substance use.

SCHOOL RISK FACTORS

Negative School Culture and Climate

The *Malignant Neglect* report describes features of the school environment—school structure and policies, academic goals, curricula, teacher qualifications and attitudes, administrative support, level of parental and community involvement, availability of extracurricular activities, and the general characteristics of the student population—that all have an influence on substance use among students as well.

Chang et al. (2018) reviewed the literature and found that the learning climate affects learners' motivation and self-confidence, and that it can increase success levels and decrease anti-social behavior. As teacher interest in a positive school climate increases, the percentage of students who use substances decreases. They also found that teacher empathy and appreciation of a student's uniqueness were also related to positive changes in motivation and engagement, which had an impact on learning climate.

Chang et al. note that, as failure to abstain from drug use may be attributed to lack of motivation, a positive classroom climate is related to motivation for adopting expected, prosocial behavior. Jaynes et al. also reviewed this literature and found that school climate (i.e., including level of peer-to-peer respect, level of respect for teachers by students, level of respect for students by teachers, and clarity of the rules) significantly impact rates of adolescent substance use.

Gaete et al. (2018) describe a sense of belonging, or school membership, as a concept of students' perceptions about whether they feel accepted, respected, included, and supported by others in the school social environment. It is also defined as the perception of social bonds with other school members, something that has implications in terms of self-identity and commitment. They say that students who feel less supported and respected by teachers and peers and less part of the school, may feel isolated, depressed, or anxious resulting in a higher risk of using drugs, and failing in school.

School Disconnectedness

The flip side of belonging is disconnectedness. Moon et al. (2020) found that the quality of the school relationship, defined as the perception of teacher support and school belonging, was associated with the initiation, escalation, and/or reduction of self-reported involvement in health risk behaviors, including substance use.

Goulet et al. (2020) found that student disengagement is a significant risk factor for further psychosocial maladjustment. They say that issues such as school dropout, grade retention, academic failure, and lack of discipline in the classroom have all been associated with negative psychosocial outcomes, such as school dropout and substance abuse. School disengagement is also found to be related to the initiation and escalation of drug use over the course of adolescence (Bachman et al. 2008).

Gaete et al. determined that a sense of school belonging, or membership, influences the way students become interested and engaged in everyday school activities and is recognized as an important factor in school achievement, retention, and participation of vulnerable students in their schools. Henry et al. (2012) found that students' school connectedness at age fourteen predicted alcohol and drug use two years later, and that a lower GPA in sixth grade was associated with the escalation of drug use over the course of junior high school (seventh to ninth grade) among rural youth.

Truancy is also an indication of disconnectedness. Henry et al. also found that truancy was associated with the likelihood of initiating alcohol and marijuana use, and cigarette smoking among at-risk, urban youth. They point to low levels of school bonding and academic achievement at ages twelve to thirteen predicting serious delinquency and drug use one year later. These factors can be precursors to dropping out of school altogether.

Dropping Out of School

The prognosis for students who drop out is not good. For those who drop out and have a substance use problem, it is even worse. The *Malignant Neglect* report found that high school students who use alcohol or other drugs frequently were up to five times more likely than other students to drop out of school. Students who use marijuana before age fifteen are three times likelier to drop out of school before age sixteen, and twice as likely to be frequent truants. And adolescents who use marijuana weekly are almost six times likelier to cut class or skip school compared to those who do not (60 percent vs. 11 percent, respectively).

Goulet et al. (2020) state that high school dropout and substance abuse in adolescence are among the serious adaptive difficulties that can have disastrous consequences for their future life course. They summarize studies that indicate that adolescents who dropout or abuse substances have:

- More difficulties in their socio-professional integration,
- are more socially isolated, may experience more physical and mental health problems,
- are more likely to develop risky sexual attitudes and behaviors early in life, and
- are more likely to be associated with juvenile and adult crime (p.689).

Goulet et al. cite numerous individual risk factors that have been associated with school dropout and substance abuse which can be grouped into two main categories: externalized difficulties and internalized difficulties. Their review found support for externalized behavioral difficulties, such as delinquent, opposing, aggressive, and hyperactive behaviors, as linked to substance abuse and dropping out. Regarding internalized difficulties, they found support for internalizing behaviors such as depressive and anxious symptoms, to be associated with later school dropout risk and substance abuse.

Other factors that educators need to be aware of when it comes to substance use, and the dangers of dropping out of school, include peer and family factors. Goulet et al. also concluded that negative peer experiences (e.g., social rejection, exclusion from the peer network) and peer victimization (e.g., different types of bullying, including verbal and physical) are associated with a higher risk of school dropout and substance abuse in late adolescence.

Henry et al. remind us that once youth drop out of school, they leave the control of the school environment, and they are often difficult to reach in the community. Dropping out of school, however, they say, is only the end of the more general process of school disengagement, a process that typically begins earlier in the educational career. Interestingly, they report that dropout status itself was not related to later involvement in delinquency, but rather, factors leading up to dropping out were predictive. These are the factors educators can be mindful of and address early on to avoid this negative outcome.

In addition to disengagement and truancy, low academic achievement also contributes significantly to dropping out. The CDC results from the Youth Risk Behavior Survey (YRBS, 2015) provide evidence of a significant association between alcohol use behaviors and academic grades. The charts in figure 8.1 show the direct correlation between substance use of alcohol and marijuana and academic grades.

Presence of Drugs in School

As the *Malignant Neglect* report found, more than half of all teens and 60 percent of high school teens—9.5 million high school students and almost five million middle school students—reported that drugs are used, kept, or sold at their schools. And there was a very wide disparity between school staff perceptions and student perceptions of the availability and access to substances in school.

The Mrug et al. (2010) review found that higher smoking rates in middle schools may facilitate individual students' smoking through increased availability of cigarettes, and perceptions of smoking as normative and acceptable (and friendship opportunities with cigarette-smoking peers). School-level alcohol and cigarette use was more strongly related to individual use for students whose parents reported poorer parenting practices (less nurturance, more harsh and inconsistent discipline) in relation to other parents. School

Health Risk Behaviors, by type of academic grades earned
- United States, Youth Risk Behavior Survey, 2015

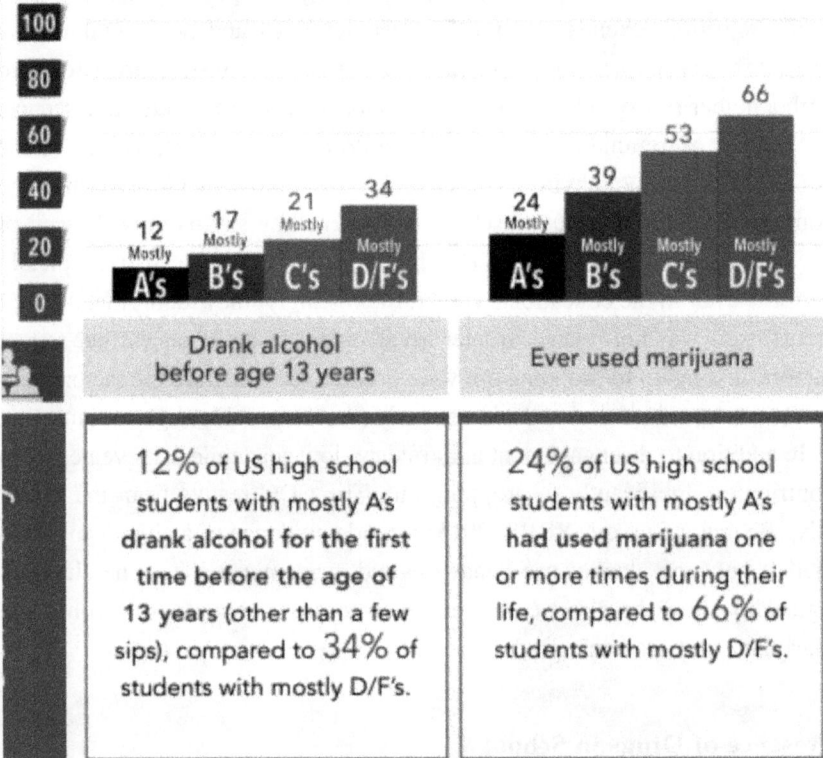

100
80
60
40
20
0

Drank alcohol before age 13 years

12 Mostly A's
17 Mostly B's
21 Mostly C's
34 Mostly D/F's

Ever used marijuana

24 Mostly A's
39 Mostly B's
53 Mostly C's
66 Mostly D/F's

12% of US high school students with mostly A's drank alcohol for the first time before the age of 13 years (other than a few sips), compared to 34% of students with mostly D/F's.

24% of US high school students with mostly A's had used marijuana one or more times during their life, compared to 66% of students with mostly D/F's.

Figure 8.1   CDC Academic Grades and Alcohol and Marijuana Use 2015. *"Making the Connection: Health Risk Behaviors and Academic Grades." U.S. Department of Health and Human Services. Centers for Disease Control and Prevention.* https://www.cdc.gov/healthyyouth/health_and_academics/pdf/DASHfactsheetHealthRisk.pdf.

cultures that do not promote strong anti-substances stance and have lax enforcement of existing policies send the wrong message to all students.

Perception of Risk

The *Malignant Neglect* report also found that students are more likely to smoke, drink, or use drugs when they believe that the harm associated with use is low. For example, adolescents who believe there is no risk, or only a slight risk of harm in smoking marijuana once a month, are six times likelier to be current marijuana users than teens who believe there is a moderate or great risk of harm (18.5 percent vs. 3.1 percent, respectively).

They don't just outgrow this use, either. Alarmingly, the report's authors also found that relatively few students who experiment with a substance discontinue its use, illustrating their lack of concern over harm—or their already acquired dependency:

> Among students who have ever tried cigarettes, 85.7 percent (2.1 million) are still smoking in the twelfth grade. Of those who have ever been drunk, 83.3 percent (2.1 million) are still getting drunk in the twelfth grade. Of those who have ever tried marijuana, 76.4 percent (1.4 million) are still using it in the twelfth grade...Among students who have ever tried cigarettes, been drunk, or used marijuana or cocaine, the overwhelming majority are still smoking, getting drunk and using these drugs by their senior year. (p.11)

For example, Vanden Toren et al. (2021) point to a study of adolescents who once have used inhalants who also tend to use, or continue to use, other substances and progress to dependence. These adolescents perceived the inhalant, nitrous oxide, as not having the status of being a drug and saw it as more innocent than alcohol or marijuana. They found that approximately 90 percent of previous users, and 24 percent of participants who had never used before, indicated that they would or maybe would like to use nitrous oxide again.

ADDITIONAL CONSIDERATIONS

School Transitions

Research has found certain academic periods to be of greater concern than others. This information is very important for strategically targeting initiatives which can make the most difference at the right time. The *Malignant Neglect* report notes that though some students begin using and abusing substances as early as the fourth grade, a significant jump in the proportion of students using substances for the first time occurs during the transition to middle school, between fifth and sixth grades.

Eighth-grade students are more than twice as likely to have used cigarettes daily for the first time in the sixth grade as in the fifth grade (2.8 percent vs.

1.2 percent) and nearly three times as likely to have been drunk for the first time (4.5 percent vs. 1.6 percent). These trends continue to show up in more recent reports of student substance use. The transition to high school is the other transition period that educators and parents need to pay attention to.

School Violence

Sadly, some schools are plagued with school violence. Overall school violence exposure and adolescent substance use were highly correlated, and an increased frequency of witnessing violence at school was related to increased frequency of substance use (Milligan et al., 2012). Sullivan et al. (2007) suggest that exposure to violence results in numerous negative outcomes for youth, including substance use and those who report having witnessed violence at a greater frequency also report higher levels of substance use.

Witnessing violence is related to increased frequencies of substance use as well. Kilpatrick et al. (2000) found that witnessing violence is among the most influential risk factors for substance use, almost tripling the risk of use for adolescents. The Milligan et al. (2012) research review also found that witnessing violence and substance use may share a common set of risk factors. Witnessing violence is a strong risk factor for poor overall adolescent adjustment, as this exposure often results in feelings of powerlessness, insecurity, and fear, whereby substances are used as a coping method.

Suicide Risk

Suicide is the second leading cause of death among youth and young adults (Moon et al., 2020). Moon's review of the literature found that low school connectedness is also correlated with several health risk behaviors, including substance use, bullying, and suicide thoughts/attempts. There are critical associations between suicidal behavior and relationships (e.g., parental monitoring), community (e.g., school academic engagement), and individual factors (e.g., substance use). They found the incidence of one-year suicide attempts for high schoolers is 7.4 percent and for suicidal ideation (thoughts), the rate is 17 percent.

A positive, significant association between substance use and suicide behaviors among adolescents was also found. Moon et al. found gender differences exist in substance use behaviors as well, with females more likely to use alcohol as their primary drug in comparison to their male counterparts. Girls also reported higher rates of other drugs as the primary substance, including amphetamines, cocaine, and opiates.

SCHOOL PROTECTIVE FACTORS

Goulet et al. (2020) maintain that an understanding of the major risk and protective factors associated with risks of school disengagement and substance abuse is necessary if we are to truly have an impact on reducing use. They advocate for the development of risk indexes that could serve as an early warning system, a universal assessment in early adolescence.

Connectedness/Belonging

The *Malignant Neglect* report's authors say that students who feel attached to or connected with their school use cigarettes, alcohol, and marijuana less frequently than students who do not feel as connected. Feeling connected with school is related to the overall school environment, including positive student-staff interactions, relationships among students, and a sense of student empowerment.

They also say that administrators, teachers, and other school staff may not realize that the nature and quality of the school environment and students' attitudes toward their school probably have more of an impact on student substance use and problem behaviors than do any curriculum-based prevention programs. Such school characteristics that associated with reduced student substance use include:

- Promoting and supporting high levels of student attachment to school.
- providing clear and consistent expectations for student behavior.
- offering smaller school sizes.
- connecting students and their families to well-coordinated support services; and
- actively engaging parents in their children's education
- encourages student attachment to school,
- more individual attention within smaller schools,
- helps coordinate support services for students and their families and
- insists on parental involvement in students' education (p. 54).

The 2009 CDC report concluded that school connectedness is second in importance, after family connectedness, as a protective factor against emotional distress. The report identifies six evidence-based strategies that schools could implement to increase school connectedness, along with specific actions that can be taken to implement each of the strategies (see figure 8.2). This report emphasizes that children and adolescents' beliefs about themselves and their abilities are shaped by how they perceive that the adults in their lives care about them and are involved in their lives, which is part of school connectedness.

The structure of the school setting can also be reviewed. The CDC report also suggests considering structuring the school so that teachers stay with the same students for three years in elementary and middle school and two or more years in high school. This can provide better continuity in learning and might allow the development of stronger teacher–student relationships, which are at the heart of connectedness, belonging, and engagement.

Student Engagement

School engagement is the meaning, importance, or interest in the educational material and activities. Moon et al. (2020) suggest that school-based relationships may be more important than educational learning engagement. Larusso et al. (2008) concur. They found that high teacher support and high teacher regard for student perspectives were associated with lower levels of substance use among students. They advised that teachers and other school professionals need to balance the discipline function with the support function of care, personal attention, and regard for students' perspectives.

Peer Relations/Friendship

In addition to teacher–student and adult–student school relationships, we know that peer relationships are vitally important to a student's sense of belongingness and engagement. The *Malignant Neglect* report recommends helping students build supportive peer groups and learning how to resist negative peer pressures. They recommend that school curriculum programs should seek to help students provide support to each other to resist substance use and abuse and build skills to resist peer pressure.

The Report maintains that peer education programs can provide information, challenge incorrect attitudes, confront unhealthy behavior, and get

Promoting School Connectedness

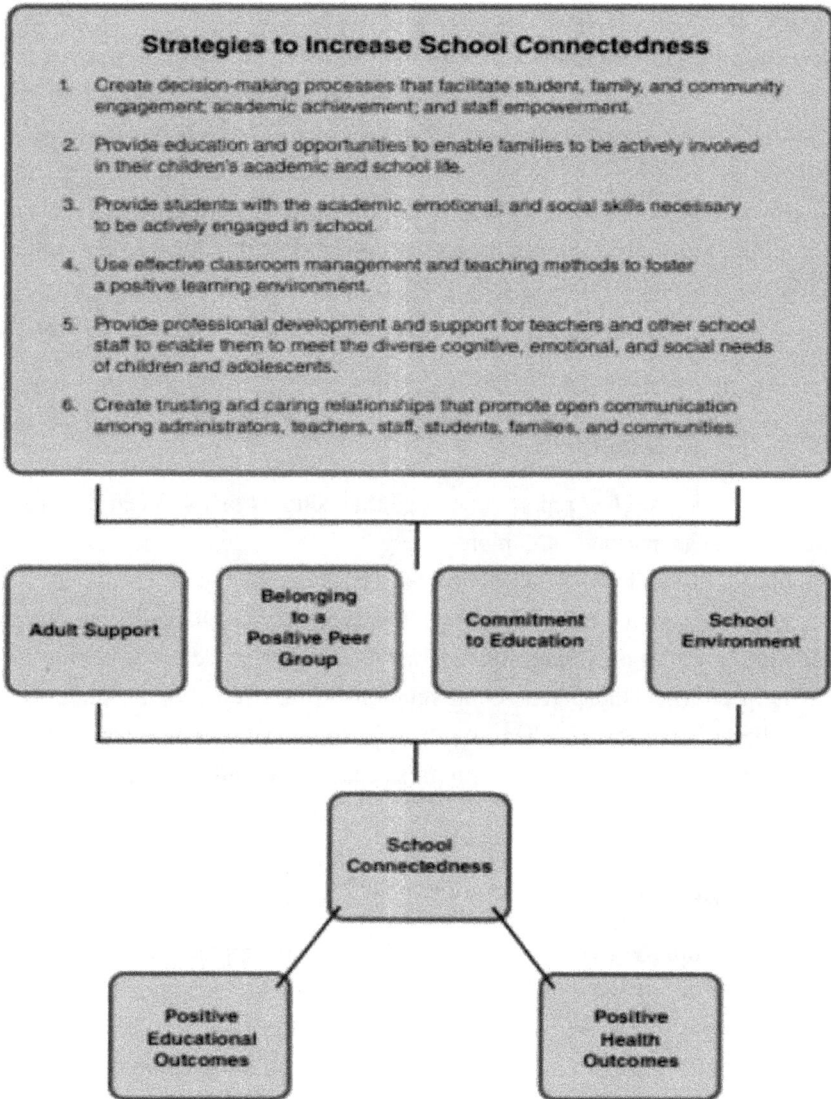

Figure 8.2 Promoting School Connectedness. *"School Connectedness: Strategies for Increasing Protective Factors Among Youth."* Centers for Disease Control and Prevention's (CDC) Division of Adolescent and School Health (DASH). Atlanta, GA: U.S. Department of Health and Human Services; 2009. https://www.cdc.gov/healthyyouth/protective/pdf/connectedness.pdf.

peers' help, if needed. Such programs can help create positive social norms, and disabuse students of inaccurate, and often exaggerated, claims regarding the prevalence of substance use among their peers. It notes that the "Friends Don't Let Friends Drive Drunk" appears to have been helpful in making the concept of designated drivers commonplace at parties and social gatherings and could perhaps be a model campaign for other harmful behaviors.

Some schools have programs that train students to be conflict mediators and in other leadership roles. Peer leaders can be an important part of prevention initiatives as they often have more credibility and influence than school staff. This chapter's Promising Program highlights an example of a program built around the concept of positive peer leadership and influence to prevent substance use.

Parent Involvement

The *Malignant Neglect* report concluded that schools that succeed in engaging parents as partners are more likely to see academic success among students and declines in substance use. Schools that involve parents by encouraging, or even requiring parental participation in students' homework and studying, not only help students achieve better academic performance, but help enhance the parent–child relationship as well. For example, one study described elsewhere here involved just regular electronic communication on the child's behavior and progress each week and noted a decrease in substance use.

Schoolwide Commitment

The *Malignant Neglect* report also calls for developing the capacity in each school to design and implement effective prevention and intervention efforts. They say that schools should develop the capacity to ensure that substance abuse prevention and intervention efforts are chosen "on the basis of research-based evidence, implemented correctly, integrated into the school environment and instructional program, and evaluated for their efficacy in reducing substance use among students in the school" (p.63).

They advocate for providing strong no-use messages every year from preschool through the twelfth grade, tailored to the age, culture, and sophistication of the child. These messages should be intensified at the transitions from elementary to middle school and from middle to high school when students are at increased risk for substance use. Schools should make every effort to incorporate these messages not only into specific prevention programs, they recommend, but into health and other academic curricula and school-sponsored social settings.

Schools also need to develop, and consistently and fairly enforce, strong and common-sense substance use policies that prohibit the possession, sale, or use of substances on school property or at school-sponsored events. There needs to be clear consequences for non-compliance that assure continued education and access to treatment.

Chang et al. (2018) note that when the messages are clear and consistent about the harms of substance use, and they learn peer refusal skills, students' decisions can change:

> When young people perceive drug use as harmful, they reduce their level of use [[14]]. Social influence of drug use [[15]], decisional balance [[16]], and drug use resistance self-efficacy [[17]] have been found to be effective components of drug prevention programs. Decisional balance is important in changing motivations and involves assessing the pros and cons of changes in behavior before embarking on behavioral changes [[18]]. (p. 2)

They describe one highly recognized evidence-based program that covers many of the protective factors identified here, called Life Skills Training (LST), described in this chapter's Promising Program section.

Evidence-Based Curricula

The list of topics emerging from this review of research is very broad. Topics important to be covered include:

- Communication skills
- Decision making skills
- Goal setting
- Problem solving
- Stress management
- Emotional Regulation/Coping skills
- Conflict resolution skills

- Social skills
- Self-management
- Refusal skills
- Assertiveness
- Mindfulness
- Cooperation and Teamwork

There is an extremely valuable matrix of evidence-based programs (Appendix A. The School Mental Health Matrix) cross-referenced by topic and behavior to assist school leadership teams in selecting initiatives customized to the needs of the local school community.

Pentz (2014) says that most school-based prevention programs—whether for prevention of substance use, conduct problems, obesity, or bullying—focus on behavioral skills training within a classroom instructional structure. They include the cognitive side of skill acquisition but tend to neglect the emotional side. They recommend attending to the emotional cues for behavior, and self-awareness, self-management, and social awareness, as well as the more explicit cognitive strategies related to behavior, in skills training programs.

The bottom line is to be sure that when matching a program to the unique and specific needs of a given school community, careful attention is paid to the research base demonstrating effectiveness of the program. In addition to a matrix of evidence-based programs, Appendix A. identifies various organizations that provide helpful assessment and evaluation information on the validity and reliability, as well as the appropriate target groups, for a variety of prevention and intervention programs.

Early Warning System and Programs for Students at Risk

There are warning signs for dropping out of school, warning signs that show up even years before a students get to that point. Henry et al. (2012) strongly advocate for an early warning system, identifying known predictors of disengagement and dropping out. They advocate for a school warning system that can predict not only dropping out but also other problem behaviors during middle and late adolescence. Such a disengagement warning system based on official records that schools already keep would provide important information for designing and targeting interventions.

Students who evidence school risk factors, especially multiple school risk factors, during the middle school years are prime candidates for interventions designed to enhance school engagement. Henry et al. found that, when they do exist, early identification, assessment, referral, follow-up, and support services often are available only to those identified as having the most severe problems. Broadening this net may capture students at even earlier stages, where the help can make the most difference.

It is also critical to consider early warning systmes for students at risk of substance use and suicide. Moon et al. (2020) state that, given the gender differences, the association between substance use and suicide behaviors and the predictors—parental monitoring and school engagement—may also differ by gender. Students who report feeling socially connected with their school show lower rates of suicide ideation (i.e., thoughts) than those who feel disconnected. They found multiple studies emphasizing the importance of protective school environments and the ability of these positive, supportive climates aiding in reducing adolescent suicide behaviors.

Environment

The 2009 CDC Report concluded that the climate at school is influenced by such factors as policies related to discipline, opportunities for meaningful participation, and teachers' classroom management practices. A positive school environment is characterized by caring and supportive interpersonal relationships; opportunities to participate in school activities and decision making; and shared positive norms, goals, and values. In addition, the report notes, schools that have higher rates of participation in extracurricular activities during or after school tend to have higher levels of school connectedness.

A positive school environment is also characterized by the both the sense of control in the building and the physical environment. Jaynes (2014) advises school leaders to pay attention to the physical environment. An environment's lack of proficiency at social control is strongly communicated by environmental cues. Jaynes found that more than 30 percent of U.S. schools report extensive disrepair, impacting over fourteen million students in those schools. What the physical environment looks like speaks volumes to those within it about how much they are cared for.

Linkages to Community Resources

And, finally, because schools cannot fight the substance use problem alone, school leaders must reach out and lock arms with every possible resource the community has to offer students and their families. When there is a paucity of treatment options for adolescents, especially urban adolescents, schools in concert with other community leaders can advocate for more resources. Too many students who need help do not get it.

Schools can assemble lists of community resources and reach out and establish partnerships for referral, and for leveraging the work that each entity is doing in this area. The American Pediatric Association, for example, says that pediatricians can serve as a resource for patients and their families and offer primary support (i.e., universal approaches designed to target all patients or potential users before a problem occurs) and secondary support (i.e., approaches targeted at patients who have screened positive for high-risk behaviors such substance use) prevention.

For the schools' part, the APA's Council on Student Health (2007) suggests that it is also important for students who have used substances to be assigned at least one trusted adult who is available in the school building to help them if they feel they need it. This adult or another school health professional, school administrator, or designated staff member should be assigned to work with the student's pediatrician and rehabilitation personnel to communicate the student's progress and work together in that student's best interest.

The wider community has a responsibility also and that will be the focus of chapter 9.

PROMISING PROGRAM: LIFE SKILLS TRAINING

As described on its website, Botvin *Life Skills Training* (LST) is a research-validated substance abuse prevention program proven to reduce the risks of alcohol, tobacco, drug abuse, and violence by targeting the major social and psychological factors that promote the initiation of substance use and other risky behaviors. This comprehensive program provides adolescents and young teens with the confidence and skills necessary to successfully handle challenging situations.

Developed by Dr. Gilbert J. Botvin, a leading prevention expert, Botvin *Life Skills Training* is backed by over thirty scientific studies and is recognized as a Model or Exemplary program by an array of government agencies including the U.S. Department of Education and the Center for Substance Abuse Prevention.

Botvin *Life Skills Training* promotes healthy alternatives to risky behavior through activities designed to:

- Teach students the necessary skills to resist social (peer) pressures to smoke, drink, and use drugs
- Help students to develop greater self-esteem and self-confidence
- Enable students to effectively cope with anxiety
- Increase their knowledge of the immediate consequences of substance abuse
- Enhance cognitive and behavioral competency to reduce and prevent a variety of health risk behaviors

The *Life Skills Training* program consists of three major components that cover the critical domains found to promote drug use. Research has shown that students who develop skills in these three domains are far less likely to engage in a wide range of high-risk behaviors. The three components are: Drug Resistance Skills, Personal Self-Management Skills, and General Social Skills.

The *Life Skills Training* is designed for elementary school students, middle/ junior high school students, and high school students. It has been evaluated and proven to be effective with white middle-class students, ethnic minority students (primarily African American and Hispanic), inner-city urban populations, suburban and rural populations.

CONCLUDING THOUGHTS

While acknowledging that school personnel cannot be expected to be addiction counselors, this chapter lays out several hopeful and important elements that are within educators' control, both in the classroom and in the school. Just the association between teacher commitment to improved school climate and student engagement is huge.

School professionals have the power to create, or enhance, a community of connection. They have the privilege of observing students for (sometimes) many hours of the day and observe things that no one else in their lives observe, not their families, or their doctors, or their neighbors. This knowledge is invaluable, when coupled with understanding of the signs and symptoms of substance use, and the possible reasons behind that use. Leveraging that knowledge with effective, evidence based programs can make such a huge difference for so many students and families.

REFERENCES

Bachman, J. G., O'Malley, P. M., Schulenberg, J. E., Johnston, L. D., Freedman-Doan, P., & Messersmith, E. E. (2008). *The Education-drug Use Connection: How Successes and Failures in School Relate to Adolescent Smoking, Drinking, Drug Use, and Delinquency*, xviii, 435 pp. New York, NY: Taylor & Francis Group/ Lawrence Erlbaum Associates.

Botvin Life Skills Training Program, National Health Promotion Associates. https://www.lifeskillstraining.com

Brown, E. C., Catalano, R. F., Fleming, C. B., Haggerty, K. P., & Abbott, R. D. (2005). Adolescent Substance Use Outcomes in the Raising Healthy Children Project: A Two-Part Latent Growth Curve Analysis. *Journal of Consulting and Clinical Psychology,* 73(4), 699–710. https://doi.org/10.1037/0022-006X.73.4.699

Centers for Disease Control and Prevention. (2009). *School Connectedness: Strategies for Increasing Protective Factors Among Youth.* Atlanta, GA: U.S. Department of Health and Human Services.

Centers for Disease Control and Prevention. (2009). *Making the Connection.* U.S. Department of Health and Human Services. DASHFactSheetDrugUse.pdf

Chang, C.-C., Liao, J.-Y., Huang, C.-M., Hsu, H.-P., Chen, C.-C., & Guo, J.-L. (2018). Evaluation of the Effects of a Designated Program on Illegal Drug Cessation among Adolescents Who Experiment with Drugs. *Substance Abuse Treatment, Prevention & Policy*, 13, 1–N.PAG. https://doi.org/10.1186/s13011-017-0139-9

Council on School Health, American Academy of Pediatrics; Committee on Substance Abuse, American Academy of Pediatrics, Mears, C. J., & Knight, J. R. (2007). The Role of Schools in Combating Illicit Substance Abuse. *Pediatrics*, 120(6), 1379–1384. https://doi.org/10.1542/peds.2007-2905. PMID: 18055689.

Dudovitz, R. N., Chung, P. J., Reber, S., et al. (2018). Assessment of Exposure to High-Performing Schools and Risk of Adolescent Substance Use: A Natural Experiment [published correction appears in JAMA Pediatr. 2021 May 1;175(5):538]. *JAMA Pediatrics*, 172(12), 1135–1144. https://doi.org/10.1001/jamapediatrics.2018.3074

Fisher, S., Zapolski, T., Al-Uqdah, S., Stevens-Watkins, D., Arsenault, C., & Barnes-Najor, J. (2019). Person-Environment Fit, Substance Use Attitudes, and Early Adolescent Substance Use. *Substance Use & Misuse*, 54(4), 628–638. https://doi.org/10.1080/10826084.2018.1531426

Gaete, J., Rojas, G., Fritsch, R., & Araya, R. (2018). Association between School Membership and Substance Use among Adolescents. *Front Psychiatry*, 9, 25. https://doi.org/10.3389/fpsyt.2018.00025. PMID: 29479322; PMCID: PMC5812301.

Goulet, M., Clément, M.-E., Helie, S., & Villatte, A. (2020). Longitudinal Association Between Risk Profiles, School Dropout Risk, and Substance Abuse in Adolescence. *Child & Youth Care Forum*, 49(5), 687–706. https://doi.org/10.1007/s10566-020-09550-9

Griffin, K. W., Lowe, S. R., Acevedo, B. P., & Botvin, G. J. (2015). Affective Self-Regulation Trajectories during Secondary School Predict Substance Use among Urban Minority Young Adults. *Journal of Child & Adolescent Substance Abuse*, 24(4), 228–234.

Henry, K. L., Knight, K. E., & Thornberry, T. P. (2012). School Disengagement as a Predictor of Dropout, Delinquency, and Problem Substance Use During Adolescence and Early Adulthood. *Journal of Youth and Adolescence*, 41(2), 156–166. https://doi.org/10.1007/s10964-011-9665-3. Epub 2011 Apr 27. PMID: 21523389; PMCID: PMC4516271.

Jaynes, S. D. (2014). Using Social Disorganization Theory to Guide Substance Abuse Prevention among Adolescents: Implications for Educators. *Journal of At-Risk Issues*, 18, 35–34.

LaRusso, M. D., Romer, D., & Selman, R. L. (2008). Teachers as Builders of Respectful School Climates: Implications for Adolescent Drug Use Norms and Depressive Symptoms in High School. *Journal of Youth and Adolescence*, 37(4), 386. https://doi.org/10.1007/s10964-007-9212-4

Lee, K. T., & Vandell, D. L. (2015). Out-of-School Time and Adolescent Substance Use. *The Journal of Adolescent Health: Official Publication of the Society for Adolescent Medicine*, 57(5), 523–529. https://doi.org/10.1016/j.jadohealth.2015.07.003

Malignant Neglect: Substance Abuse and America's Schools. (2001). National Center on Addiction and Substance Abuse at Columbia University. 633 Third Ave., 19th Floor, New York, NY 10017-6706 (22). Tel: 212-841-5255; Fax: 212-956-8020; Web site: http://www.casacolumbia.org

Milligan, E. W., Radunovich, H. L., & Wiens, B. A. (2012). School Violence Exposure and Adolescent Substance Use: A Rural Investigation. *Graduate Student*

Journal of Psychology, Department of Counseling and Clinical Psychology, Vol. 14. Teachers College, Columbia University.

Moon, S. S., Kim, Y. J., & Parrish, D. (2020). Understanding the Linkages between Parental Monitoring, School Academic Engagement, Substance Use, and Suicide among Adolescents in U.S. *Child & Youth Care Forum*, 49(6), 953–968.

Mrug, S., Gaines, J., Su, W., & Windle, M. (2010). School-level Substance Use: Effects on Early Adolescents' Alcohol, Tobacco, and Marijuana Use. *Journal of Studies on Alcohol and Drugs*, 71(4), 488–495. https://doi.org/10.15288/jsad.2010.71.488

Penney, J., Dargan, P. I., Padmore, J., Wood, D. M., & Norman, I. J. (2016). Epidemiology of Adolescent Substance Use in London Schools. *QJM*, 109(6), 405–409. https://doi.org/10.1093/qjmed/hcv171. Epub 2015 Sep 26. PMID: 26412803.

Pentz, M. A. (2014). Integrating Mindfulness into School-Based Substance Use and Other Prevention Programs. *Substance Use & Misuse*, 49(5), 617–619. https://doi.org/10.3109/10826084.2014.879796

Van den Toren, S. J., van Grieken, A., & Raat, H. (2021). Associations of Socio-Demographic Characteristics, Well-being, School Absenteeism, and Substance Use with Recreational Nitrous Oxide Use Among Adolescents: A Cross-sectional Study. *PLoS ONE*, 16(2), 1–14. https://doi.org/10.1371/journal.pone.0247230

Chapter 9

Understanding the Role of the Community in Addressing Student Substance Use

INTRODUCTION: THE ROLE OF THE COMMUNITY

As important as school professionals are in the lives of students, they only impact about six hours per day, so family and community play extremely influential roles in a student's overall social and emotional development. This chapter focuses on the wider spheres of influence: the neighborhood and community.

What resources are available in our wider communities? Do any local groups or organizations offer prevention programming or parent education? Are there specific options and programs for adolescents who need treatment? Are they evidence based and of good quality? What aspects of our communities might be exacerbating the problem?

And does the school have any relationships with these groups? Is there at least a list of who and where they are to share with a family that does seek help? And if there are few or no resources in the wider community, what can be done about that? Whose responsibility is it anyway? Where does the leadership come from to take on this challenging community-wide issue? And, when there is interest in doing something, what are the necessary steps to get started?

Moon et al. (2020) suggest considering the impact of community from a framework addressing such factors from several levels: at the societal, community, relational, and individual levels. Societal factors include social and cultural norms, policy, and other laws, while community-level influences are regional and encompass local schools, health care, neighborhood centers, and workplaces. The community is often where important political and economic decisions are made about priorities and resources.

Most research focuses on risk factors of problem behaviors at the level of individuals, but decisions regarding prevention policy are frequently made at the community level (Feinberg, 2012). Feinberg says that children and families are influenced by the culture, norms, and social relations of their communities. He notes that it is important to remember that communities may differ, not only in the overall level of risk or outcomes but also in the relations between risk factors and outcomes, which is important to keep in mind when making policy decisions.

RISK FACTORS

Overall Risks

Burrows-Sanchez and Hawken (2007) describe both community and neighborhood factors which include such things as geographical characteristics, local and state laws, socioeconomic status, population density, crime rates, and attitudes toward substance abuse. They say community risk factors for adolescent substance use include adult and community norms that favor drug use, lax drug laws, and high availability of substances.

They observed that when the legal age of drinking was increased back in the 1980s, fewer alcohol-related traffic incidents were reported. Similarly, they point to higher taxation of alcohol as related to overall decreases in consumption. Additional factors include disorganized and unsafe neighborhoods. Factors that contribute to disorganization and lack of safety include crime, poverty, and failure to maintain buildings and homes.

The Indiana University's Center for Health Policy report, *Community Conditions Favorable for Substance Use* (2018), found that prominent risk factors include, but are not limited to:

- Availability of alcohol and other drugs
- Availability of firearms
- Community norms and laws favorable toward drug use, firearms, and crime
- Transitions and mobility

- Low neighborhood attachment and community disorganization
- Poverty or extreme economic deprivation (pp. 4–6).

In their review of the literature, the report's authors found that even the perception of availability was associated with drug use. They also found studies that established a positive relationship between the availability of firearms and the prevalence of substance use, and that legislation, enforcement, and community dynamics combine to influence the local accessibility of drugs and weapons.

This report also documented the fact that communities with high rates of mobility appear to be linked to an increased risk of drug and crime problems. These problems occur more frequently in communities or neighborhoods where people have little attachment to the community. Other community factors identified in this report include a lack of social cohesion, weak infrastructure, and limited resources for prevention or intervention.

Access to Substances

Regarding access to substances, Steen's (2010) most consistent finding associated with use was access to substances. Steen said the percent of adolescents reporting easy access to the substance explained 55 percent of the variance reported odds of alcohol use, 62 percent of the variance of cigarette use, and 80 percent of the variance in the odds of marijuana use.

Steen concluded that, while perception of easy access by an individual is a risk factor for that individual, it is also risky to live in an environment where a large portion of other adolescents believe the substance is easy to obtain. When a large percentage of adolescent's report being able to obtain a substance, this most likely represents high overall access within the environment at all levels and becomes an indicator of overall supply.

Socioeconomic Status

The HBFF *Emerging Trends Report* (2018) describes how characteristics of the environment influence adolescent substance use. Described as an "equal-opportunity destroyer," the report states that some forms of substance use during adolescence, like cigarette smoking, are consistently associated with socioeconomic disadvantage. Other forms such as excessive drinking appear to disproportionately affect upper-middle-class families.

High school seniors whose parents had a college degree were more likely to have gotten drunk in the last month than seniors whose parents had not graduated high school. Adolescents whose parents were more educated were less likely to be smokers than adolescents whose parents had less education. The report concluded that no one group is immune from the risk of starting to use substances. Adolescents living in all types of communities might be at risk for substance use for different reasons.

The *Malignant Report* (2001) found that the availability of alcohol or illicit drugs in neighborhoods, adverse economic conditions, and high crime rates all increase the risk of youth substance use and consequent poor academic performance. The physical appearance of neighborhoods also sends messages about community tolerance for substance use and delinquency. Students who say that there is a lot of crime in their neighborhood are more likely than those who say there is not to report that they currently use substances.

Characteristics such as low socioeconomic status and high residential mobility impact neighborhood cohesion, support, and control, and can lead to an environment with less community adult supervision and monitoring of youth (Handley et al., 2015).

The Handley et al. research review on these issues found:

- evidence that children, adolescents, and adults living in disadvantageous neighborhoods have greater exposure to substances and more opportunities to use
- elevated levels of alcohol and drug use among individuals living in disadvantaged neighborhoods
- a higher neighborhood unemployment rate enhanced adolescent risk for marijuana use initiation.
- young adults living in deteriorating neighborhoods were more likely to use marijuana than individuals living in more **stable** and less disadvantaged neighborhoods.

The Hadley et al. study of neighborhood disadvantage included diverse indicators such as exposure to unemployed adults loitering, gang activity, low household income, and easy access to drugs within the neighborhood. Thus, adolescents in the Handley et al. study, living in neighborhoods marked by drug use and sales, violence, and the lack of safety, were more likely to approve of drug use and less likely to view drug use as harmful, which in turn predicted higher levels of adolescent drug use.

Lee et al. reviewed research on poverty and substance use during early childhood and found they are related to a greater likelihood of substance use during transition to adulthood They observed that parents' ability to provide positive parenting strategies might be compromised by chronic stress resulting from poverty and economic problems. They found that individuals with a lower socioeconomic status had a higher prevalence of cigarette use, but lower prevalence of alcohol use or other illicit drugs.

There is some mixed research on a link between low socioeconomic status and substance use as well. Fagan et al. (2015) reviewed thirty-four studies that examined the effects of neighborhood structural (i.e., economic disadvantage, mobility) and social (e.g., social networks, tolerance of substances) factors on the likelihood of any adolescent tobacco, alcohol, and marijuana use. Whereas 18 percent of the studies reported a negative relationship between community socioeconomic status and alcohol use by adolescents, 14 percent of studies showed the opposite effect, and 68 percent did not find a significant relationship.

Violence

Exposure to community violence has been linked both to several internalizing and externalizing symptoms (Lofving-Gupta et al., 2018). These researchers say that both substance use and the problem behavior associated with it increased similarly along with severity of violence exposure. This association is not gender specific. Age is another important factor regarding the prevalence of exposure, as well as the effects of it. Older children tend to report a higher prevalence of such exposure and seem to react with more externalizing symptoms compared to younger ones.

Lofving-Gupta et al. suggest that engagement in high-risk behaviors, like substance use, may represent a way of coping with negative effects following violence exposure for adolescents. For example, one study of young adults they reviewed concluded that individuals with PTSD had four times higher risk of developing substance use disorder than those without the diagnosis.

They identified a strong association between witnessing violence and substance use, with some research finding that this association was stronger with witnessing violence, compared to victimization.

Regarding violence, gender, and substance use, Lofving-Gupta determined that boys report more episodes of victimization, as compared to girls. Girls, they say, may be less exposed to community violence, as compared to boys, but they may be likely to experience more trauma than males. They found that boys tend to react with more externalizing behaviors, whereas the girls to a higher degree respond with internalizing symptoms following exposure to community violence.

Community Disengagement

Just as was seen with school disengagement, community disengagement is also associated with adolescent substance use. Pound and Campbell (2015) conducted a review of existing research on community disengagement and substance use. They found that health-related risk-taking was more likely among the following young people:

- those with insufficient ties to their community
- those living in societies without formal rites of passage
- those who are isolated from mainstream society
- those whose lives are overly regulated or circumscribed
- those who suffer discrimination
- those who have low social status
- those born into a risk-taking environment.

PROTECTIVE FACTORS

Protective factors include safe environments for residents, high standards for adolescents, and a range of positive community activity (Burrows-Sanchez and Hawkin, 2007). They found that strong and positive bonds to the community serve as a protective factor against substance use and other problem behaviors for adolescents. Adolescents who feel positive connections with their community are at less risk for substance abuse than those adolescents who do not.

These connections do not magically happen. In addition to a desire to address this urgent community problem, action requires policies, needs assessment, investment, enforcement, engagement, and coalition building. There are many hopeful models and practices that community leaders, who are really committed to doing something about adolescent substance use, can draw upon. The CDC has a slogan to inspire: Address It Today. Prevent It Tomorrow (figure 9.1).

Policy

A comprehensive approach to prevention designed to reduce risk factors, while enhancing protective factors in communities, is a promising approach for the prevention of adolescent problem behaviors and the promotion of positive youth development (Arthur et al., 2010). Policies are needed for initiatives to disseminate prevention research, to encourage data-driven prevention

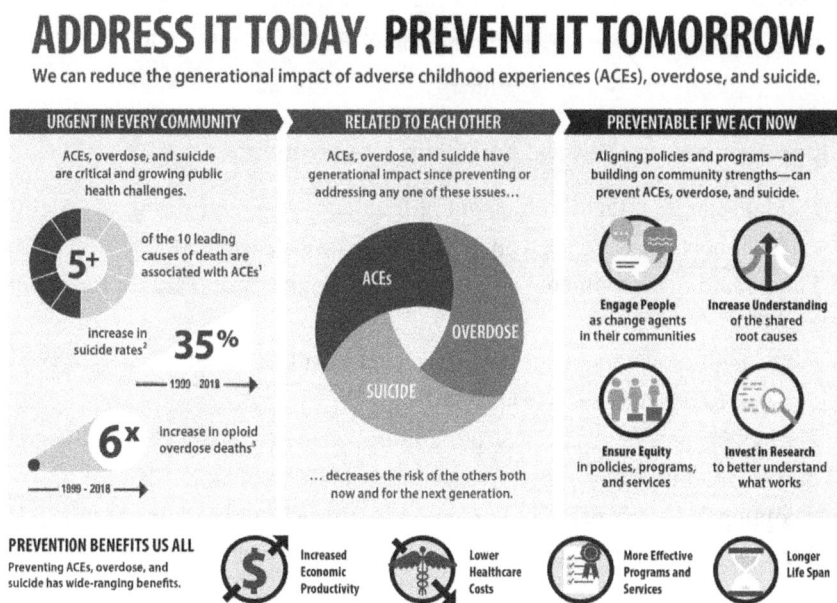

ADDRESS IT TODAY. PREVENT IT TOMORROW.
We can reduce the generational impact of adverse childhood experiences (ACEs), overdose, and suicide.

URGENT IN EVERY COMMUNITY

ACEs, overdose, and suicide are critical and growing public health challenges.

5+ of the 10 leading causes of death are associated with ACEs[1]

increase in suicide rates[2] **35%**

1999 — 2018

6× increase in opioid overdose deaths[3]

1999 - 2018

RELATED TO EACH OTHER

ACEs, overdose, and suicide have generational impact since preventing or addressing any one of these issues...

ACEs

OVERDOSE

SUICIDE

... decreases the risk of the others both now and for the next generation.

PREVENTABLE IF WE ACT NOW

Aligning policies and programs—and building on community strengths—can prevent ACEs, overdose, and suicide.

Engage People as change agents in their communities

Increase Understanding of the shared root causes

Ensure Equity in policies, programs, and services

Invest in Research to better understand what works

PREVENTION BENEFITS US ALL
Preventing ACEs, overdose, and suicide has wide-ranging benefits.

Increased Economic Productivity

Lower Healthcare Costs

More Effective Programs and Services

Longer Life Span

[1] https://www.cdc.gov/vitalsigns/aces/index.html
[2] https://www.cdc.gov/nchs/products/databriefs/db362.htm
[3] https://www.cdc.gov/nchs/data/databriefs/db356-h.pdf

https://www.cdc.gov/injury/priority/index.html

APHA
AMERICAN PUBLIC HEALTH ASSOCIATION

CDC
CENTERS FOR DISEASE CONTROL AND PREVENTION

Figure 9.1   CDC APHA Infographic. *"CDC APHA Infographic and Description."* Centers for Disease Control and Prevention, National Center for Injury Prevention and Control. (Page last reviewed: December 15, 2020). https://www.cdc.gov/injury/priority/CDC -APHA-Infographic.html.

planning, and to mobilize community stakeholders to utilize tested, effective strategies to prevent adolescent drug use and related problems.

The *Malignant Neglect Report* presents several policy areas and opportunities for both local communities and for state and federal governments:

Opportunities for Communities

- Community agencies, in partnership with schools, can establish confidential hotlines where parents and students can call for advice on how to handle substance abuse concerns and get help.
- Communities can create family resource centers in cooperation with schools that provide health, education, and social service resources for parents as well as students.
- Local businesses can work with schools to create before and after school programs that provide mentoring and opportunities for youth to participate in academic, artistic, cultural, and recreational and work programs.
- Local governments, neighborhood organizations, parents and local businesses can work together to improve the community environment.

Opportunities for Federal and State Governments

- Fund research on the development of treatment programs designed specifically to meet the needs of youth.
- Fund additional treatment services to close the one million child treatment gap.
- Fund additional independent research and evaluation of what motivates children to use and not to use drugs.
- Strengthen and enforce laws prohibiting sales of cigarettes and alcohol products within the vicinity surrounding school boundaries.
- Adopting federal legislation like the Drug Abuse Education, Prevention and Treatment Act of 2002 (p. 9).

Communities can legislate, advocate, fund, and promote interventions and programs that can better help children and families in crisis. Beal et al. (2019) discuss the need for legislative action to promote the use of assessments of adversity and support trauma-informed care, which has occurred in several states. This, they say, demonstrates the importance of the work focused on reducing adolescent substance use, with the long-term goal of improving lifelong health and well-being.

As an example, the state of Washington funded the Washington Family Policy Council. This Council mobilized collaborative community response to complex ACE (adverse childhood experience)-related social problems. This community empowerment approach is an empirically supported model of ACE Response, identified as among the first of its kind in the country, specifically addressing ACEs and their consequences at the community level. The Family Policy Council acted as a leading interagency council partnering with forty-two local affiliates.

The Council founded collaborative community partnerships, restructured natural supports, and improved services and policies necessary to reduce the rates of seven major ACE-related social problems identified in the community, including substance use. They found ways of working to build community capacity and reduce ACEs which generated locally tailored strategies. Their estimated cost savings was $55.87 million in 2009–2011.

Mallet et al. (2015) also advocate for community juvenile justice initiatives, such as effective Teen Court diversion programs. They say we must continue to advocate on behalf of these most at-risk and disenfranchised young people to stem the tide of recidivism and deterioration. Doing so will increase the chance of positive outcomes for both these adolescents and the wider community as well.

Needs Assessment

Advances in community substance use prevention have led to an emerging best-practice model called *community diagnosis*, in which communities systematically identify risk factors compared to national and state norms, and then select preventive interventions targeting those elevated risk factors (Feinberg et al., 2012). The community diagnosis approach is being done in communities through state and federal policies and programs.

This approach forms the basis of the Center for Substance Abuse Prevention's strategic prevention framework and community prevention policy initiatives sponsored by the federal government. For example, doing such diagnosis is a critically important element of the Communities that Care (CTC), highlighted as this chapter's Promising Program.

Investment

The Center for Health Policy Report (2018) calls for more investment in public health funding as a remedy for the adolescent substance use (and other) problem. This report finds that, regarding mental and behavioral healthcare system investments, the United States has some of the worst mental and behavioral healthcare systems of any developed nation.

This report calls for investment in funding streams, service delivery capacities, and an adequate workforce of substance abuse treatment and recovery systems as paramount to curbing substance use and abuse. It notes that the cost-benefit ratios for early treatment and prevention programs for addictions and mental illness programs speak for themselves: a $1 investment yields $2 to $10 savings in health costs, criminal and juvenile justice costs, educational costs, and lost productivity.

As evidence of the success of community-based initiatives, they point to long-term analyses showing a consistent track record for substance use outcomes in communities with a federal Drug-Free Communities grant from 2002 to 2012. The prevalence of past thirty-day use of alcohol, tobacco, and marijuana declined significantly among both middle school and high school students:

> The prevalence of past 30-day alcohol use dropped the most in absolute percentage point terms, declining by 2.8 percentage points among middle school students and declining by 3.8 percentage points among high school students. The prevalence of past 30-day tobacco use declined by 1.9 percentage points among middle school students, and by 3.2 percentage points among high school students from DFC grantees' first report to their most recent report. Though significant, the declines in the prevalence of past 30-day marijuana use were less pronounced, declining by 1.3 percentage points among middle school students and by 0.7 percentage points among high school students. [27] (p. 9)

Enforcement

To be successful, community initiatives must include consistent enforcement of laws and regulations. The Karki et al. (2012) research review, for example, indicated that implementing regulatory actions (policies and laws), developmental prevention intervention, early screening and brief intervention, and harm reduction methods might reduce the use of alcohol, tobacco, and other drugs.

As reported, access to substances appears to be strongly associated with substance use. Policies that impose barriers to access should receive greater attention in the field of adolescent substance use prevention. Steen's (2010) study results provide support for policies that restrict the supply of alcohol, cigarettes, and marijuana. Taxes on cigarettes and alcohol can provide a financial barrier to adolescent use. Legal barriers may also restrict access, particularly if enforcement activities are prioritized, Steen concludes.

Pound and Campbell (2015) found that, in terms of smoking, regulatory interventions such as increasing the price of tobacco, marketing restrictions, and mass media interventions are known to have an impact on smoking prevention and cessation among youths. They recognize that support for effective controls on the tobacco industry, and the alcohol and food industries, is a big challenge, but is also important due to the impact of marketing of unhealthy products and lifestyles on adolescents.

Community Connectedness and Cohesion

Just as in school communities, connectedness and cohesion deeply affect members of a community. Su and Supple (2018) found that neighborhood cohesion was protective in relation to adolescent substance use profiles. Specifically, neighborhood cohesion was associated with adolescents' lower risk of use of multiple substances. They say that adolescents' perception of neighborhood cohesion might reflect the overall quality of the neighborhood environment (e.g., levels of social controls, availability of alcohol and drugs).

Pound and Campbell discuss the need for interventions to integrate young people in danger of becoming disconnected, rather than drive them away. They suggest targeted interventions that support vulnerable young people, as well as universal interventions that aim to tie young people more closely to their communities. Interventions that enable them to contribute actively to their communities would not only be likely to increase their confidence and sense of achievement, they maintain, but would help to recast young people as active, caregiving members of their communities, rather than as potentially troublesome dependents.

Pound and Campbell summarize the following community measures that can increase community connectedness and decrease adolescent risk-taking:

- Strong social bonds that tie young people to their communities.
- increased social status, including sufficient freedom to exercise creativity.
- a reduction in levels of inequality and discrimination.

- rites of passage (or their contemporary equivalent) to mark the transition to adulthood (pp. 75–78).

Community Coalitions

Community coalitions are a popular strategy for mobilizing communities to disseminate effective interventions designed to promote public health and prevent adolescent problem behaviors such as alcohol, tobacco, and other drug use; delinquency; violence; and health-risking sexual behavior (Arthur et al.). There is encouraging evidence that community prevention coalitions can succeed at achieving public health goals.

Community coalitions also have been advocated as a mechanism for mobilizing communities to engage in prevention and health promotion efforts because they can bring together diverse community stakeholders to address a shared goal (Center for Health Policy, 2018). Activating a coalition of stakeholders could hold promise for coordinated, widespread change in preventive services across organizations and agencies in a community, including the dissemination of tested, effective strategies.

The benefit of coalition building is enormous, especially when tacking an enormous community problem—shared responsibility, leveraging each member's resources and expertise, increasing the effectiveness of each coalition member's contributions, and more. And as can be seen with the Drug-Free Community grants and model programs, the investment of time and energy pays dividends.

High-Quality, Culturally Responsive Prevention and Intervention

Advances in prevention science over the past two decades have produced a growing list of tested and effective programs and policies for preventing adolescent substance use, say Arthur et al. Yet they maintain that widespread dissemination and high-quality implementation of effective programs and policies in communities have not yet been achieved.

When the problem is within the family, the community is the only other place for adolescents to turn. When there is substance use, the McCoy et al. (2020) study found that positive support within the community, defined as supportive adults in the neighborhood and access to activities outside of school, such as youth group and clubs, served as a protective factor against alcohol and marijuana use in the face of increased adversities in the household.

McCoy found that community support reduces the likelihood of substance use in the face of increased exposure to adverse events in the household. Yet impoverished neighborhoods are least likely to have the resources to provide opportunities such as clubs or sports to youth. They emphasize the importance of providing such support and resources, which can significantly reduce risk of adolescent substance use. Educating community members about the risks of adolescent alcohol and marijuana use may be especially fruitful, they say.

Universal substance use prevention strategies for all of a community's young people can be an important mechanism for transmitting societal norms on the substance use and for developing skills to make and implement safer decisions about their own use or in situations where others are using (Midford, 2010). Prevention programs that engage young people have the best chance of achieving and maintaining benefit. Midford notes that these programs also offer the potential of creating a more sympathetic environment for complementary systemic strategies, such as restrictive advertising of legal drugs.

Media influences on adolescents are ever-present, with positive images of substance use in ads and movies and on social media. These have powerful impacts on adolescents. Yet the Das et al. (2016) review found that coordinated widespread community-based interventions *can* effectively counter such messages. They say that mass media campaigns involving a solid theoretical basis, formative research in designing the campaign messages, and message broadcast have shown positive impacts on use of substances such as cigarettes, given that these were of reasonable intensity and done over extensive periods of time.

Figure 9.2 presents a trendline of prevention messages between 2002 and 2015, showing a decline. If communities are to prevent initiation of substance use and reduce current levels, messages must reach young people to counter the barrage of pro-substance use messages they receive every day.

Regarding prevention in communities with high stress, Arthur et al. found that to succeed under such contexts, resilient youth need to develop high levels of self-regulation, control, and competence. These traits enable these

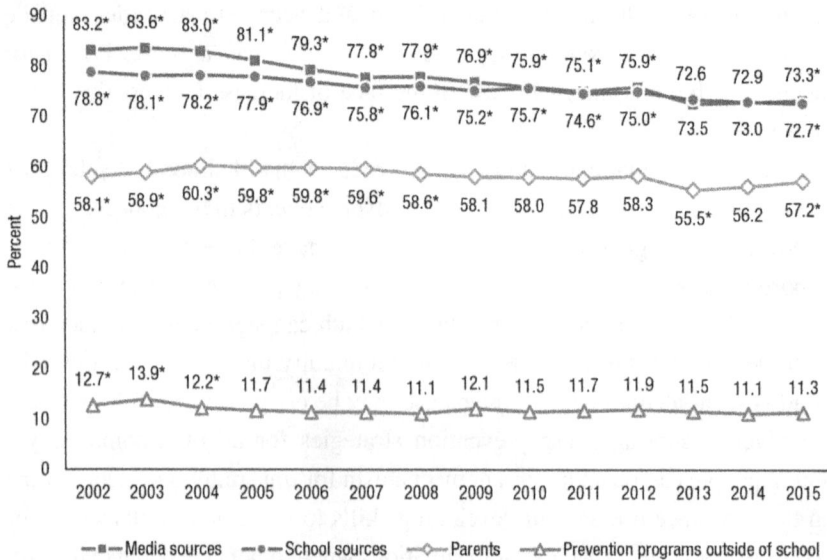

Figure 9.2 Trends in Exposure to Substance Use Prevention Messages in the Past Year among Adolescents Aged Twelve to Seventeen: 2002–2015. *Lipari, R.N. Exposure to substance use prevention messages among adolescents. The CBHSQ Report: October 3, 2017. Center for Behavioral Health Statistics and Quality, Substance Abuse and Mental Health Services Administration, Rockville, MD.* https://www.samhsa.gov/data/sites/default/files/report_3380/ShortReport-3380.html.

adolescents to avoid risky behaviors common in high-poverty neighborhoods, such as substance use, delinquent behaviors, and school failure. Addressing the physiological cost of maintaining the high levels of self-regulation needed to succeed in the face of persistent life adversity (i.e., self-efficacy) is an important consideration as well, they suggest.

PROMISING PROGRAM

According to its website, Communities that Care (CTC) is a system for planning and marshaling community resources to address problematic behavior, such as aggression or substance use, in adolescents. It has five phases to help communities work toward their goals. The CTC system includes training events and guides for community leaders and organizations.

CTC is a coalition-based prevention system that activates community stakeholders to collaborate on the development and implementation of a science-based community prevention system. The main goal is to create a "community prevention board" comprising public officials and community leaders to identify and reduce risk factors while promoting protective factors by selecting and implementing tested interventions throughout the community.

Arthur et al. (2010) evaluated Pennsylvania's implementation of CTC. They describe the CTC process which provides a structure for

- engaging community stakeholders.
- establishing a shared community vision regarding the healthy development of young people.
- data collection and reporting tools for assessing the prevalence of risk and protection, substance use, delinquency, and violence in communities.
- prioritizing risk and protective factors for community action; and
- tools for matching prioritized risk and protective factors with tested and effective preventive interventions.

CTC guides the coalition to create a strategic prevention plan designed to address the community's profile of risk and protection with tested, effective programs. CTC assists the coalition in:

1. assessing community readiness to implement the system.
2. getting organized and trained to use CTC.
3. assessing community levels of risk, protection, and health and behavior outcomes.
4. creating a community action plan.
5. implementing the plan and monitoring and evaluating program implementation and outcomes.

The evaluation data described by Arthur et al. also indicate that the CTC system helps community coalitions achieve the qualities of effective prevention coalitions. The CTC coalitions studied were more likely than prevention coalitions (in the study's control communities) to assess community prevention needs using epidemiologic data; to build the capacity of coalition members to implement science-based approaches to prevention; to develop clear, written community prevention plans; to implement tested, effective prevention programs; and to monitor and evaluate the effects of their programs on participants.

The evaluations concluded that implementation of the CTC system can produce significant, population-level effects in reducing the prevalence of adolescent drug use and delinquency in the community.

By marshalling resources, focusing on specific problems, and selecting evidence-based interventions, the CTC can reduce community-wide risk factors that lead to reductions in adolescent delinquent behaviors. Developers say takes two to five years for communities to notice a marked reduction in risk factors, and five to ten years to observe substantial decreases in adolescent substance use and delinquency.

CONCLUDING THOUGHTS

The phrase "It Takes a Village" can be heard a lot. The village creates that sense of community, of connectedness that the research in this chapter documents as necessary in a neighborhood as it is in a school. For, just as one teacher cannot do this alone in a school, one school or community cannot successfully tackle the issue of adolescent substance use by itself. There needs to be a safety net, an infrastructure, for students and families, made up of all the elements of that community.

Unfortunately, such an infrastructure does not work as well for students and families in lower-income neighborhoods. The pandemic put this situation regarding public health in stark relief. So, now efforts must be redoubled to institute the necessary changes to address these unconscionable disparities.

And still, there are things that can be done, short of a societal overhaul, that can make a difference. Initiatives such as community coalitions focusing on parent education, and community-level prevention and intervention programs have proven to make a difference. Communities can provide students with resources and supports to help them overcome the many challenges they face, especially in low-income communities, with commitment, leadership, and action.

Every family should have the opportunity to get help when needed. And the starting point can be the school community, a community resource that any family can get access to. And when students and families turn to school staff, they need to be able to offer them something: support, resources, programs, referrals, both from the school system and the larger community. Is your community or school ready to do that?

REFERENCES

Arthur, M. W., Hawkins, J. D., Brown, E. C., Briney, J. S., Oesterle, S., & Abbott, R. D. (2010). Implementation of the Communities That Care Prevention System by Coalitions in the Community Youth Development Study. *Journal of Community Psychology*, 38(2), 245–258. https://doi.org/10.1002/jcop.20362

Burrow-Sanchez, J. J., & Hawken, L. S. (2007). *Helping Students Overcome Substance Abuse: Effective Practices for Prevention and Intervention* (May 9, 2007). New York, NY: The Guilford Press.

Center for Health Policy. (2018). *Community Conditions Favorable for Substance Use*. Indianapolis, IN: Indiana University.

Centers for Disease Control. Address it Today, Prevent it Tomorrow Graphic. Retrieved from: CDC APHA Infographic & Description | Priority | CDC, 2022.

Chen, E., Miller, G. E., Brody, G. H., & Lei, M. (2015). Neighborhood Poverty, College Attendance, and Diverging Profiles of Substance Use and Allostatic Load in Rural African American Youth. *Clinical Psychological Science: A Journal of the Association for Psychological Science*, 3(5), 675–685. https://doi.org/10.1177/2167702614546639

Communities that Care, The Center for Communities that Care, School of Social Work, University of Wisconsin. http://communities that care.ne

Cordova, D., Mendoza Lua, F., Muñoz-Velázquez, J., Street, K., Bauermeister, J. A., Fessler, K., Adelman, N., Neilands, T. B., & Boyer, C. B. (2019). A Multilevel mHealth Drug Abuse and STI/HIV Preventive Intervention for Clinic Settings in the United States: A Feasibility and Acceptability Study. *PLoS ONE*, 14(8), 1–24. https://doi.org/10.1371/journal.pone.0221508

Fagan, A. A., Wright, E. M., & Pinchevsky, G. M. (2015). A Multi-level Analysis of the Impact of Neighborhood Structural and Social Factors on Adolescent Substance Use. *Drug and Alcohol Dependence*, 153, 180–186. https://doi.org/10.1016/j.drugalcdep.2015.05.022

Feinberg, M. E. (2012). Community Epidemiology of Risk and Adolescent Substance Use: Practical Questions for Enhancing Prevention. *American Journal of Public Health*, 102(3), 457–468. https://doi.org/10.2105/AJPH.2011.300496

Handley, E. D., Rogosch, F. A., Guild, D. J., & Cicchetti, D. (2015). Neighborhood Disadvantage and Adolescent Substance Use Disorder: The Moderating Role of Maltreatment. *Child Maltreatment*, 20(3), 193–202. https://doi.org/10.1177/1077559515584159

Hazelden Betty Ford Foundation. (2018). Does Socioeconomic Advantage Lessen the Risk of Adolescent Substance Use? Retrieved from: https://www.hazeldenbettyford.org/education/bcr/addiction-research/socioeconomic-advantage-edt-818

Karki, S., Pietila, A.-M., Lansimies-Antikainen, H., Varjoranta, P., Pirskanen, M., & Laukkanen, E. (2012). The Effects of Interventions to Prevent Substance Use among Adolescents: A Systematic Review. *Journal of Child & Adolescent Substance Abuse*, 21(5), 383–413.

Lee, C. T., PhD, Joseph McClernon, F., PhD, Kollins, S. H., PhD, Prybol, K., BS, MPH, & Fuemmeler, B. F. MPH. (2013). Childhood Economic Strains in Predicting Substance Use in Emerging Adulthood: Mediation Effects of Youth Self-Control and Parenting Practices. *Journal of Pediatric Psychology*, 38(10), 1130–1143. https://doi.org/10.1093/jpepsy/jst056

Lipari, R. N. (2017). *Exposure to Substance Use Prevention Messages among Adolescents*. The CBHSQ Report: October 3, 2017. Center for Behavioral Health Statistics and Quality, Substance Abuse and Mental Health Services Administration, Rockville, MD.

Löfving-Gupta, S., Willebrand, M., Koposov, R., Blatný, M., Hrdlička, M., Schwab-Stone, M., & Ruchkin, V. (2018). Community Violence Exposure and Substance Use: Cross-cultural and Gender Perspectives. *European Child & Adolescent Psychiatry*, 27(4), 493–500. https://doi.org/10.1007/s00787-017-1097-5

Malignant Neglect: Substance Abuse and America's Schools. (2001). *National Center on Addiction and Substance Abuse at Columbia University*, 633 Third Ave., 19th Floor. New York, NY 10017-6706 (22). Tel: 212-841-5255; Fax: 212-956-8020; Web site: http://www.casacolumbia.org.

McCoy, K., Tibbs, J. J., DeKraai, M., & Hansen, D. J. (2020). Household Dysfunction and Adolescent Substance Use: Moderating Effects of Family, Community, and School Support. *Journal of Child & Adolescent Substance Abuse*, 29(1), 68–79.

Pound, P., & Campbell, R. (2015). Locating and Applying Sociological Theories of Risk-taking to Develop Public Health Interventions for Adolescents. *Health Sociology Review*, 24(1), 64–80. https://doi.org/10.1080/14461242.2015.1008537

Steen, J. A. (2010). A Multilevel Study of the Role of Environment in Adolescent Substance Use. *Journal of Child & Adolescent Substance Abuse*, 19(5), 359–371.

Su, J., Supple, A. J., & Kuo, S. I.-C. (2018). The Role of Individual and Contextual Factors in Differentiating Substance Use Profiles among Adolescents. *Substance Use & Misuse*, 53(5), 734–743. https://doi.org/10.1080/10826084.2017.1363237

Chapter 10

Making a Difference

Connection, Engagement, Resilience, and Hope

COMMITTING TO ENHANCING
PROTECTIVE FACTORS

The evidence presented here has demonstrated that substance use disorders increase the risk for academic failure and unemployment and involvement in crime as well as an overall poor quality of life. These potentially lead to a perpetuation of these and other problem behaviors in future generations. These consequences have been found to be more costly to society in the long run than sound prevention that improves parenting practices, improves school bonding and success, and prepares young people to have healthy relationships (Sloboda, 2012).

In this chapter, we turn to the common themes around the protective factors in addressing student substance use. As demonstrated, substance use is pervasive, especially for students at risk of experiencing poverty, trauma, family dysfunction, and psychological distress. Bozzini et al. (2021) say that focusing on protective factors could play a key role when exposure to risk is unavoidable and essentially constant—a reality for too many of our students. Figure 10.1 presents an overview of the protective factors as they relate to the topics covered here.

The protective factors discussed here relate to Bossini's three categories of protective variables: (1) dispositional attributes: individual differences, such as high self-efficacy; (2) family attributes, such as parental support and affection; and (3) extrafamilial circumstances, such as support from other adults

Protective Factors At-A-Glance

	Screening	Attachment	Culturally Responsive Practices	Parent Education	Emotional Regulation Strategies	Staff Training	Academic Support	Early Intervention	Refer Out as Need	Fair Rule Enforcement	Social Skills	Refusal Skills	Assertive Commun	Evidence Based Prevent.	Stress Mgt
Adolescent Substance Use	x	x	x	x	x	x	x	x	x		x	x	x	x	x
COD: Trauma	x	x	x	x	x	x	x	x	x		x	x	x	x	x
COD: ADHD	x	x	x	x	x	x	x	x	x		x	x	x	x	x
COD: Conduct Disorder	x	x	x	x	x	x	x	x	x		x	x	x	x	x
COD: Anx/Dep	x	x	x	x	x	x	x	x	x		x	x	x	x	x
Family			x	x	x	x		x	x	x	x			x	x
Peers			x	x		x		x		x	x	x		x	
School	x		x	x	x	x	x	x	x	x	x	x	x	x	
Community	x		x	x					x	x				x	

Figure 10.1 Protective Factors At-A-Glance. *Author created.*

or strong community integration. They note that substance use varies among adolescents. Effects of risk and protective factors on substance use vary, depending on adolescents' circumstances and use patterns.

While there is a tremendous cost to the individual, the family, and the community, there is also evidence that investment in initiatives emphasizing and advancing the protective factors outweighs the cost of that investment. Midford (2010) claims that drug education results consistently in a reduction in drug use, albeit small, and produces a saving of $5.60 for every dollar spent, indicating that a universal approach to prevention for young people is of benefit to society. Such an approach will not eliminate drug use swiftly, but it does contribute to incremental reduction across the whole youth population.

Midford identifies four elements of programs that influence substance use:

- Information on the consequences of use combined with the development of decision-making skills and self-efficacy through participation and practice.
- resistance training to counter pressures to use substances.
- normative information on the acceptability and prevalence of use among age peers as a validation of conservatism.
- and broader social skills training to improve self-esteem and social competence, so drug use is less attractive (p. 1593).

Midford says the new generation of drug education programs, based on social learning theory, are more rigorous than previous efforts and they demonstrably change substance use behavior. Midford attributes this to the benefits of two additional components (that have been addressed in this volume): a more general social-skills component and a component providing normative information on drug use by young people.

Compton et al. (2019) also maintain that through a commitment to interventions, policies, and practices that increase protective factors and diminish risk factors, the number of individuals liable to develop substance misuse and its resulting consequences, including addiction and overdose, may be reduced.

There are three common approaches to prevention: "universal," "selective," and "indicated." Universal programs are designed for, and applied to, everyone; selective programs are delivered to specific adolescents based on their risk of developing a substance use disorder; and indicated programs are targeted at adolescents experiencing early signs of substance use problems.

Universal programs offer the advantage of avoiding the stigma that can occur through singling out high-risk individuals, and these programs have the potential for greater effects and dissemination at the population level (Newton et al., 2017). In terms of delivery location, Newton et al. say that school-based programs are ideal settings, offering both the infrastructure to deliver curriculum-based drug education and the appropriate social and learning environment to address risk factors in a developmentally appropriate way. Schools present a unique opportunity to reach large audiences while also keeping costs low.

No matter the location of an initiative to target adolescent substance use, there must first be an over-riding passion and commitment to addressing it, to ensuring an emphasis on increasing protective factors and reducing risk factors, and investing only in proven, evidence-based programs to have the best chance for successful prevention or intervention—and for saving lives.

TAKING ACTION

When a school or community does take the initiative to address the problem of youth substance use, there are guidelines and protocols and programs which can increase the chances of effectiveness. Evidence-based drug abuse prevention programs delivered to entire communities typically have multiple components (Griffin and Botvin, 2010). These often include a school-based component, family, or other components, along with mass media campaigns, public policy initiatives, and other types of community organization and activities.

Community-based programs that deliver a coordinated, comprehensive message about prevention can be effective in preventing adolescent substance use. Federal, state, and local grants are often available to support community coalitions that want to work to address this issue. Many community-based programs that have been shown to be successful have a community coalition behind it, leveraging the strength and power of each organization into one mighty force to fight for their children.

At the school level, action requires a team. Concerned staff can come together and conduct a needs assessment and identify ways that universal, selective, and targeted programs can be incorporated into the existing structure and/or determining what additional structures and resources may be

Table 10.1 How Risk and Protective Factors Affect People in Five Domains

Risk Factors	Domain	Protective Factors
Early Aggressive Behavior	Individual	Self-Control
Lack of Parental Supervision	Family	Parental Monitoring
Substance Abuse	Peer	Academic Competence
Drug Availability	School	Anti-drug Use Policies
Poverty	Community	Strong Neighborhood Attachment

NIDA. 2020, May 25. What are risk factors and protective factors? Retrieved from https://nida.nih.gov/publications/preventing-drug-use-among-children-adolescents/chapter-1-risk-factors-protective-factors/what-are-risk-factors on 2022, June 17

necessary. Creating an action plan on implementing the planned strategy and then ensuring implementation, evaluation, and follow-up are necessary. Staff should be provided time to engage in this important work.

FOCUSING ON CONNECTEDNESS AND QUALITY ATTACHMENTS

Social bonding includes warmth, affective relationships, and commitment (Bossini et al., 2021). Prevention while also fostering safe, stable, and nurturing relationships and environments enables children to learn empathy, impulse control, anger management, and problem solving can have a protective effect (Compton et al., 2019). They believe that prevention interventions can ameliorate what would otherwise be a toxic environment—even without changing the environment.

When it comes to addressing connectedness with children experiencing trauma, Masten and Coatsworh (1998) recommend the ARC (Attachment, Regulation, Competency). The ARC model consists of:

1. building secure **A**ttachments between child and caregivers(s).
2. enhancing self-**R**egulatory capacities; and
3. increasing **C**ompetencies across multiple domains.

This model could well apply to any student experiencing the psychological distress and inability to control their behavior. The very first element is attachment to a care giver. This attachment, whether that be a teacher, church leader, or other adult, can be a lifeline for many students who feel they have no one to talk to. Such an attachment builds over time so that when students need to turn to someone for inspiration or support, that influential person is right there for them. Students are then more open to the second and third parts of the model, enhancing coping skills and competencies.

Building resilience happens in the context of caring and attachment. This element is at the top of the list of external protective factors presented in figure 10.1. The caring adult provides the adolescent access to the opportunities and resilience skills they need to internalize their worth and value and learn to regulate their emotions and self-soothe when experiencing distress. This relationship also offers the student hope, hope that things can be better, that they will be able to handle challenging situations in healthy ways.

USING EVIDENCE-BASED PREVENTION STRATEGIES

Sloboda et al. (2012) discuss the opportunity those who work with adolescents have and the promise of prevention:

> We believe the majority of individuals who will eventually follow a trajectory involving problematic substance use have some differentiating and distinguishable characteristics prior to their earliest use of psychoactive substances. These predisposing characteristics facilitate an individual's following an escalating problematic substance use pathway. Predisposition, however, does not mean predestination but only increased susceptibility or vulnerability. This presents the critical opportunity to address these susceptibilities early enough that the problematic use never develops. This is the promise of prevention and the ultimate importance of understanding risk and protective factors. (p. 947)

Compton et al. (2019) speak to this promise by noting that, across childhood and adolescence, the risk factors that predispose someone to later substance use are common and shared with several other negative health outcomes. Because of this, prevention interventions may affect a wide range of behavioral and health outcomes, not just substance use. By altering the child's or adolescent's trajectory at critical ages and thereby reducing many negative outcomes, they found, such programs can thus be both effective and cost-effective, producing a large return on investment.

School-based prevention programs that have been tested and proven effective focus on building drug resistance skills, general self-regulation, social skills, and/or changing normative expectations regarding inaccurate beliefs about the high prevalence of substance use, according to Griffin and Botvin (2010). The most effective programs, they say, are highly interactive in nature, skills-focused, and implemented over multiple years.

Use of evidence-based programs and fidelity in their use have been identified as vitally important to effective implementation of prevention programs. Newton et al. (2017) identified one way of achieving high fidelity: the use of interactive delivery techniques, such as the Internet. Such programs, they say, can improve consistent program delivery; increase accessibility and sustainability; improve student engagement through the inclusion of audio-visual elements; and provide personalized and tailored feedback.

Chen et al. (2015) find that targeting behavioral vulnerability is not sufficient. They argue that interventions need to focus on resiliency, especially for children living in difficult situations. These children repeatedly face uncontrollable life stressors, which typically cannot be managed through the kinds of active-coping efforts that facilitate academic success. They advocate for resiliency training and for coping efforts that involve acceptance and accommodation of the self to the stressor combined with endurance of adversity with strength, finding meaning in difficult situations and maintaining optimism as most beneficial.

IMPLEMENTING EVIDENCE-BASED SKILLS TRAINING

Just as attachment is a central element to the ARC model, so too are competence and emotional regulation, the other elements of this three-part ARC model. Skills identified as important for adolescents struggling with substance use include:

- Resiliency
- Resistance/refusal skills
- Stress management
- Emotional regulation
- Problem solving
- Decision making
- Conflict resolution

- Social skills
- Self-efficacy
- Communication/assertiveness
- Self-control
- Goal setting
- Mindfulness

In addition to resiliency, resistance and refusal skills training programs teach adolescents ways to recognize situations where they are likely to experience peer pressure to smoke, drink, or use drugs. Students are taught ways to avoid or otherwise effectively deal with these high-risk situations. Griffin et al. call for interventions designed with the goal of increasing adolescent's awareness of the various social influences that support substance use, and teaching them specific skills for effectively resisting both peer and media pressures to use substances.

Prevention approaches also need to include content and activities to correct inaccurate perceptions regarding the high prevalence of substance use. Educating adolescents about actual rates of use, which are almost always lower than the perceived rates, reduce perceptions regarding the social acceptability of drug use, say Griffin et al. These approaches attempt to undermine adolescents' popular, but inaccurate, beliefs that substance use is considered acceptable and not particularly dangerous.

And, finally, Griffin et al. say that effective competence-enhancement approaches teach some combination of the following life skills:

- general problem-solving and decision-making skills.
- general cognitive skills for resisting interpersonal or media influences.
- skills for increasing self-control and self-esteem.
- adaptive coping strategies for relieving stress and anxiety using cognitive coping skills or behavioral relaxation techniques.
- general social skills and general assertive skills (p. 7).

The most effective competence-enhancement programs teach personal and social skills and emphasize the application of the skills to situations related to substance use, as well as how they may be used in other important situations. These same skills can be used for dealing effectively with the many challenges students confront in everyday life, which will serve students for the rest of their lives.

INCORPORATING PARENT ENGAGEMENT AND EDUCATION

Family-focused interventions are said to be the most effective interventions for preventing adolescent substance use with an average effect size two to nine times greater than the size of school-based interventions that focused solely upon young people (Kumpfer et al., 2003). Expanding school-based prevention programs to include parenting components could increase prevention outcomes (Newton et al., 2017). These researchers acknowledged, however, that the two approaches could be complementary, as in combination they produce an additive effect. They suggest there is a strong rationale for combined programming.

For example, Newton et al. conducted a review of parent-only interventions that demonstrated some beneficial effect for substance use outcomes in young people. They conducted an extensive research review of prevention programs for students and parent and found that about 90 percent of the programs that met their inclusion criteria demonstrated significant intervention effects in terms of delaying or reducing adolescent alcohol and/or other drug use in at least one trial.

Bergman et al. (2019) conducted a two-year, randomized controlled trial to test whether parent-teacher communication reduces use among middle school adolescents in low-income, minority families. Their intervention consisted of weekly messages to parents detailing their child's missed assignments and behavior problems, which were obtained from the online gradebook. Parents were sent messages any week that the student had any missed assignment or behavior problem.

These researchers found evidence that providing actionable information to parents about their child's academic performance can reduce adolescents' engagement in substance use. In a sixteenth-month follow-up period from the beginning of seventh through the end of eighth grade, use of alcohol or marijuana was cut by 44 percent (10.2 percent vs. 18.2 percent). They argue that this initiative capitalizes on the growing use of the online gradebook used in schools nationwide and, using existing school software, involves minimal cost.

ASSURING EVIDENCE-BASED
INTERVENTION AND TREATMENT

Interventions

When it comes to interventions and treatment for students with substance use problems, the good news is that there is evidence of quality treatment approaches for adolescents diagnosed with a substance use disorder. Das et al. (2016) reviewed interventions for smoking/tobacco use, alcohol use, drug use, and combined substance abuse and found effective programs for each type of substance. For alcohol, for example, school-based alcohol interventions including personalized feedback, moderation strategies, identification of risky situations, and goal setting, are associated with reduced frequency of drinking.

Regarding drug use, Das et al. found that school-based interventions based on a combination of social competence and social influence approaches show protective effects in preventing drugs and marijuana use. Among the interventions targeting combined substance abuse, they found school-based primary prevention programs that include antidrug information combined with refusal skills, self-management skills, and social skills training are effective in reducing marijuana and alcohol use among adolescents.

Treatment

Winters et al. (2009) reviewed the research on several approaches to treatment of adolescent substance use. Outpatient treatment is the predominant setting in which adolescents receive drug treatment. They found that among adolescents receiving treatment for a substance use disorder, it can be expected that from one-third to one-half are likely to return to some drug use at least once within twelve months following treatment.

They identified common themes in treatment programs. They teach skills to resist the triggers associated with the individual's drug use pattern, address life functioning issues that likely contributed to the onset and maintenance of the drug use (e.g., mental health, family issues), and identify and build upon a youth's strengths. Their review was organized around the strategies or approaches including:

- 12-step-based treatment,
- family-based interventions,

- behavioral therapy,
- cognitive behavioral therapy (CBT),
- motivational-based therapy (motivational enhancement/interviewing),
- electronic and web-based therapy, and
- pharmacotherapy approaches.

The following is a summary of their findings on effectiveness of these approaches:

12-Step Facilitation

Two-thirds of treatment programs utilize these basic principles of 12-step treatment as part of their approach. At the twelve-month follow-up, 53 percent of the treatment completers reported abstinence or minor relapse (used once or twice) compared to 15 percent for those who didn't complete treatment, and to 27 percent for a waiting-list group.

Family Therapy

The family therapy approach seeks to reduce an adolescent's use of drugs and correct the problem behaviors that often accompany drug use by addressing the mediating family risk factors such as poor family communication, cohesiveness, and problem solving. Family therapy showed the largest substance use reductions.

Behavior Therapy

Behavior therapy targets actions and behaviors presumed to be influenced by one's environment, including modeling, rehearsal, self-recording, stimulus control, urge control, and written assignments. Substance use significantly decreased over the course of the treatment for the behavioral treatment group with 73 percent reporting abstinence during the last month of treatment compared to only 9 percent of the comparison group.

Cognitive Behavior Therapy (CBT)

Cognitive Behavior Therapy (CBT) encourages adolescents to develop self-regulation and coping skills. Techniques commonly used include the identification of stimulus cues preceding substance use, the use of strategies to avoid situations that may trigger the urge to use, and skill development for refusal techniques, communication, and problem solving.

Motivational Interviewing (MI)

MI utilizes a non-confrontational approach to assist the adolescent in exploring their use. They are encouraged to examine the pros and cons of their use and to create goals to help them achieve a healthier lifestyle. They receive personalized feedback that respects their freedom of choice regarding his/her own behavior. The research on MI is encouraging. Importantly, the authors say these findings have occurred in multiple settings including schools, juvenile, and emergency departments.

Technology

Recognizing that most adolescents have access to mobile devices, access increases the possibility of reaching adolescents. Computer-based interventions and text-messaging resources have become embraced and accepted as a promising and effective technology-based health tools for preventing, treating, and supporting with study results showing promise: lowering rates of impairment, improving functioning, decreasing risk behaviors, and increasing adherence to or compliance with therapeutic/recovery regimens.

Medication

Medications approved by the U.S. Food and Drug Administration can be used to treat addiction to opioids, alcohol, or nicotine in adults, but there are no approved medications to treat marijuana, cocaine, or methamphetamine addiction, and no medications are currently approved to treat adolescents.

Winters et al. conclude that that family therapy, behavioral therapy, CBT, and MET were among the treatment types showing the largest substance use reductions. The most convincing and consistent comparative effectiveness finding, they say, was for family therapy. They say these analyses, though they note are far short of definitive, suggest that treatments are relatively effective across a wide range of adolescents differing in terms of demographics and problem severity.

GUARANTEEING CULTURALLY RESPONSIVE
PROGRAMS AND PRACTICES

In a promising sign of the times, virtually every single research article reviewed for this book concluded by saying that preventions, interventions, and/or treatment must recognize and value the culture and diversity of the adolescents and families involved. As has been shown here, there are cultural differences involved in substance use, in access to substances, in the perceptions of use, in perceptions of treatment, in responsiveness to treatment, and in effects of different environments.

Failure to address this diversity will result in failure of the programming. On the other hand, leadership ensuring culturally responsive practices, grounded in knowledge, understanding and respect for the ethnic and cultural diversity of students and their families will only enhance and increase the effectiveness of these programs. Understanding gender differences where appropriate, appreciating the acculturation gap of immigrant families, and accommodating for special needs will only strengthen the bonds, the connectedness, the engagement schools are striving for, and significantly increase the value of these efforts.

THE IMPACT OF THE COVID-19 PANDEMIC
ON ADOLESCENT SUBSTANCE USE

Many news articles describe the impact of the COVID-19 pandemic on the use of substances and on the mental health of adolescents. A study of 8,000 adolescents, (Pelham et al., 2021) found the overall prevalence of substance use did not change significantly during the first six months of the pandemic. They did find higher rates of substance use when students were in school (vs. out of school), whether that schooling was online or in-person/ hybrid, however. Thus, they said, even online schooling may maintain greater contact with peers that facilitates access to substances and social use contexts.

Pelham et al. found that adolescents in families that experienced loss of income or material hardship during the pandemic were more likely to use substances. Also at elevated risk of use were youth with pre-existing externalizing and/or internalizing problems or whose parents used substances. Stress, depression, and anxiety were associated with use, even when adjusting for the pre-pandemic level of internalizing problems.

Ji-Tong et al. also remind us just how much COVID-19 has altered lives, especially adolescents and young adults who lost their emotional and social support systems and may be suffering. In their work, they found large percentages of adolescents afraid of getting the disease, who were anxious about the health of their families, and who were worried about housing and food insecurity. Additionally, almost half of their survey respondents reported anxiety and a quarter reported depression, numbers significantly higher than pre-Covid numbers.

PROMISING PROGRAM: RECOVERY HIGH SCHOOLS

As stated, there is a high relapse rate among adolescents who face great challenges when attending school during or after treatment. They are warned away from their using friends and they may be stigmatized and shunned by non-using peers. Even knowing how to relate and respond to peers given newfound sobriety can be challenging for adolescents returning from treatment. Yet increasing social interaction with non-substance-using peers is associated with greater odds of remission and recovery. This can be done at a recovery high school.

Recovery high schools are an alternative high school option that provides recovery support and a protective environment for students with substance use disorders and related behavioral, emotional, or mental health needs. Recovery high schools provide services supporting both the academic and therapeutic needs of students. These schools attempt to support recovery and academic achievement by creating connectedness and building social and recovery capital in a context with clear pathways to success.

According to Winters et al. (2009) review of the literature, certain elements are common:

1. Building a base of peer/family connection, social structures, accountability, psychoeducational information, and recovery resources;
2. Repairing/replacing disconnected or unhealthy peer, family, and authority relationships and minimizing contact with high-risk peers during school hours;

3. Providing students the opportunity to meet other students with similar histories and goals and to practice skills, including how to have sober fun;
4. Identifying and responding to behaviors indicating potential substance use or the symptoms of a co-occurring disorder by taking advantage of smaller school environments and specialized staff;
5. Requiring participation in support and mutual aid groups outside school to promote contact with additional positive peers and mentors; and
6. Providing an individualized, accredited curriculum taught by licensed teachers to give students a chance to stay on-course for earning a high school diploma.

Results at six months compared adolescents attending a recovery high school (RHS) following treatment to non-RHS students who had received similar treatment. Researchers found that RHS students were twice (59 percent versus 30 percent) as likely to report complete abstinence from alcohol, marijuana, and other drugs at the six-month follow-up. RHS students reported significantly fewer days of marijuana use (nine days compared to twenty-six days in the past three months), and RHS students reported significantly less absenteeism from school.

Given such promising results, it is surprising that there are only thirty-six recovery high schools in the United States today. Committing to changing this reality and establishing a recovery high school in every community, and alternative peer groups in every middle and high school, should be a top priority for everyone who cares about adolescents today.

CONCLUDING THOUGHTS

In December 2021, U.S. surgeon general Dr. Vivek Murthy issued an alarm about the youth mental health crisis, which was significant before the COVID-19 pandemic and now exacerbated by it. He said:

> Mental health challenges in children, adolescents, and young adults are real and widespread. Even before the pandemic, an alarming number of young people struggled with feelings of helplessness, depression, and thoughts of suicide—and rates have increased over the past decade. The COVID-19 pandemic further altered their experiences at home, school, and in the community, and the effect

on their mental health has been devastating. The future wellbeing of our country depends on how we support and invest in the next generation. (HHS, December 2021, p. 4)

So many adolescents struggle with substance use trying to address mental health issues. A disproportionate number of them struggle with the co-occurring disorders described here: ADHD, trauma, anxiety, depression, poverty, and more. Unfortunately, only one of ten individuals needing treatment ever gets it. Some of the reason for that is their own denial. For some, it's a lack of resources and access. Yet for some others, it is due to the terrible stigma addiction still has today, instead of being recognized as a mental health disorder.

Treatment programs for those in active addiction focus on both education about substance use, and on individual and group counseling. So many of the recommendations reported here are part of such treatment, from connectedness, to focus on resilience and self-efficacy, and to optimism. And these are all recommended protective factors for supporting students struggling with substance use as well.

This volume has presented a synthesis of the findings on adolescent substance use prevention and intervention. These findings offer direction and hope. They offer direction on so many of the protective factors that can be incorporated, or enhanced, as well as evidence-based strategies and programs that can be integrated into a school's curricula.

These findings also offer hope. Hope for supporting and investing in the next generation. Hope that education professionals can make an even bigger—sometimes even lifesaving—difference in the lives of the students they care for and care about, and their families. Hope that the profession can be a big part of reducing the suffering and pain of future generations—and improving their lives. And isn't that what it's all about?

REFERENCES

Bergman, P., Dudovitz, R. N., Dosanjh, K. K., & Wong, M. D. (2019). Engaging Parents to Prevent Adolescent Substance Use: A Randomized Controlled Trial. *American Journal of Public Health*, 109(10), 1455–1461. https://doi.org/10.2105/AJPH.2019.305240

Bozzini, A. B., Bauer, A., Maruyama, J., Simões, R., & Matijasevich, A. (2021). Factors Associated with Risk Behaviors in Adolescence: A Systematic Review. *Revista brasileira de psiquiatria (Sao Paulo, Brazil: 1999)*, 43(2), 210–221. https://doi.org/10.1590/1516-4446-2019-0835

College for Behavioral Health Leadership. It Beings with You: Resilience Protective and Risk Factors. Retrieved from: Resilience | Change4Health.

Compton, W. M., Jones, C. M., Baldwin, G. T., Harding, F. M., Blanco, C., & Wargo, E. M. (2019). Targeting Youth to Prevent Later Substance Use Disorder: An Underutilized Response to the US Opioid Crisis. *American Journal of Public Health*, 109, S185–S189. https://doi.org/10.2105/AJPH.2019.305020

Das, J. K., Salam, R. A., Arshad, A., Finkelstein, Y., & Bhutta, Z. A. (2016). Interventions for Adolescent Substance Abuse: An Overview of Systematic Reviews. *The Journal of Adolescent Health: Official Publication of the Society for Adolescent Medicine*, 59(4S), S61–S75. https://doi.org/10.1016/j.jadohealth.2016.06.021

Griffin, K. W., & Botvin, G. J. (2010). Evidence-based Interventions for Preventing Substance Use Disorders in Adolescents. *Child and Adolescent Psychiatric Clinics of North America*, 19(3), 505–526. https://doi.org/10.1016/j.chc.2010.03.005

HHS, U. S. Health and Human Services. U.S. Surgeon General Issues Advisory on Youth Mental Health Crisis Further Exposed by COVID-19 Pandemic. December 2021. Retrieved from: surgeon-general-youth-mental-health-advisory.pdf (hhs.gov)

Kumpfer, K. L., Alvarado, R., & Whitesideh, O. (2003). Family-based Interventions for Substance Use and Misuse Prevention. *Substance Use & Misuse*, 38, 1759–1787.

Masten, A. S., & Coatsworth, J. D. (1998). The Development of Competence in Favorable and Unfavorable Environments: Lessons from Research on Successful Children. *American Psychologist*, 53(2), 205–220. https://doi.org/10.1037/0003-066X.53.2.205

Midford, R. (2010). Drug Prevention Programs for Young People: Where Have We Been and Where Should We Be Going? *Addiction*, 105(10), 1688–1695. https://doi.org/10.1111/j.1360-0443.2009.02790.x

Newton, N. C., Champion, K. E., Slade, T., Chapman, C., Stapinski, L., Koning, I., Tonks, Z., & Teesson, M. (2017). A Systematic Review of Combined Student- and Parent-based Programs to Prevent Alcohol and Other Drug Use Among Adolescents. *Drug & Alcohol Review*, 36(3), 337–351. https://doi.org/10.1111/dar.12497

NIDA. (2020, June 2). Principles of Adolescent Substance Use Disorder Treatment. Retrieved from https://www.drugabuse.gov/publications/principles-adolescent-substance-use-disorder-treatment-research-based-guide/principles-adolescent-substance-use-disorder-treatment on 2021, November 21.

Pelham, W. E. 3rd, Tapert, S. F., Gonzalez, M. R., McCabe, C. J., Lisdahl, K. M., Alzueta, E., Baker, F. C., Breslin, F. J., Dick, A. S., Dowling, G. J., Guillaume, M., Hoffman, E. A., Marshall, A. T., McCandliss, B. D., Sheth, C. S., Sowell, E. R., Thompson, W. K., Van Rinsveld, A. M., Wade, N. E., & Brown, S. A. (2021). Early Adolescent Substance Use Before and During the COVID-19 Pandemic: A Longitudinal Survey in the ABCD Study Cohort. *Journal of Adolescent Health*, 69(3), 390–397. https://doi.org/10.1016/j.jadohealth.2021.06.015. PMID: 34452728.

Sloboda, Z., Glantz, M. D., & Tarter, R. E. (2012). Revisiting the Concepts of Risk and Protective Factors for Understanding the Etiology and Development of Substance Use and Substance Use Disorders: Implications for Prevention. *Substance Use & Misuse*, 47(8/9), 944–962. https://doi.org/10.3109/10826084.2012.663280

Winters, K. C., Botzet, A. M., Fahnhorst, T., Stinchfield, R., & Koskey, R. (2009). Adolescent substance abuse treatment: A review of evidence-based research. In C. G. Leukefeld, T. P. Gullotta, & M. Staton-Tindall (Eds.), *Adolescent substance abuse: Evidence-based approaches to prevention and treatment*, 73–96. Springer Science + Business Media. https://doi.org/10.1007/978-0-387-09732-9_4

Yau, J. J., & Nager, A. L. (2021). Adolescent and Young Adult Stress and Coping during COVID-19: The Utility of a Pediatric Emergency Department Screener. *International Journal of Emergency Medicine*, 14(1), 41. https://doi.org/10.1186/s12245-021-00359-4. PMID: 34315406; PMCID: PMC8314256

Appendix A

Selected Reviews of Evidence-Based Programs

CDC: High Risk Substance Use in Youth | Adolescent and School Health | CDC

CDC Drug Free Communities: Drug-Free Communities Support Program | Drug Overdose | CDC Injury Center

Child Welfare Information Gateway: Evidence-based practice registries list evaluated programs and practices to prevent child abuse and neglect, violence, juvenile delinquency, substance abuse, and other community concerns.

Find It Toolkit: University of Washington Addictions, Drugs and Alcohol Institute ADAI: Finding Substance Abuse Resources in WA State (uw.edu)

National Adolescent and Young Adult Health Information Center: Guide to Evidence-Based Programs for Adolescent Health: Programs, Tools: Evidence-Based-Guide.pdf (ucsf.edu)

National Institute of Health: Evidence-Based Interventions for Preventing Substance Use Disorders in Adolescents Evidence-Based Interventions for Preventing Substance Use Disorders in Adolescents (nih.gov)

National Institute of Justice Drug Abuse Prevention and Education: Rated Programs and Practices: Drug Abuse Prevention and Education— Rated Programs and Practices | CrimeSolutions, National Institute of Justice (ojp.gov)

New York State Office of Addiction Services and Supports: early intervention programs to help youth who exhibit elevated risk factors and are using substances, as well as educational and multi-component programs which focus on improving risk and protective factors at home and in the community: Evidence-based Prevention Programs | Office of Addiction Services and Supports (ny.gov)

SAMSHA: 20190719-samhsa-finding_evidence-based-programs-practices .pdf

University of WI What Works: Evidence-Based Program Registries— What Works Wisconsin—Effective Programs and Resources for Children, Youth and Families

U.S. Department of Education Office of Safe and Drug-Free schools Grants: Archived: Programs/Initiatives—OSDFS

Yannacci, J. and Rivard, J. (April, 2006) Matrix of Children's Evidence Based Interventions, Center for Mental Health Quality and Accountability, NASMHPD Research Institute. https://www.co-occurringdisrodersnys.org

Appendix B

NIDA *Principles of Adolescent Substance Use Disorder Treatment*

National Institute of Drug Abuse (NIDA) Principles of Adolescent Substance Use Disorder Treatment

1. **Adolescent substance use needs to be identified and addressed as soon as possible.** Drugs can have long-lasting effects on the developing brain and may interfere with family, positive peer relationships, and school performance. Most adults who develop a substance use disorder report having started drug use in adolescence or young adulthood, so it is important to identify and intervene in drug use early.
2. **Adolescents can benefit from a drug abuse intervention even if they are not addicted to a drug.** Substance use disorders range from problematic use to addiction and can be treated successfully at any stage, and at any age. For young people, any drug use (even if it seems like only "experimentation"), is cause for concern as it exposes them to dangers from the drug and associated risky behaviors and may lead to more drug use in the future. Parents and other adults should monitor young people and not underestimate the significance of what may appear as isolated instances of drug taking. A relapse signals the need for more treatment or a need to adjust the individual's current treatment plan.
3. **Routine annual medical visits are an opportunity to ask adolescents about drug use.** Standardized screening tools are available to help pediatricians, dentists, emergency room doctors, psychiatrists, and other clinicians determine an adolescent's level of involvement (if any) in

tobacco, alcohol, and illicit and nonmedical prescription drug use. When an adolescent reports substance use, the health care provider can assess its severity and either provide an onsite brief intervention or refer the teen to a substance abuse treatment program.

4. **Legal interventions and sanctions or family pressure may play an important role in getting adolescents to enter, stay in, and complete treatment.** Adolescents with substance use disorders rarely feel they need treatment and almost never seek it on their own. Research shows that treatment can work even if it is mandated or entered into unwillingly.

5. **Substance use disorder treatment should be tailored to the unique needs of the adolescent.** Treatment planning begins with a comprehensive assessment to identify the person's strengths and weaknesses to be addressed. Appropriate treatment considers an adolescent's level of psychological development, gender, relations with family and peers, how well he or she is doing in school, the larger community, cultural and ethnic factors, and any special physical or behavioral issues. Many adolescents who abuse drugs have a history of physical, emotional, and/ or sexual abuse or other trauma.

6. **Treatment should address the needs of the whole person, rather than just focusing on his or her drug use.** The best approach to treatment includes supporting the adolescent's larger life needs, such as those related to medical, psychological, and social well-being, as well as housing, school, transportation, and legal services. Failing to address such needs simultaneously could sabotage the adolescent's treatment success.

7. **Behavioral therapies are effective in addressing adolescent drug use**. Behavioral therapies, delivered by trained clinicians, help an adolescent stay off drugs by strengthening his or her motivation to change. This can be done by providing incentives for abstinence, building skills to resist and refuse substances and deal with triggers or craving, replacing drug use with constructive and rewarding activities, improving problem-solving skills, and facilitating better interpersonal relationships.

8. **Families and the community are important aspects of treatment.** The support of family members is important for an adolescent's recovery. Several evidence-based interventions for adolescent drug abuse seek to strengthen family relationships by improving communication and improving family members' ability to support abstinence from drugs. In

addition, members of the community (such as school counselors, parents, peers, and mentors) can encourage young people who need help to get into treatment—and support them along the way.

9. **Effectively treating substance use disorders in adolescents requires also identifying and treating any other mental health conditions they may have.** Adolescents who abuse drugs frequently also suffer from other conditions including depression, anxiety disorders, attention-deficit hyperactivity disorder (ADHD), oppositional defiant disorder, and conduct problems. Adolescents who abuse drugs, particularly those involved in the juvenile justice system, should be screened for other psychiatric disorders. Treatment for these problems should be integrated with the treatment for a substance use disorder.

10. **Sensitive issues such as violence and child abuse or risk of suicide should be identified and addressed.** Many adolescents who abuse drugs have a history of physical, emotional, and/or sexual abuse or other trauma. If abuse is suspected, referrals should be made to social and protective services, following local regulations and reporting requirements.

11. **It is important to monitor drug use during treatment.** Adolescents recovering from substance use disorders may experience relapse, or a return to drug use. Triggers associated with relapse vary and can include mental stress and social situations linked with prior drug use. It is important to identify a return to drug use early before an undetected relapse progresses to more serious consequences. A relapse signals the need for more treatment or a need to adjust the individual's current treatment plan to better meet his or her needs.

12. **Staying in treatment for an adequate period of time and continuity of care afterward are important.** The minimal length of drug treatment depends on the type and extent of the adolescent's problems, but studies show outcomes are better when a person stays in treatment for 3 months or more. Because relapses often occur, more than one episode of treatment may be necessary. Many adolescents also benefit from continuing care following treatment, including drug use monitoring, follow-up visits at home, and linking the family to other needed services.

13. **Testing adolescents for sexually transmitted diseases like HIV, as well as hepatitis B and C, is an important part of drug treatment.** Adolescents who use drugs—whether injecting or noninjecting—are

at an increased risk for diseases that are transmitted sexually as well as through the blood, including HIV and hepatitis B and C. All drugs of abuse alter judgment and decision making, increasing the likelihood that an adolescent will engage in unprotected sex and other high-risk behaviors including sharing contaminated drug injection equipment and unsafe tattooing and body piercing practices—potential routes of virus transmission. Substance use treatment can reduce this risk both by reducing adolescents' drug use (and thus keeping them out of situations in which they are not thinking clearly) and by providing risk-reduction counseling to help them modify or change their high-risk behaviors.

Source: Principles of Adolescent Substance Use Disorder Treatment | National Institute on Drug Abuse (NIDA) https://nida.nih.gov/publications/principles-adolescent-substance-use-disorder-treatment-research-based-guide/principles-adolescent-substance-use-disorder-treatment

About the Author

Deborah Lynch taught in urban elementary and high schools for twenty years. She also worked as an assistant director of the Educational Issues Department of the American Federation of Teachers. She was instrumental in the award of a $1.3 million MacArthur grant for an education reform and teacher leadership initiative to the Chicago Teachers Union and served as its president from 2001 to 2004. Lynch earned a PhD in public policy from the University of Illinois at Chicago, was a professor in the College of Education at Chicago State University for ten years., and is now Professor Emeritus there. She also holds a master's degree in addiction studies and is a certified addiction counselor with the Hazelden Betty Ford Foundation. She is president of the Serenity Academy Board of Directors, a nonprofit organization committed to advancing alternative peer groups (APGs) and recovery high schools.

About the Author